# PRAISE FOR *STRANDED IN THE SKY*

"Of all the tales told of that infamous day in 1941, Philip Jett's is probably the most unique. *Stranded in the Sky* is really three stories: the exclusive experience of traveling the Pacific in a luxury flying clipper, hopping remote islands in lavish comfort; the gripping drama of daring escapes through hostile skies as the Japanese navy swept through the region on December 7th; and the interwoven history of Pan American Airways from its pre-war creation to pioneering successes to bankruptcy in the 1990s. Vivid descriptions of far flung island outposts like Midway and Wake were particularly interesting to this Pacific traveler. Jett's thoroughly researched book was a pleasure to read and an education for anyone interested in the Pacific war and commercial aviation history." —DAVID W. JOURDAN, AUTHOR OF *LAST MAN DOWN: USS NAUTILUS AND THE UNDERSEA WAR IN THE PACIFIC*

"This was a fascinating read for me. It captures history that I want to preserve for my grandchildren. The stories were so vivid that I imagined I was back on Wake Island in 1941 with my mother, father, and brother." —PHIL COOKE, SON OF JOHN COOKE, JR., PAN AM AIRPORT MANAGER

"An absorbing and revealing account of a little-known episode at the outbreak of America's war with Japan. Who even gave a thought to the fact that luxury airliners would be in the air and flying into the middle of the maelstrom in the Pacific at the time Japanese forces attacked Pearl Harbor and other Allied targets in December, 1941? I, for one, certainly hadn't. Philip Jett's book will appeal to those who enjoy well told, true WWII stories, as well as aviation buffs and those who, like myself, can't resist taking a step back in time." — STEPHEN DANDO-COLLINS, AUTHOR OF *THE BIG BREAK: THE GREATEST AMERICAN WWII POW ESCAPE STORY NEVER TOLD*

# STRANDED
## IN THE SKY

# ALSO BY PHILIP JETT

---

*Taking Mr. Exxon: The Kidnapping of an Oil Giant's President*

*The Death of an Heir: Adolph Coors III and the
Murder That Rocked an American Brewing Dynasty*

The Untold Story of Pan Am Luxury Airliners
Trapped on the Day of Infamy

# STRANDED
## IN THE SKY

## PHILIP JETT

TURNER
PUBLISHING COMPANY

TURNER PUBLISHING COMPANY
Nashville, Tennessee
www.turnerpublishing.com

Cover and book design by William Ruoto

Library of Congress Cataloging-in-Publication Data
Names: Jett, Philip, author.
Title: Stranded in the sky : the untold story of Pan Am luxury airliners
    trapped on the day of infamy / Philip Jett.
Other titles: Untold story of Pan Am luxury airliners trapped on the day of
    infamy
Description: Nashville, Tennessee : Turner Publishing Company, [2023] |
    Includes bibliographical references and index.
Identifiers: LCCN 2022026734 (print) | LCCN 2022026735 (ebook) | ISBN
    9781684429363 (paperback) | ISBN 9781684429370 (hardcover) | ISBN
    9781684429387 (epub)
Subjects: LCSH: Pearl Harbor (Hawaii), Attack on, 1941. | World War,
    1939-1945—Campaigns—Pacific Area. | Pan American World Airways,
    inc.—History. | World War, 1939–1945—Aerial operations, Japanese. |
    World War, 1939–1945—Pacific Area. | Pacific Clipper (Airplane) |
    Philippine Clipper (Airplane) | Anzac Clipper (Airplane) | Hong Kong
    Clipper (Airplane) | Transpacific flights—History—20th century.
Classification: LCC D767.92 .J48 2023  (print) | LCC D767.92  (ebook) | DDC
    940.54/26693—dc23/eng/20221018
LC record available at https://lccn.loc.gov/2022026734
LC ebook record available at https://lccn.loc.gov/2022026735

Printed in the United States of America

*In Memory of Dad*

# CONTENTS

# PREFLIGHT BRIEFING

To be caught in mid-air over the vast expanse of the Pacific with a
precious cargo of humans . . . in a sudden war is no pleasant thing.
—*The Kansas City Star*, December 21, 1941

The second bell has just sounded, which means it's time for you to voyage into the past to the Golden Age of air travel. You will soon exit the Pan American Airways System (Pan Am) terminal in San Francisco and board Pan Am's gigantic seaplanes called "flying boats"—the *Anzac, Hong Kong, Pacific,* and *Philippine Clippers*—the largest and most luxurious planes of the era. Many aviation experts contend that Pan Am's flying boats were the most magnificent planes of all time:

> There was a time, believe it or not, when people actually fell in love with airplanes. They didn't just go from here to there by air, they went in style. None of this three-abreast, elbow-in-your-ribs stuff that passes for air comfort today. No cramped legs when the seat forward suddenly reclines against the knees behind, making a tall man feel like a sardine wedged into a too-small can. Even the jumbo jets haven't revived the honest-to-god luxury that was.

Once onboard your flying boat, Pan Am stewards will treat you as royalty for the duration of your voyage, whether you are flying to the Orient, the Antipodes, the Philippines, or a South Pacific isle along the way. You will experience how the affluent and influential passengers reveled in the grandeur of those magnificent planes and the exotic destinations that their wealth or high-paying careers accorded them. You will eat four-course meals, consume the best selection of wine and liquor, and witness sights that have been imagined by many but viewed by only a fortunate few.

Yet I must warn you. You will be flying over the Pacific Ocean on December 7, 1941. On that infamous day, the Empire of Japan attacked Pearl Harbor, Hawaii, and several other Pacific locations— including Midway Atoll, Wake Island, Guam, and Manila—used by Pan Am for layovers and refueling stops. In a flash, all frivolity will disappear and you will join other passengers thrust into the first day of the Pacific War who were forsaken with only the slimmest hope of safely returning home.

To avoid confusion during your adventure, you should note that there is a difference not only in the time of day but in the dates for: (1) the US mainland, Hawaii, and Midway Atoll, which are east of the International Date Line; and (2) all other relevant locations mentioned in this book, such as Wake Island, Guam, the Philippines, Macau, Hong Kong, Singapore, Canton Island, Fiji, New Caledonia, New Zealand, and Japan, which are west of the International Date Line. For instance, if I were to lob a stone above the surf of Hawaii on December 31, it would hit the water on January 1 at Wake Island or Hong Kong. I reference the differences in date occasionally, but to avoid tiresome repetitive alerts, keep in mind that Hawaii, Midway Atoll, and the continental United States are a day behind other pertinent locations mentioned.

In addition, because these flights took place in December 1941 at a time when the Empire of Japan became an enemy of the United States of America, I have been sensitive to the concern that many of the quoted words, terms, and phrases used by individuals, newspapers, and magazines from that period may be offensive to people today. Therefore, I have substituted other words or phrases inside brackets in order that the quote may be used to further the story without use of the pejorative expressions.

While this is a work of narrative historical nonfiction, I believe that I have stayed as true to the facts as possible while recounting the tales of these men and women in a manner worthy of their experiences during that frightful time. I relied on primary and secondary sources to tell this story and attempted to locate corroboration for all sources. All too often I have discovered that resources, whether interviews, books, magazines, internet articles, or other sources, contain inaccuracies or falsehoods that have been perpetuated to such an extent that they gain an artificial credibility. I hope none squeezed through my strainer of truth.

I have not created any dialogue or changed facts to suit my story or make it more thrilling: it's thrilling enough as it is, as your voyage across the Pacific will soon confirm. Children and grandchildren of many of the crew and passengers named in this book helped me build and shape their ancestors, down to the brand of cigarettes they smoked. They also recalled anecdotes retold—verbally or through diaries and letters—by those onboard. I occasionally deduced scenes when direct information was unavailable; for instance, seating one passenger with another so that I could use the scene to factually describe a passenger or an event. These liberties are tiny clouds floating in a vast sky of facts. From transcendent planes and exotic locations to interesting people and courageous pilots and crews, this is my account of their fascinating story. It has never been told exactly as set forth herein.

And now it is time for you to board. Enjoy your trip, and good luck. May divine providence be with you as it was with the Pan Am passengers on that fateful day in December 1941, a day that not only lives in infamy, but in the hearts and minds of those who lived to tell the story—and what a story it is.

"It is one of the most interesting stories to come out of the war."
—Argus News Service, February 20, 1942

# PROLOGUE

---

The Great Depression had entered its seventh year. By 1935, over twenty percent of the American workforce was unemployed and poverty had hit all-time highs. Shanty towns and soup lines populated every major city despite President Roosevelt's New Deal. Gloom and hopelessness pervaded as citizens lost confidence in the United States. To add to the misery, baseball legend Babe Ruth retired in June, and America's beloved humorist Will Rogers was killed in a plane crash in August. People needed heroes. They needed a rebirth of American prestige. On Friday, November 22, 1935, arising from the sea to the clouds of heaven, a Pan American Airways seaplane would deliver both.

===

More than 100,000 people braved the cold San Francisco Bay winds to witness the historic event that November along a shoreline that stretched from Oakland to the east and the Embarcadero, North Beach, and Presidio to the west. Warmed by their Sunday-best coats, hats, and scarves, along with the swelling suspense that surged through their veins, the onlookers bristled with excitement as a band played "The Star-Spangled Banner" and fireworks exploded over the bay where an old masted clipper ship floated symbolically at anchor. Following numerous speeches of dignitaries that droningly mimicked the ones spoken previously, a gigantic luxury seaplane—or, more precisely, a flying boat, like none ever seen before—called the *China Clipper* taxied into the bay and prepared for takeoff. Minutes later, to the crowd's delight, the four engines roared and propelled the flying boat ever faster along the bay, trailed by streams of water that sprayed high along each side of the plane's fuselage to create a marvelous wake of white foam. It was then, as if directed in some colossal chorus, that the thousands of onlookers erupted into wild cheers and applause, waving their hats, hands, and handkerchiefs, while the herculean flying boat broke free of the water's surface and gradually, yet majestically, sailed into the air. The crowd's jubilation advanced like a tsunami that resonated along the bay's cusp as the airplane "spread her silver wings against the setting sun" and embarked upon a long and hazardous voyage to the mysterious Orient. Only a handful of aviation pioneers in modified single-engine airplanes had ever made the intended voyage successfully—most had not—and never had a commercial airliner contemplated, much less attempted, the perilous journey until that day.

The intended route would span an astonishing 8,200 miles to Manila in the Philippines over a dangerous and isolated expanse of the Pacific Ocean—stretching across one-third of the Earth's circumference. Pan American Airways System—increasingly known as Pan Am—intended to complete the voyage in six and a half days, with stops at its newly constructed marine bases in Honolulu, Midway Atoll, Wake Island, and Guam, accomplishing in less than a week what had previously taken three weeks by ocean liner.

The headline in the *Times* of San Mateo captured the day's momentous event: "World Pauses to Watch Sailing of Clipper Ship on Historic Pacific Hop." Not to be outdone, the *San Francisco Examiner* reported that "suggestive of the experience of Flash Gordon, time and space will be annihilated today by the departure of the Pan-American Airways giant airliner . . . for Manila." In addition to newspaper headlines and radio broadcasts, the historic event would

*China Clipper* flying over unfinished Golden Gate Bridge. *Pan American Air Ways*, Supplement No. 2, November 22, 1935, 9; U. Miami PAA. SFO Museum, San Francisco (SFOM).

be captured on film. Universal Newsreel and Fox Movietone News had installed movie cameras inside Pan Am's flying boat and on a small biplane that escorted the big clipper out of the harbor. The black-and-white films would be projected on silver screens to captivated audiences around the world—a world that suddenly seemed much smaller.

Pan Am's first flight across the Pacific Ocean would not carry passengers. Instead, this was the inaugural flight of a regularly scheduled mail route from San Francisco to Manila. The lucrative airmail route would eventually be extended to Hong Kong and Singapore. The flying boat's first passenger flight to Manila would occur a year later when more than three thousand of the wealthiest would vie for only fifteen seats, with blue bloods, businessmen, and Hollywood celebrities vainly attempting to charter the entire plane.

Hailed as the Paul Bunyan of the sky that "rivals the vivid imagination of Jules Verne," the technological marvel that would accomplish this incredible feat had been conceived by Pan Am's CEO and founder, Juan Trippe, and his friend and Pan Am consultant, Charles Lindbergh. Constructed by the Glenn L. Martin Company (later part of Lockheed Martin), the M-130 flying boat was a large fixed-wing seaplane that took off and landed upon water using the belly of its large fuselage rather than separately attached floats or pontoons. Its name—*China Clipper*—had been selected by Juan Trippe, who as a young man had cultivated a fascination with the sea and the old clipper sailing ships. He bestowed the unique aircraft moniker "clipper" on all Pan Am planes and used naval terms for the crews like captain, first officer, navigator, and engineer.

For days afterward, hourly and daily reports of the *China Clipper*'s progress filled radio bulletins and newspaper headlines. Everyone wanted to know where the indomitable flying boat was and whether it would make it to Manila and return safely. Six and a half days later, the *China Clipper* landed successfully in Manila Bay to the cheers of thousands and delivered tens of thousands of pieces of mail, including a letter from President Franklin D. Roosevelt to the president of the Philippines, a feat of supreme dispatch. Following a two-day rest, the pilot and crew boarded the *China Clipper* once again and reversed course, island-hopping across the Pacific on their way back to California. They completed the long return flight without incident, landing in the bay at Alameda on December 6, 1935. The exhausted men had flown 123 hours and 12 minutes and traversed 16,420 miles of ocean in 14 days. It was an unparalleled achievement in world history at the time.

The auspicious voyage had also succeeded in making Pan Am a household name. The international airline whose "clippers" bore their names and the blue-and-white Pan Am logo on their fuselages became the unofficial standard-bearer of the United States around the world. Instantly, thousands of merchants exploited the name *China Clipper* and the seaplane's design for their products. Almost anything that could be sold displayed the clipper's name or image—from coloring books, children's toys, and board games to cereal, beer, and motor oil. Everyone and everything connected with Pan Am suddenly possessed superstar status. As one copilot remarked, "We never paid for a drink again."

Pan Am CEO Juan Trippe appeared on the cover of *Time* magazine twice, and Pan Am flying boats appeared on the cover of *Life* magazine twice. Not only did news and technological magazines cover Pan Am, but so did fashion and home magazines. There was even a Hollywood film, *China Clipper*, distributed in 1936 by Warner Brothers, starring Humphrey Bogart as the pilot, released to coincide with the clipper's inaugural passenger flight. Other films soon followed, with the clippers appearing anywhere from a major role as in *Charlie Chan at Treasure Island* to a single spoken line in *Casablanca*. The Pan Am board of directors and shareholders relished the attention showered on the airline. Clippers became part of not only American culture, but culture around the world. It seemed that everyone wanted to fly aboard Pan Am clippers, or, for those who could not afford the exorbitant fares, dreamed of doing so.

For the next six years, Pan Am purchased larger and more luxurious flying boats to travel across the Pacific. Besides Honolulu and Manila, Pan Am would fly to Macau, Hong Kong, and Singapore. Auckland, New Zealand, was added in 1940. The airline also completed regularly scheduled passenger flights across the Atlantic Ocean beginning in 1939. These routes were all in addition to those that for a decade had carried passengers and cargo to Alaska, Mexico, the Caribbean, and South and Central America. Borrowing from a Norwegian fairy tale popular at the time, Pan Am flew thousands of passengers and hundreds of thousands of pounds of mail across millions of miles "east of the sun and west of the moon." Its

passenger and mail routes covered an astonishing sixty-two countries and colonies around the world, during a period when competing US airlines never left the North American continent.

And at last, the Great Depression was nearing its end. There seemed
to be no bounds to what Pan Am and Americans could do. The sky
wasn't even the limit any longer. Then came December 7, 1941.

The Imperial Japanese Navy task force had sailed 3,500 miles eastward from Japan across a rough and treacherous North Pacific
Ocean. After twelve days and nights, the Japanese armada reached
their destination in total secrecy on the morning of Sunday, December 7, 1941. From a point 230 miles directly north of Oahu in the
Hawaiian Islands, at 6:00 a.m., 183 Japanese bombers and fighter
planes took off from the task force's aircraft carriers to the cheers
of "banzai (hurrah)!" The first wave of attackers sped toward their
target: the US Pacific Fleet moored in Pearl Harbor near Honolulu,
along with nearby US Army Air Forces bases. A second wave of 167
attack planes would follow not far behind.

At 7:49 a.m., still undetected as enemy aircraft, the massive formation of Japanese planes passed over Waimea Bay on the northern tip of Oahu, zigzagging between mountains and roaring over
the heads of laborers toiling in pineapple fields. The formations
quickly split to follow their assigned routes that would lead them
to US airfields and to Pearl Harbor. During the final minutes, crew
members checked their machine guns and bombsights. Some would
be releasing torpedoes, others dropping high-altitude bombs, while
others would dive at their targets and release their bombs at close
range. Just as the Japanese fighters and bombers neared their targets,
Cmdr. Mitsuo Fuchida, who was in command of all the attacking
planes, shouted the coded signal over the radio that indicated complete surprise had been achieved: "Tora! Tora! Tora!"

Of the seventy-five thousand soldiers, sailors, and Marines stationed at Pearl Harbor, Sunday morning found many aboard their ships nursing hangovers from Saturday night's liberty. Of those awake, some prepared for Sunday worship aboard their ships, while other young men planned to meet girls on Waikiki Beach. Then suddenly from the sky without warning, just as the ships' bugles commenced sounding eight o'clock Colors, Japanese warplanes led by Cmdr. Fuchida commenced their relentless and deadly attacks. "Like a hurricane out of nowhere, my torpedo planes, dive bombers, and fighters struck suddenly with indescribable fury," Fuchida recalled.

Though Pearl Harbor was the top prize of the Japanese air and naval assault, the Empire of Japan executed a coordinated attack that December 7 (December 8 across the International Date Line) against other specified targets in the Pacific: Midway Atoll, Wake Island, Guam, the Philippines, Singapore, Hong Kong, Malaya (later to become part of the new nation of Malaysia), Borneo, and Thailand, many of which housed Pan Am marine bases for its transpacific clippers.

Three Pan Am luxury flying boats, with their affluent and influential passengers aboard, cruised across the Pacific sky that morning, and a fourth prepared to do so, all unaware of the attacks being orchestrated by the Empire of Japan that would thrust the United States into another world war:

The *Philippine Clipper* had just departed Wake Island for Singapore.
The *Pacific Clipper* had taken off from Honolulu on its way to New Zealand.
The *Anzac Clipper* had left San Francisco and was preparing to land at Honolulu.
The *Hong Kong Clipper* was nearing takeoff from Hong Kong for Manila.

Much of the US Pacific Fleet would soon be ablaze and sinking at Pearl Harbor, while rows of mangled and burning US fighter planes and bombers would be strewn across the ground, never having had the chance to take off. Within hours, defenses on other American, British, and Dutch islands would be fully engaged in a futile effort to repel the Japanese onslaught. Though few US military planes were available to take off and join the fight, any US plane in the region would be shot down by the Japanese without hesitation—including Pan Am's luxury flying boats caught in the first day of war in the Pacific. With US military assistance out of the question, Pan Am crews and their frightened passengers had no choice but to survive the best they could, if they could.

This is their story. It begins two days before Thanksgiving, on November 25, 1941.

# STRANDED
## IN THE SKY

## CHAPTER 1

# DESTINATION HONOLULU

The Embarcadero and Market Street were bustling at noon on Tuesday, November 25, 1941. It was lunchtime for San Franciscans and time for many of the locals and tourists to visit the brimming shops and cafes before withdrawing into their homes for a long Thanksgiving weekend. With Christmas only four weeks away, patrons and idlers alike braved the wind and cold to fill the festively decorated sidewalks and get a jump on shoppers who'd dawdle till December.

Behind them rose the Port of San Francisco's hallmark 245-foot clock tower above the Ferry Building where ferries arrived and departed daily. Though commuter boats that once made nearly two hundred chock-full trips a day still steamed across the bay to Alameda and Oakland, they were boarded less frequently, and their routes to Sausalito and Vallejo had closed entirely. The magnificent Golden Gate and San Francisco–Oakland Bay Bridges now supported most of the commuter traffic by automobile and train. Many called it progress; others cried out for the old ferryboats of the past whose sputtering wakes had cast a charm along the coastline of eastern San Francisco.

Progress had also spawned Treasure Island, which now occupied a portion of San Francisco Bay that for centuries had been but treacherous shallow water. Though not the secret island of buried treasure described in Robert Louis Stevenson's 1883 adventure novel, it was named for the tale scribed by the famous writer who'd

Golden Gate International Exposition at Treasure Island with new Pan Am terminal and clipper in Clipper Cove. SFOM.

lived in San Francisco sixty years earlier. The 385-acre flat island had been forged from tons of boulders and filled with sand and silt dredged from the bay in time for the Golden Gate International Exposition, which had opened two years earlier in 1939. Aside from crooner Bing Crosby singing to a crowd of sixty thousand, Pan American Airways had been by far the paramount attraction at the two-year world's fair.

Earlier that same morning, in the bay off the shore of that tiny man-made landmass, tourists and locals with time on their hands staked claims to seats in the grandstand at Pan Am's new terminus. Reporters, hoping for a photograph and an interview of a celebrity, like Fred Astaire or Greta Garbo, jockeyed for enviable positions at the doorways. Some toted large cameras strapped to their shoulders or smaller box cameras, while others carried pads and pencils. The raucous crowd proved that a takeoff of a Pan Am clipper was still an event anywhere, especially at Treasure Island, despite the dank darkness of predawn. For there, in tranquil water dubbed Clipper Cove, rested the Jumbo of all airplanes—Pan Am's *Pacific Clipper*, moored and waiting with its gangway secured for a 7:15 a.m. departure to Honolulu within the exotic Hawaiian Islands.

Named after the vast ocean over which it flew and landed, the *Pacific Clipper* was one of the newest of Pan Am's whopping Boeings, a Model B-314A flying boat, having made its maiden flight over the Pacific only six months before. It was unquestionably the leviathan of the sky. "[Like all the big Boeings] it is an elegant operation, a kind of combination airplane, cruise ship, hotel and restaurant . . . a great tradition of Pullman service carried to the airborne ultimate, a wonderful bird—at home in the air or on the water."

Sightseers maintained a steady eye on the "wonderful bird" as they eagerly waited in darkness amid a stiff bay wind. The weather was fair and would reach into the sixties later in the day, but chilly darkness had culled many of those who would otherwise have attended the morning's goings-on.

Most preferred to witness takeoffs in the late afternoon, as was customary for Pan Am clippers departing Treasure Island for Honolulu. On those flights, passengers slept in berths as the clippers flew overnight and made a morning landing. That's because despite having floodlights lining the wings, Pan Am typically scheduled its clippers to land during daylight to avoid boats and other obstructions that might lurk in the water. With foul weather grounding the

Frank "Mac" McKenzie. National Library of New Zealand.

*Pacific Clipper* and other clippers the day before, however, Pan Am's flight schedulers called for a takeoff at the crack of dawn to ease the congestion. The unusual occurrence would be the first daylight flight from the West Coast to Honolulu landing after nightfall. And so, the observers sat in the cold and darkness and waited for takeoff.

The crew and passengers also waited, albeit within a warm, Art Moderne–style terminal building topped with a glass control tower and two adjacent gigantic hangars. Among those waiting was a modestly tall, thin man in a starched white shirt and beige sport coat holding a lit cigarette in one hand and a telephone receiver in the other. He had just dialed his wife's sister in Alameda, with whom he'd dropped his golden-haired eleven-year-old daughter, Doreen, the night before. He wanted to say goodbye before his little girl went to school and before he departed on the *Pacific Clipper*. He told his daughter Doreen, who didn't cry anymore when her daddy left on long trips, to be a good girl and mind her elders and to have the very best Thanksgiving. Then following a difficult goodbye for both father and only child, he hung up the complimentary telephone in the Pan Am lounge and picked up his fedora.

Frank McKenzie, often called Mac by his familiars, was a forty-three-year-old engineer, formerly with Curtiss-Wright in Alameda. Mac had proven to be exceedingly capable at Pan Am and at present carried the haughty official title Construction Superintendent for the Pacific Division, though most often he was simply called the chief engineer. Mac had overseen the construction and maintenance of Pan Am's marine facilities in the Pacific since 1935. He now found himself enjoined to journey to Manila in the Philippines and oversee work on the clipper marine base at Cañacao Bay in Cavite Harbor. The typically unflappable engineer was itching to get underway as he sat silently enjoying the morning newspaper shrouded by smoke budding from draws on his cigarettes. He had been requisitioned just two days before Thanksgiving, a not altogether unusual occurrence, but this year's holidays were most important to him for reasons that he shared with only those closest to him. Mac's goal, no, his utmost desire, was to complete his work in Manila as quickly as his skills would allow and return to Alameda. He had promised Doreen that he'd be back in time for Christmas.

Mac moved one step nearer to that goal when at last the moment had arrived for the crew to board the clipper. The crew always boarded before the passengers. A high-pitched brass bell rang out a single time, reminiscent of one aboard a naval vessel, to signal the crew that it was time to board. It was the "first bell."

"Members of the crew of the *Pacific Clipper* will please go aboard," directed a voice over the loudspeaker inside the terminal offices and lounge.

The clipper's captain and his first officer stepped out of the terminal ahead of nine other crew members as they marched in pairs, with the assistant steward being the odd man bringing up the rear. Those who lined the terminal's departure area and the grandstand

Black Cadillac Fleetwood stretch limousines with drivers. Pan American Airways, *New Horizons*, Vol. 8, No. 6, June 1937, 20; U. Miami PAA.

appreciated the spectacle displayed by the flight crew—adorned in their crisp naval officer–styled uniforms with gold-striped cuffs and white-peaked caps, carrying briefcases as they walked in choreographed lockstep looking straight ahead, military style. One steward on a number of Pan Am clipper flights recalled that when someone was not walking in unison with the others, "You'd holler, 'You're out of step!'"

Like an enormous twenty-two-legged caterpillar steadily vanishing through a side hatch, the flight crew entered the flying boat and manned their stations. Each crew member commenced performing all-important preflight checks and engine tests as the passengers continued to relax and smoke in the terminal's lounge.

With the exception of military men and Pan Am employees like

Mac, most passengers on Pan Am clipper flights were aristocrats or influential—usually both—and were treated as such. Some had arrived at the Pan Am terminal on Treasure Island that morning by black Cadillac Fleetwood stretch limousines that had collected them from their hotels. Pan Am employees often said, "There's only one class of passenger on clipper flights—first class." It was no wonder. The price of a single round-trip ticket to the Orient or the Antipodes, a ticket which usually unfolded from a passenger's nose to his toes, approached $2,000 (that's worth an astounding $40,000 today). The median home value in 1941 was around $3,000.

"You would be amazed if you could see the typical Clipper passengers," construction supervisor Harry Olson would write his wife aboard a Pan Am clipper days later. "A very . . . exotic lot. Every nationality in the world."

There were Hollywood film stars such as Errol Flynn, Henry Fonda, Desi Arnaz and Lucille Ball, Douglas Fairbanks Jr., Fay Wray, Ingrid Bergman, and Orson Welles. Famous playwrights and authors like George Bernard Shaw, H. G. Wells, and Ernest Hemingway also boarded, and there were Alexander Graham Bell, world boxing champion Jack Dempsey, and the US president's son Jimmy Roosevelt.

In addition to those famous for appearing on celluloid film or in sensational print, a continual stream of foreign ambassadors and envoys such as Russian ambassador Maxim Litvinov and Japanese diplomat Saburō Kurusu boarded Pan Am's clippers, preferring their comfort and speed at the financial expense of their governments. Kurusu had flown to the US onboard the *Hong Kong*, *China*, and *California Clippers* two weeks earlier to attend several meetings in Washington, DC, in the hope of alleviating Japan-US trade and expansionist tensions. Even President Franklin Roosevelt would board a Pan Am clipper in January 1943 to meet British Prime Minister Winston Churchill at the Casablanca Conference in North Africa. It would be the first time a US president made a transoceanic flight. The president would celebrate his 61st birthday while on board.

"The Clippers have been the best international club in the world," *Life* magazine wrote. "Dues are high but there is excellent conversation in four languages."

Though all passengers were considered first class, a select few received the designation "VIP" and were granted even greater consideration. The *Pacific Clipper* would carry its share of VIPs on the continuation of its scheduled flight to Auckland, which would soon connect at Honolulu. Like always, the big Boeing carried top military brass—or "gold braids," as they were called—who always expected heightened veneration. Then there was Sir John Percival Madsen, who was taking the clipper home to Sydney, Australia, after having been tapped on the shoulder with a sword by King George VI at Buckingham Palace in honor of his work in radiophysics. The newly dubbed knight had been absent from home since May. Muriel Heagney also was returning to Sydney. Ahead of her time, she'd flown to New York City where she attended the International Labor Organization convention. She was a distinguished activist for women's rights, particularly the right to equal pay. Alice Jackson also would be aboard. She was the editor of *Australia Women's Weekly*, a magazine of national circulation within the Land Down Under, who was returning to Australia after months in London, having had an audience with Queen Elizabeth (the Queen Mother) and having interviewed the Duchess of Kent. Then there was the Pan Am mainstay that included corporate executives representing their oil, mining, banking, and manufacturing interests, who may have considered themselves VIPs but were deemed merely first class by Pan Am. Of late, however, more and more passengers were gold braids, owing to the increasing concern over the Empire of Japan's military buildup in the Pacific.

At seven o'clock that morning, with the crew's checks complete and the four massive engines' shining propellers spinning slowly, a bell rang out twice, followed by the command over the loudspeaker: "Passengers for the *Pacific Clipper* will please go aboard."

Dressed in their finest, as most anyone going anywhere did

during that era, the passengers strode leisurely along a concrete path flanked by manicured shrubs to the shimmering *Pacific Clipper* that floated patiently in the cove. It was turning into a marvelous morning. Remnants of a feathery gray fog mixed with the chilled scent of salty bay water were gradually giving way to the warmth of dawn's sunshine. A near equivalence of men and women formed the line of passengers along the windswept pathway. Mac, though anxious to board, lingered near the rear out of deference to the paying passengers. He tended to look down as he leisurely stepped forward, the whole extravagance of boarding having become fairly routine to him. He'd seen it all a hundred times.

Men in overcoats held their hats while women grasped their fluttering dresses near the knee to prevent an embarrassing incident caused by the propellers' whirling gusts. More than one halted their stroll for only a moment to adjust their eyeglasses or to turn and take in the uniquely futuristic experience. Most waved at folks who were there to see them off. A few of the ladies blew kisses in fun as men waved their hats overhead. A feeling of celebritydom may have overcome a few as the hordes of spectators waved and shouted enthusiastically from the grandstand beneath the lights, snapping photos of everything in their camera lens's angle of view. The commotion loosely resembled the hullabaloo of a film's premiere in Hollywood, devoid of the red carpet. "A Clipper departure [to Hawaii] is a gay event," read a Pan Am article, "with Hawaiian music flooding the terminal, which is thronged with tourists, business people, service personnel and friends and relatives who have come to wish them bon voyage."

A snappily uniformed purser wearing white gloves directed passengers to step across a gangway connected to the starboard-side stabilizer that rested atop the water (called a sponson) in order to enter the main hatch of the airplane. Two stewards waited there, each smartly dressed in a white shirt and vest, black pants and tie, and a white jacket trimmed with a black collar, cuffs, and buttons. Demonstrating a warm smile and a professional voice, the stewards

Passengers boarding across a sponson onto a clipper. Cradle of Aviation Museum, Garden City, New York. U. Miami PAA.

greeted each passenger and assisted them inside the seaplane as the other travelers awaited their turns.

The stewards strategically seated everyone inside the plane to provide the proper ballast. The *Pacific Clipper* could carry up to seventy-four passengers, or, if flying overnight, thirty-six passengers who could sleep in berths. It could have carried more but was constricted by a maximum takeoff weight of 82,500 pounds, consisting mostly of precious fuel necessary to reach Hawaii, which at a distance of 2,403 miles was the longest stretch in the challenging Pacific overseas route. If burdened beyond its weight limit, the innovative flying boat would become nothing more than a motorboat, cruising on the bay, unable to separate itself from the water's surface. So weight was carefully measured and double-checked. Only seventy-seven pounds of luggage per passenger, with a substantial charge for each extra pound, were permitted to be stowed in the baggage compartment above the lounge and behind the crew's quarters. No heavy baggage was permitted in the cabins: only hats, coats, briefcases, haversacks, vanity cases, and small packages could be taken onboard. To determine the exact takeoff weight, a steward weighed everything and everybody inside the terminal before boarding. Those unhappy with their body's density, whether it be too slight or too plentiful, were granted no courtesy, except to be weighed out of view of the others.

Once inside the magnificent metallic fusion of bird and fish, some women gently unpinned and surrendered their hats to a steward, who stowed them in boxes near the rear of the plane. Some men likewise handed their fedoras over. Mac, who'd been waiting until everyone else boarded, tossed his cigarette to the ground and stepped inside. The stewards as well as the crew knew Mac; some better than others. He regularly traversed the Pacific and was a fixture at all Pan Am marine bases along the routes to the Orient and the Antipodes, the name given to countries in the Southern Hemisphere by those in the Northern. For those who hadn't seen Mac in the terminal, they extended their usual warm greetings with firm handshakes. Some welcomed him aboard with a little more consideration than their usual virile salutations, knowing that Mac had recently lost his wife. Still, the Scottish-born engineer spouted a large smile below his pencil moustache and returned the greetings with a hearty Celtic accent.

The magnificence of Pan Am's big flying boats like the *Pacific Clipper* had understandably waned in Mac's eyes after logging thousands of hours in the air, but for the other passengers it was a luxurious and technological sight like no other. The awe of those escorted inside the flying palace for the first time may have been audible as their heads swiveled back and forth like oscillating fans. "A Clipper had a personality of its own; it had a certain style," read one

A couple in the deluxe compartment of a Boeing B-314. *Pan American Air Ways,*
Vol. 10, No. 1, March 1939, 13; U. Miami PAA.

magazine. "Her interior was like that of no other airplane," bow-tied
journalist H. R. "Bud" Ekins wrote.

And for good reason. A famous New York theatrical designer,
Norman Bel Geddes, had designed the interior of the Boeing flying boats and employed his own Streamline Moderne Art Deco
throughout. Pan Am assigned Bel Geddes the task of keeping weight
to a minimum in his design, which meant applying novel aluminum

alloys and plastics and even synthetic polymers for furniture, berths, walls, and carpet. Glass was no longer used in the sixty-five windows, but lightweight plastic. Accordion-pleated shades on rollers covered each plastic window. Cushions were made of Australian horsehair and latex. The cabins featured straight walls and a flat ceiling rather than simply following the curvature of the fuselage. Art Deco–style sconces lined the walls that were laced with zippered soundproof and fireproof upholstery overlaid with a world atlas design. Glistening stars adorned each lounge chair, and black walnut lined the doors of the "lady's powder room" and the "gentleman's retiring room." Three additional lavatories with hot and cold running water were positioned about the aircraft. A water fountain was available at both the front and rear of the plane. For those wanting something stronger to drink, they could sit at a bar and order cocktails or sodas. And there was the grand dining room with five black walnut tables on which the finest china, glassware, and silver services would be placed to await the most exquisite meals ever served in the air. "Setting the dining room was first class," Pan Am steward Sam Toarmina recalled. "The tablecloths and napkins were of elegant linen. Tasteful sterling silverware and spotless glasses complemented the bone china."

The wealthy often desired that their clipper flight include not only opulence, but privacy. To achieve that wish, more than one of the seven luxurious passenger cabins could be purchased to create a grand private stateroom, which meant that instead of paying a fare of $2,000 for a single seat, the passenger might pay $10,000 or more for the entire cabin (nearly $200,000 today). If that wasn't adequate, aft lay a "deluxe compartment" used by the ultimate flyer who wanted privacy with the utmost luxury, often dubbed the Bridal Suite, complete with a pull-out three-seat davenport; a loveseat; black walnut side and coffee tables; writing and dressing tables covered in leather with stools, lights, and a mirror; a washbasin concealed beneath a beige Micarta tabletop; and a wardrobe

Passengers in the deluxe compartment. *Pan American Air Ways, Supplement* "The Yankee Clippers Sail Again," March 1939, 16; U. Miami PAA.

closet with hangers, all at a price commensurate with the superior accommodations, of course.

Now properly seated within such lavish and state-of-the-art surroundings, the time had arrived for the passengers to cease their admiration of the plane's interior long enough to prepare for takeoff. It was 7:15 a.m., and the sun had streaked the sky with swaths of orange, purple, and yellow, clearly revealing the water's colorful surface to the pilots. The stewards made certain that loose articles were stowed away and safety belts checked before handing out chewing gum and cotton balls to ease the impending pain of altitude change. With the steward's call up to the bridge that all was secure, the clipper's captain announced over the intercom: "The cabin is secure and we're ready for takeoff."

The captain directed the first engineer, seated behind him, to increase engine speed. On command, the plane's propellers spun faster, pulling the plane away from shore. Passengers who'd not traveled by clipper often felt a bit unnerved by the rumbling of the engines that rattled their cabins as the seaplane sailed slowly along the bay's surface. The captain, who employed skills on the water much different from those in the air, made a tight half turn right and again left to check the rudder. The flying boat then cruised along the bay and slowed again, which caused its nose to dip deeper into the water. The captain turned the plane once more. The clipper was at the head of its lane; it was time for takeoff.

"Full power!" called out the captain to his engineer. He then pulled hard on the throttles, and the seaplane's four "Twin Cyclone" engines thundered. Passengers stiffened and gripped anything that was near. Some likely muttered a short prayer as the speed

A Boeing B-314 during takeoff. Pan American World Airways, *Clipper*, Vol. 14, No. 7, July 1955, 1; U. Miami PAA; Cradle of Aviation Museum, Garden City, New York.

intensified, propelling the plane along the bay faster and faster, as water sprayed past their windows and pounded the underbelly of the plane. Others grinned big-eyed with excitement. Mac, on the other hand, likely chewed his gum and continued reading, perhaps glancing out at the view, though just as likely not. In barely half a minute, the nose section of the plane raised up "on the step," where the plane comfortably skimmed along the surface of the water. Then seconds later, without warning, the flying boat lifted majestically from the salt water into the velvety air, leaving some stomachs behind on the bay's surface. For those who'd never been in Pan Am's luxury planes before, and even for those who had, the sensation was exhilarating.

Stomach butterflies soon gave way to wonder as the grandiose view gradually revealed itself below them—the Bay Bridge, Coit Tower, Fisherman's Wharf, Golden Gate Bridge. "For a while everyone plasters his nose to the windows to see below the beautiful delicate bridges of San Francisco and that sturdy rock—that modern *Château d'If* Alcatraz . . . where Al Capone was," wrote Clare Boothe Luce, author, journalist, and wife of Henry Luce, the publisher of *Time*, *Life*, and *Fortune* magazines. With each foot of altitude, the sights grew fainter. "Far behind us was a packed mass of buildings in a haze—a white and lovely city, San Francisco, at the nation's gate. She was fading fast," Dorothy Kaucher, who'd flown on the *Hawaii* and *China Clippers*, wrote.

With everyone now resting in their seats chewing their gum and yawning wide while the plane continued its steady climb beyond the clouds, the stewards helped some passengers adjust their seats and passed out pillows. The plane ride was remarkably relaxing. "Most of the time your flight will be as smooth as riding in your family car," boasted a Pan Am clipper brochure. "As roomy as the [zeppelin] *Hindenburg* and as steady as a rock," wrote journalist Bud Ekins.

Half an hour later, with gum and cotton balls removed and collected and the smell of eggs, bacon, and sausage filling the tropospheric air inside the unpressurized cabin compartments, the passengers smiled with delight as a steward announced: "Breakfast is served."

## CHAPTER 2

# TROUBLE BREWING

Months earlier, in January 1941, Admiral Isoroku Yamamoto, commander in chief of Japan's Combined Fleet, had formulated a comprehensive and risky attack plan against the US Pacific Fleet in Pearl Harbor, along with simultaneous attacks against American, British, and Dutch interests throughout the Pacific. To that end, the Japanese Imperial Navy's six aircraft carriers—*Akagi*, *Kaga*, *Sōryū*, *Hiryū*, *Shōkaku*, and *Zuikaku*—had lifted anchor and set sail from Hitokappu Bay (now Kasatka Bay) in the Kuril Islands, Japan, at 6:00 a.m. on November 25, 1941, Hawaiian time, after a kickoff party aboard the *Akagi*.

Incredibly, US Naval Intelligence had lost track of the carriers that had been anchored in Japanese waters. "When carriers are not heard from . . . they are likely in port," reported Adm. Kimmel's chief intelligence officer, Lt. Cmdr. Edwin Layton, in Hawaii. The only carriers on the move, according to US Naval Intelligence, were the ones heading toward Southeast Asia. This prompted American and British military leaders to erroneously believe that an attack solely on the Malay Peninsula and Thailand or perhaps the Philippines was imminent. In response, the Americans and British steadfastly abided by entrenched notions of fair play and simply waited for Japan to fire the opening salvo. Only then would the US Navy move to halt the looming Japanese offensive.

As the American and British military waited, uninformed and confident, the largest flotilla ever assembled in modern warfare to that date was closing in on the Hawaiian Islands. The massive Japanese attack force that stretched for miles in the North Pacific consisted of thirty-two surface vessels. At the attack group's core were the six aircraft carriers loaded with 420 torpedo planes, bombers, and fighter aircraft and countless torpedoes and armor-piercing bombs. Two battleships, four cruisers, eleven destroyers, and nine oil tankers, along with thirty-five submarines, supported the carriers. Aboard these vessels were hundreds of young men who worshipped their emperor and would proudly die for him and the Empire of Japan. All were speeding across the Pacific—undetected.

⸻

Saburō Kurusu and Japan's ambassador to the United States, Adm. Kichisaburō Nomura, sat in the Japanese embassy in Washington, DC, a Neo-Georgian-style house built ten years earlier. Looking out a grand rear window upon an exotic tea house surrounded by landscaped gardens and the whisper of rippling water, the gregarious Kurusu considered the challenging task to which he'd been appointed "special envoy" by Prime Minister Hideki Tōjō in Tokyo. As he lolled within the tranquil yet walled and secure compound in the US capital, he realized that Tōjō was poised for a fight and this was likely the last chance for peace with the United States. "I realize the difficulty of my task," Kurusu said upon first arriving in the US, "but I still have a fighting chance to make a success of my mission."

Small-statured with round glasses and a graying moustache, special envoy Kurusu had flown halfway around the world to reach Washington, DC, much of it aboard Pan Am's *China Clipper*. Having been in Washington for the past two weeks, Kurusu and Japanese Ambassador Nomura had already met with US Secretary of State Cordell Hull. Nomura liked Hull and the feeling was mutual, though Hull cared little for Kurusu, who he believed was cheerily elusive. Nonetheless, Kurusu was a career professional and as honest as any diplomat. Surprisingly, he possessed a genuine affinity for the American people. He had lived all over the world, including Chicago, where he met his American wife of Japanese descent and where two of his three children had been born. He even used American slang regularly: for instance, telling a reporter that "I wish I could break through the line and score a touchdown," referring to reaching a peace agreement. It was because of his American ties and his lifelong work as a diplomat that he had been placed in charge of persuading President Franklin Roosevelt to accept Japan's peace terms.

Dressed in black overcoats and fedoras, Kurusu and Nomura had personally delivered those peace terms to Secretary of State Hull on November 20, just five days before the Japanese attack force set sail. The terms were short and simple . . . and irresoluble: the United States must cease military aid to the Republic of China, ignore Japan's military presence in French Indochina, and resume full trade relations with Japan, particularly the shipment of oil to the fuel-starved country.

Kurusu didn't realize it, but when he and the ambassador delivered the memorandum, Hull had already read Tokyo's peace terms the day before. The US Army and Navy intelligence offices had been intercepting coded diplomatic messages labeled "PURPLE" between Tokyo and Ambassador Nomura's embassy in Washington for several months as part of the US cryptanalysis project called "MAGIC." In fact, the United States decoded and read the intercepted diplomatic messages faster than the diplomats inside the Japanese embassy could. This capability only applied at that time to messages sent over diplomatic channels, not military ones. Once the PURPLE messages were decoded, they were passed along to a very select list of US officials, which included Secretary Hull. When Kurusu gained entrance into the secretary of state's office and handed him the conditions of peace, Hull read them with the appearance of great interest as if reading them for the first time, so as not to give away MAGIC's ability to decrypt and decode PURPLE messages.

Six days later, on November 26, the day before Thanksgiving in the United States, Nomura and Kurusu were summoned to the offices of Secretary Hull, where they met once again for just over an hour. Hull relayed President Roosevelt's stringent reply to Japan's November 20 peace terms: the United States would unfreeze Japanese funds in the US and resume trade with Japan, including delivering oil needed only for civilian use, *provided that* "the Government of Japan will withdraw all military, naval, air and police forces from China and Indochina . . . and will not support any government in China other than the National Government of the Republic of China." Despite his skills of obfuscation and amiable persuasion, a saddened Kurusu told Hull that he'd deliver the message, but said, "If this is the idea of the American government, I don't see how an agreement is possible. Tokyo will throw up its hands at this."

Though all men exited the meeting smiling for the press corps, they remained silent. It was no secret that peace negotiations had reached a stalemate.

Prime Minister Tōjō, who had doggedly rattled his saber while Kurusu worked to attain peace with the United States, immediately made his position obvious during a radio broadcast in Tokyo. "So long as the United States maintains an attitude of obstructing Japan's policy to establish a new East Asiatic order . . . we have to conclude that the United States lacks faith and sincerity in preserving the peace . . . and if anything breaks out, the United States must bear the whole responsibility."

President Roosevelt traveled to his Warm Springs, Georgia, getaway for a Thanksgiving respite as Secretary Hull and the rest of the American people commenced enjoying their long Thanksgiving holiday. As families gathered around their crowded dinner tables and gave words of thanks over delightful home-cooked feasts, none could have imagined that a massive Japanese attack force that would start a long and bloody war was already underway—one that would leave empty chairs and saddened hearts at the following year's tables.

## CHAPTER 3

# EAT, READ, AND DOZE

The *Pacific Clipper* cruised over open seas as the drone of its engines faded, masked by the rising echoes of voices and laughter from within. Many passengers had relocated to the festal lounge to savor a robust American-style breakfast, the aroma of which filled the opulent fuselage—coffee, tea, and freshly squeezed juices; assorted dry cereals, cold cuts, fruit, eggs, bacon and sausage; pastries, croissants, toast, and marmalade. While the passengers ate and chatted, sharing where they'd been and where they were going, the two stewards stood nearby like sentries at their posts, observing their airborne guests with unwavering smiles. Besides possessing expertise in first aid and managing food and passengers, stewards kept up with current events in case they were engaged in conversation while catering to the passengers' needs.

Except for the omnipresent stewards, the clipper's crew attempted to remain invisible to the passengers. They ate separately from them, sometimes grabbing a bite near the galley or in the crew's quarters above the passenger cabins, where they slept. The only exception was when the captain dined at the VIP table, much like the captain of a naval ship; a "PR chore" that most pilots would have preferred to skip. Some Pan Am employees like Mac favored associating more with members of the crew than with the passengers. Technically, Mac wasn't allowed to go up on the bridge, because it would have violated Pan Am's safety rules. Whether he sneaked up to the bridge

The "bridge" of a Boeing B-314 with pilot, copilot, navigator, radioman, and engineer. Pan American Airways, *New Horizons*, Vol. 13, No. 3, January 1943, 21; U. Miami PAA.

or not, no one would tell. The "bridge" was Pan Am's naval term for the cockpit or flight deck, which, like most planes, was at the nose of the Herculean flying boat; but, unlike others, it was a full level above the main passenger cabins. A metal spiral staircase at the front of the plane connected the two levels.

As passengers sipped coffee from their white-and-blue china cups bearing the Pan Am logo, some began to realize that they were now captive for the next several hours—if not days—with total strangers, sharing both the thrills and tedium that accompanied a long transpacific flight. "Presently you turn away from the window and begin

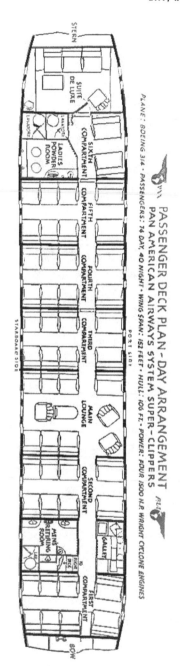

Floor diagram of the passenger area on a Boeing B-314's interior. The flight deck, crew quarters, and cargo compartments were on upper levels. U. Miami PAA.

to eye your fellow passengers with new interest and keen curiosity," Clare Boothe Luce had written for *Life* magazine the month before. The flight to Honolulu would take eighteen continuous hours. Even more: if a passenger connected in Honolulu to fly on to Singapore or Hong Kong, it could take six days, or 142 hours, in the air to cover 9,400 miles—all one way. They would have the pleasure of duplicating that marvelous-yet-wearing feat with different travelers on a return flight, though passengers typically waited to initiate that voyage after they'd enjoyed a month's tranquilizing repose in the Orient.

"Riding the Clipper is a tiresome business," construction supervisor Harry Olson wrote in a letter during one of his clipper flights from Wake Island to Honolulu. "We climb up to 10,000 feet and all we can see is clouds. When we can see the ocean below it has a hard metallic appearance, much the same as pictures you have seen of the moon. The motors drone along steadily until you are not conscious of them. They have a wonderful buffet lunch and everyone eats most of the time. Eat, read and doze. I am always glad when we come down."

Harry Olson was fairly accurate in his description, though perhaps a bit too dreary. Granted, there were few activities that a person could engage in while thousands of feet in the air, but many delighted in the recreational pursuits offered to pass the time. Besides whatever personal items the passengers carried aboard, Pan Am supplied popular books, newspapers, magazines, puzzles, and card and board games for all ages. Chess and the popular new game Monopoly were favorites during the lengthy flights, as were bridge and gin rummy played on Pan Am–logoed cards. Some passengers simply relished being aboard a Pan Am clipper, an adventure very few in the world experienced. Most people had never flown aboard any kind of airplane, large or small, let alone the most remarkable airship of all.

Seasoned business travelers like Mac had boarded the clipper prepared for a long flight. He carried books and magazines related to his major interests: aviation, fishing, and gardening. He also brought along a satchel full of Pan Am reports associated with his upcoming engineering task in Manila—various calculations, soil tests, meteorological history, tide aberrations, and blueprints. And there was the Girl Scout horseshoe-shaped charm that Doreen had given him to bring good luck during his voyages. Moreover, he had worked in a Scottish coal mine as a young man; a few hours on a luxury airliner to exotic locales certainly would not do him in.

Families that traveled usually shared a single cabin separated from the other passengers that allowed them to converse and play among themselves, though a single aisle passed through all of the cabins from stem to stern, excepting the "deluxe compartment" at the very rear of the plane. Inevitably, especially after a drink or two, a handful of passengers ventured out and commenced striking up conversations, particularly in the lounge. Sometimes passengers trolled the aisle and cabins like train conductors to seek out partners for bridge or board games or simply for conversation.

Other passengers passed the time sipping tea or cocktails and smoking cigarettes in the lounge. The special cocktail of the flight was the Clipper Cocktail, a concoction of rum, vermouth, and grenadine poured over ice. If a VIP was known to have a favorite drink, the stewards made certain that it or its ingredients were on board. The same went for cigars and cigarettes.

And then there was more food. Pan Am's famous lunch buffet was served from noon till three o'clock. One or both stewards manned the buffet table, where they carved slices of warm prime roast beef and Virginia ham, or they heated butter for freshly steamed Maine lobster. They also cut and served fresh pies and other delicious creations. The buffet was so popular among the passengers that they often returned to nibble like goldfish in their bowl until the dratted three o'clock hour arrived. Even then, many last-minute patrons carried portions back to their cabins to enjoy after the buffet was wheeled away.

The delicious breakfasts, lunches, dinners, and snacks didn't magically materialize thousands of feet in the air. Like everything at

Stewards manning the three-hour buffet. U. Miami PAA.

Pan Am, the preparation of passengers' meals was regimented and methodical. Meals were planned days in advance and took hours to prepare. The menus changed for each flight and for holiday flights, like Christmas, and carried special culinary delights.

The tasks of clipper stewards much resembled those onboard luxury trains and ocean liners, except that Pan Am required the absolute best for everyone. Shipments of fresh food and produce, as well as hard-to-find canned goods, constantly arrived at Pan Am bases by the ton from the US mainland, Honolulu, Guam, and elsewhere to keep up with passengers' appetites. Stewards served more than 35,000 meals in 1941 aboard Pan Am seaplanes, and that was only for those headed to the Orient. Another 250,000 meals were served in Pan Am hotels at Midway, Wake Island, and Guam alone.

Passengers in main dining room. Pan American World Airways, "The First 50 Years of Pan Am," 1977, 10. U. Miami PAA.

What's more, many stewards had been trained as chefs by New York City's Waldorf-Astoria Hotel to satisfy the well-defined palates of the wealthy Pan Am traveler. They learned to prepare a delicious four-course dinner consisting of sixteen different items, from appetizers to dessert.

"The food on the Clippers is grand," wrote syndicated columnist and war correspondent Ernie Pyle. "Absolutely fantastic," wrote another.

And it wasn't just the food that was superlative. The choice of beverages—soda, tea, beer, liquor, and champagne—seemed limitless. The wine selection alone appeared as if a sommelier had been secreted aboard with bottles of vintage wine from the cellar of William Randolph Hearst. "It was the last word in luxury for its time," Pan Am steward John Salmini recalled.

Dinner for the evening of November 25, 1941, aboard the *Pacific Clipper* would exemplify such culinary delights. "Like dinner at the Waldorf," a newspaper wrote, not knowing that the stewards had been trained there. It opened with celery hearts, ripe green olives, and consommé. The entrée consisted of individual baked and stuffed squab chicken, roasted Parisian potatoes, and fresh peas, along with a chef's green salad with French dressing and freshly baked French rolls. To top off the meal, pecan rolls, salted nuts, fresh fruit, assorted cheeses, and after-dinner mints were gobbled up with the utmost satisfaction.

As everyone finished their meal, perhaps with an after-dinner port, they partook of one of the most satisfying pleasures of the time—a relaxing draw on a cigarette. Even so, the use of tobacco was restricted. Boeing's placement of fuel tanks in the wings and sponsons didn't bode well for smoking throughout the aircraft. For that reason, smoking was permitted exclusively in the lounge where stewards kept the ashtrays clean, except during takeoffs and landings when smoking was prohibited altogether. Despite the fact that the plane was well-ventilated, cigars and pipes were discouraged for the comfort of the other passengers, particularly if someone registered a complaint due to its unpleasant effect on that passenger's emphysema, tuberculosis, or perfume.

Millions of cigarettes were smoked on Pan Am planes and at its hotels in 1941. Tins containing 1.5 million cigarettes, like Old Gold, Chesterfield, Lucky Strike, and Camel, not to mention cigars, were delivered that year solely to the Pan American Airways hotels at Midway, Wake Island, and Guam, only three of the hotels in the vast network of lodgings in the Pan American Airways System worldwide.

Mac was certainly one who enjoyed his scotch and Chesterfields. And being from Scotland, he had no objection to the fancy meals and refined service, though he frequently teased the stewards that no menu was complete without haggis (Scotland's national dish). And

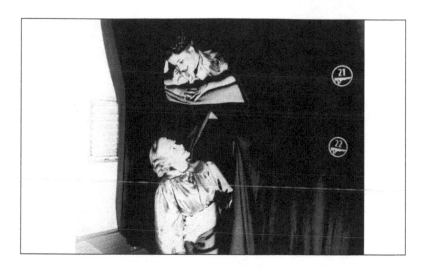

Passengers in their sleeping berths. U. Miami PAA.

he was not averse to a nap . . . or two, especially with the evening growing late.

As the outside darkness crept inside and enveloped the interior of the flying boat and its full-bellied passengers, the dimly lit sconces along the walls of the lengthy fuselage gently illuminated the cabins as passengers reposed. Because the clipper's captain expected to land in Honolulu around 9:00 p.m., the stewards did not set up sleeping berths. Normally, the clipper would have taken off from Treasure Island around 4:00 p.m. and landed in Honolulu the next morning, allowing passengers to experience the berths, but not on this flight. An overnight flight was actually enjoyable because the berths were among the nicest commercial berths on the ground, in the air, or on the sea. Each berth, enclosed in navy-colored curtains pulled and zipped tight, had its own window, air vent, reading light, call button, and hangers. And of course, there was more food—the midnight supper—sandwiches, cold cuts, and salads, tea, sodas, milk, and hot chocolate for those who remained awake.

Like most of the others, Mac caught his last glimpse of the horizon ablaze with color before the sun sank into the ocean. Another three hours and he'd be in Honolulu. Mac may have found himself gazing without thought, even though he carried a great deal on his mind. Twenty years of memories flashed across that mind—his wife, Hazle, whom he lamented more than he could bear, especially with the holidays upon him, despite the fact that she was Irish, a good-natured quip he'd cast her way sometimes just to stir her endearing laugh. And he missed his eleven-year-old daughter, Doreen, a cute little girl and his favorite Girl Scout, and she missed him too. He'd never felt so far away from her. It would be almost a month before he'd return home, hopefully in time for Christmas. He'd promised little Doreen that he'd make it this year, and he meant it. He had planned his job in Manila meticulously to ensure that he'd be back home in plenty of time, absent some *force majeure*, like an act of God—or an emperor.

## CHAPTER 4

# PARADISE OF THE PACIFIC

A single steady blast from a siren atop Aloha Tower alerted Honolulu that the *Pacific Clipper* was approaching from the US mainland. Reminiscent of the old farm bell calling everyone in for supper with its ring, the siren conjured merchants anxious to receive their deliveries, alerting the postmaster and his aides to collect thousands of pounds of mailbags from the incoming clipper. Despite the lateness of the nine o'clock evening hour, hotel buses and limousines also hurried to pick up their guests, and family and friends rushed to greet disembarking passengers. Sightseers keen on witnessing a nighttime landing at sea also raced others to the harbor.

The approaching *Pacific Clipper* circled the Middle Loch of Pearl Harbor, guided from below by battery-powered green and white bulbs on poles on top of buoys that lighted the flying boat's landing path within the loch. Despite the fact that the Boeing was equipped with bright landing lights, night landings on water were fraught with hazards and were to be avoided when possible. Sandbars, coral, and obstructions floating on or barely below the surface, as well as errant surface vessels, could damage or even destroy a flying boat and kill all those onboard. For that reason, in advance of a clipper landing, whether day or night, Panair boats (owned by Pan Am) dragged the landing area, searching for anything in the water and instructing all boats to leave the area.

A ceremony on the dock at Pearl City. Hawaii State Archives.

Following a gradual approach funneled by the green and white lights on buoys, the captain steered the clipper to a silky smooth landing, although the clipper's steel-reinforced belly did shudder a bit on contact with the water's rippled surface. Passengers were startled with delight as they watched the warm water spray past their windows, yet pleased to see the water's volume decreasing as the plane reduced speed. Within seconds, the captain eased up on the yoke, dropping the nose of the mighty seaplane and slowing the plane to a peaceful drift. The clipper then turned and ferried its weary occupants toward Pan Am's tropical marine port.

Anxious to reach the dock after eighteen hours in the air, the travelers could see the whitewashed pier and a crowd of spectators drawing nearer. Instead of an unsightly structure of steel and concrete like those of the US Navy across the loch, Pan Am's docking area melded into the Pacific island's tropical setting. Exotic flora, palm trees, white sand, and stylish buildings with palm-frond roofs staffed by tanned men in crisp white coveralls bearing blue Pan Am insignias awaited the clipper's arrival. Built on an outcropping of the Pearl City Peninsula on the Hawaiian island of Oahu, Pan Am's marine port was officiously titled Ocean Air Base Number One. Most knew the flying-boat base simply as Pearl City. It lay on the Middle Loch of Pearl Harbor, within sight of Pearl's famous Battleship Row.

With its spinning propellers advancing the flying boat leisurely toward shore, steered by the tail rudder, a hatch on the seaplane's nose popped open, and the fourth officer emerged to catch a mooring line. It was tossed by a Pan Am employee standing aboard an open motorboat that had an American flag waving wildly above its stern. With a proficiency gained through daily repetition, the beaching crew darted about the dock, grabbing ropes, pulling them tight, and tying them off, though this time under the pier's lights swarming with insects. Additional employees in two rowboats tied lines from buoys to the floating seaplane.

Once the big plane was tautly moored and anchored, the passengers were the first to disembark, through the main hatch on the starboard side, with the aid of stewards. A few minutes later, the crew exited and marched in formation along the pier, as was Pan Am's attention-grabbing ritual. Mac stepped onto the pier and shared an enthusiastic handshake with Pan Am's marine base manager, Willard "Bill" Eldridge. The island's tepid breeze and the scent of the tropical air greeted Mac and those disembarking with him. Finding themselves on a fixed and steady dock, the weary but cheerful passengers stretched their arms and legs in every direction. As they did, a hatch opened in the rear of the seaplane, and Pan Am employees unloaded

Crew members deboarding in lockstep. U. Miami PAA.

luggage onto wheeled carts, as well as hefty mailbags stuffed with parcels and letters from the continental United States and beyond.

The passengers delighted in what awaited them near the end of the floodlit boardwalk—a line of smiling native girls adorned in floral sarong dresses with flowers in their hair. Their hands and arms motioned the passengers forward with a fluidity seemingly impossible by human flesh and bones. The lovely women placed colorful Hawaiian flower leis over the passengers' heads and served them fresh pineapple juice as island music piped through the PA system—perhaps the most memorable landing for any sky traveler anywhere—at the "Paradise of the Pacific."

Passengers later shared what a sight they had seen—the lights of Honolulu as far as forty miles away as their clipper neared the Hawaiian paradise. One passenger, Alured Kelly, a wealthy Australian textile manufacturer, described the view: "Red lights on high standards around the harbor; in a brilliantly lighted background, the big navy yard and aerodromes, in the harbor a good number of warships riding at anchor, fairly close together with their riding lights on; and the streets of the harbor town gay with street lights, advertising signs, to say nothing of festoons of colored fairy lights erected for the start of the Christmas-shopping month." The commander in chief of the US Pacific Fleet at Pearl Harbor, concerned about sabotage and never envisaging a Japanese aerial bombardment, ordered that all lights throughout the harbor burn brightly during the night. The command had fortuitously fixed a dazzling beacon for the oncoming *Pacific Clipper*—as it would any approaching plane . . . or planes.

Those who'd arrived aboard the clipper were met with black Cadillac stretch limousines and drivers in black hats and ties standing ready to chauffeur them to their hotels. Most passengers sojourned at the two largest and most luxurious hotels on Waikiki Beach. At a time in Hawaii when grass huts and outrigger canoes lined the beach and exceptional lodgings were scant, the pink Spanish-Moorish-style Royal Hawaiian Hotel and the statelier Victorian-style Moana Hotel attended to every need of Pan Am's passengers and crews. Both hotels had been built by the Matson Navigation Company to grandly accommodate those traveling aboard its ocean liners, having cultivated trade and tourism in Hawaii since the age of masted schooners.

Of course, picturesque Hawaii was a destination unto itself for many travelers. Several passengers had arrived days earlier, such as a wealthy international banker and his wife, who would be taking the *Pacific Clipper* to Auckland, New Zealand, on their way to India. Mac also would be staying at the tropical island paradise for a couple of days. His flight aboard the *Philippine Clipper* wasn't scheduled to take off for Midway Atoll until Friday, November 28. Until then, he'd see to it that all cargo and work crews necessary for his upcoming construction project in the Philippines were in place and that anything else required would be shipped.

The novelty of clipper travel may have waned for Mac, but he never tired of visiting the world-famous Waikiki Beach. With Mount Leahi (Diamond Head) as its backdrop, the blinding white beach emerged from lavish green foliage with coconut trees that extended their fronds toward sparkling blue water and ivory-crested waves. It was magnificent each time Mac stepped foot on Waikiki. He'd be staying at the Moana Hotel, with its towering banyan tree that sheltered the courtyard. The hotel showcased its magnificent view of Diamond Head from the beach side and a lush green mountain range from the street. Mac planned to stretch out on a beach towel the next morning with a cold drink and a cigarette and welcome the warm sun to splash its rays down on him. It was a grand perk of working for Pan Am's Pacific Division, especially when most everyone in the States was battling winter.

However, Mac's time on Waikiki Beach lasted much longer than the two days he'd expected. In fact, his furlough lasted nine days. The *Philippine Clipper* that had been scheduled to take off from Honolulu for Midway on November 28 wouldn't even arrive in Honolulu until December 4, a full week behind schedule. Bad weather had grounded it in San Francisco; and when it had attempted to reach Honolulu on two separate take-offs, rain and gale force winds had turned it back, the first turnaround of the winter season.

So, instead of landing in Singapore on December 3, Mac's *Philippine Clipper* flight now wasn't scheduled to land at its Pacific base deep in the Orient until December 10. That gave Mac merely one week to complete his project once he arrived in the Philippines and another week to fly home to San Francisco. This would be cutting it close, but Mac was determined not to break the promise he'd made to Doreen. This would be the first Christmas that Doreen's mother wouldn't be there with her. There'd be no way that he wouldn't be there with her too.

On December 4, the *Pacific Clipper* rested on its wheeled beaching cradle outside the Pan American Airways hangar at Pearl City, yards from the *American* and *Philippine Clippers* that bobbed against the lapping waves of the loch. The *Philippine Clipper* had at last landed that morning. The three Pan Am seaplanes would be joined by the *China Clipper* that afternoon, a rare gathering of Pan Am's flying boats. The unusually bad weather between San Francisco and Hawaii had caused the bunching of the aircraft at the Hawaiian port.

With fair weather having arrived at last, the first of the four flying boats to depart Honolulu would be the *Pacific Clipper*. The beaching crew had already commenced the painstaking task of moving the herculean plane from the hangar to the concrete ramp that extended into the loch. The Boeing B-314A was impressive; a full one-third larger than the Glenn Martin *Philippine* and *China Clippers*. It stood more than three stories tall, resting on its portable undercarriage. Pan Am's Boeing flying boats were the largest transport airplanes of any kind in the world.

The *Pacific Clipper* may not have been as tall as the decade-old Empire State Building, but it seemed to the crew as if they were casting the iconic building's first three stories into the Middle Loch. Powerful caterpillar tractors (with tracks instead of tires) pulled the seaplane on its cradle toward the salty water at a speed of three miles an hour as members of the ground crew strode along all sides to survey the transfer for potential problems. It would be an hour-long undertaking. At the loch's edge, an electrical winch slowly released the taut steel cable to gradually roll the flying boat along the ramp into the seawater. The plane was tethered here and there by a collective mile of ropes as the beaching crew chief blew his whistle to signal the men to begin the next step of the launch. At long last, it was done—the *Pacific Clipper* floated on the water, moored to buoys along the dock. The ground crew locked the gangway into place and pulled the cradle ashore to be stowed back at the hangar.

A Boeing B-314 on its beach cradle. U. Miami PAA.

Pan Am's schedule for December 4 called for the *Pacific Clipper* to depart Hawaii at 8:00 a.m. for a 5,116-mile journey to New Zealand. The plane would stop at Pan Am's island bases along its Antipodes route that included British Canton Island, Suva in Fiji, and Nouméa in the French colony of New Caledonia before reaching Auckland, New Zealand. The clipper's passengers, mostly British, American, and Dutch, had arrived from myriad locales by various means of transportation. A few had flown into Hawaii on Pan Am's *American Clipper*, others on the *Philippine Clipper*, and some had sailed aboard the Matson Navigation Company's "white ships," like the SS *Lurline* and *Matsonia*.

At eight o'clock in the morning of that Thursday, December 4, on schedule, the *Pacific Clipper* took off for Auckland, with twenty-six passengers aboard. It was followed by the *American Clipper*'s departure for San Francisco that afternoon. Mac still waited for his flight to depart. At least the *Philippine Clipper* had landed at Pearl City that morning. He had seen it land with his own eyes.

─────────

When the sun rose on Friday, December 5, only two clippers floated in the Middle Loch of Pearl Harbor, waiting their turns to take off. The *Philippine Clipper* was scheduled to take off first, at 8:00 a.m., heading for Midway Atoll on its way to Singapore. It would be followed by the *China Clipper*, departing that afternoon for San Francisco.

The *Philippine* and *China Clippers* were Martin M-130 mid-sized flying boats that could carry up to forty-six passengers but typically carried no more than thirty in three ten-berth compartments during their overnight flights. On this upcoming voyage to Singapore, an overabundance of mailbags and cargo prevented the *Philippine Clipper* from flying with a full passenger manifest, to the frustration of those hoping to secure a seat. Since 1927, the US government had entered into long-term contracts with private airlines to deliver US mail along domestic routes and, in Pan Am's case, along international ones. Payment was based on payload—a specified sum per pound of mail carried via airplane to its scheduled destination. It was a lucrative undertaking for Pan Am; so profitable, in fact, that the airlines would favor mail over passengers when determining payload.

Besides mail, the *Philippine Clipper* would be laden with more than the usual amount of cargo. During the night, a procession of cargo carriers had rolled along the dock like miniature railway cars. Typical cargoes taken to Manila, Hong Kong, Singapore, and other islands along Pan Am's routes were limited only by the imagination. Items like wedding gowns, movie and news reels, seeds and cuttings, jewelry, false teeth, wooden arms and legs, and even polo balls were stowed in the flying boat's belly. On this trip, however, Pan Am had effectively chartered the flight to the US military, agreeing to carry a cargo that consisted mostly of tires and spare parts for Gen. Claire Chennault's squadron of Curtiss P-40 Warhawks fighting the Japanese in China, better known as the American Volunteer Group (AVG) Flying Tigers. That's why there were so few passengers—only nine—of whom Mac would be one. More than two hundred tubed tires had been stowed not only in the cargo hold, but in some of the rear passenger cabins from which seats, tables, and even the flooring and walls had been removed.

Like all Pan Am flights prior to takeoff, mechanics had scoured the *Philippine Clipper* the day and night before, thoroughly checking the four massive engines and the web of hydraulic and fuel lines that snaked their way throughout the clipper's expansive wings and fuselage. Revolutionary technology had produced a magnificent aircraft that could land on and take off from the Seven Seas and travel for days in all but the worst weather. In exchange for such incredible capabilities, the aircraft required constant repair and modification. "There was always lots of . . . work on the flying boats . . . in waters all over the world," a former Pan Am mechanic remembered.

Though life-insurance policies often excluded fanciful air travel because underwriters considered airplanes too risky for their insureds, Pan Am boasted an amazing safety record. Chief engineer and passenger safety zealot André Priester insisted on it. Priester was known for saying "Aviation in itself is not inherently dangerous. But . . . it is terribly unforgiving of any carelessness, incapacity or neglect." James Stahlman, owner of the *Nashville Banner* newspaper, who had been on the inaugural round-trip flight to Hong Kong aboard the *Philippine Clipper*, wrote in 1936 of the safety when flying with Pan Am: "Flying [on a clipper] is not only safe today, but it will be safe tomorrow. . . . And I'm telling you, I had more fright on that twenty-mile [automobile] trip from Cavite to Manila than I did in crossing the whole Pacific

Ocean and back." And Ernest Hemingway once told *Look* magazine: "Pan Am and I are old friends . . . I feel as safe with Pan Am as I do any morning I wake up to a good working day."

With any problems repaired ahead of takeoff, the *Philippine Clipper*'s crew had arrived early that December 5 morning to review the flight plans and weather reports. Pan Am hired and trained the best crew members of any airline, they said. "We had the cream of the crop," said Sanford Kaufman with Pan Am management. "We were hiring many young naval pilots who were also graduates of good colleges." One example of Pan Am's "good" college hiring was flight engineer John Parrish Jr., who graduated with a mechanical engineering degree from Princeton University and a master's degree from the California Institute of Technology.

A steward in the galley. Pan American Airways, *New Horizons*, Vol. 11, No. 5, February 1941, 27. U. Miami PAA.

Everyone recognized that the safety of Pan Am's passengers depended on its mechanics and top-notch pilots; but, just as important to Pan Am, the passengers' pleasure depended on the quality of the plane's stewards. "The pilots work from sun to sun, but the stewards' work is never done," stewards liked to say. And of course, just as Mac had experienced on the *Pacific Clipper*, food would be an extremely important feature of the *Philippine Clipper* flight.

As takeoff time for the *Philippine Clipper* neared, thirty-three-year-old Pan Am purser and flight steward Charles Percival "Charlie" Relyea completed stocking the seaplane's galley with the choicest cuts of steak, veal, and duck, along with the freshest fish and most succulent fruits and vegetables. He had received the menus for the flight at the morning's briefing, conducted by the ground captain. Breakfast, lunch, and dinner menus changed with each flight, varying depending on destination. Charlie was in charge of making certain he had everything needed to prepare and serve the lavish meals set out on the menus. There was no room for error, since he couldn't run out to the market ten thousand feet above the ocean.

Charlie was the perfect steward for a Pan Am flight—handsome, intelligent, energetic, jovial, the archetype of the "never met a stranger" kind of fellow—who took tremendous pride in his career with Pan Am. Always cracking a joke and making people feel comfortable thousands of feet in the air, passengers were partial to Charlie and enjoyed having him as their steward. And, not above telling a good yarn, word spread throughout the Pacific that Charlie was a "great-grandson of the last king of Hawaii"—which was impressive, considering Charlie had been born and raised in Staten Island, New York.

In preparation for the flight that morning, Charlie had learned at the morning briefing that the *Philippine Clipper* was headed for Singapore, that it would take five days and four nights, and that there'd be nine passengers and eight crew members aboard. Charlie would

Charles "Charlie" Relyea. Pan American Airways, *New Horizons*, Vol. 12, No. 9, June 1942, 24 (cropped); U. Miami PAA.

be the sole steward, since there were so few passengers. He'd received the seating assignment and a list of the flight's VIPs, of which there were none. "Let's have a good trip," the ground captain told Charlie as he walked out of the room.

Inside the well-appointed Pearl City terminal building, which resembled a large rectangular grass hut more than an international airline terminal, a sign inside the terminal notified Mac and the other passengers of the takeoff time in white letters and numerals:

**Trans-Pacific Crossing No. 1551 Philippine Clipper
Captain Hamilton Departing Pearl City 8:00 A.M.**

A similar board stood outside with a large map of the plane's route to Singapore. Some passengers stopped to be photographed standing beside the sign before boarding.

With the sounding of the first bell and then the second, the *Philippine Clipper* with everyone aboard cruised toward the mouth of Pearl Harbor, where it slowed and turned into the head of its take-off lane. With the command of "full power" and the manhandling of the rigid controls by Capt. John "Hammy" Hamilton and First Officer William "Bill" Moss, the *Philippine Clipper* skimmed the water's surface, slowly at first, then gained speed rapidly. It wasn't long, perhaps forty-five seconds, till Capt. Hamilton pulled slightly on the yoke to raise the seaplane's nose. The *Philippine Clipper* lifted off from the Middle Loch. It truly was a beautiful thing to behold. The view of the lush green Hawaiian landscape encircled by white sand and deep blue water swelled in the plane's square windows, which were jammed with the faces of those onboard.

Starboard-side passengers could clearly see Battleship Row with the tall masts of the *West Virginia, Maryland, California, Arizona, Tennessee, Oklahoma,* and *Nevada* rising like steel blue mountain peaks along the east side of Ford Island. The captain had not ordered the window shades drawn, but photographs of the harbor were forbidden as a military security measure. Those on the port side shuffled across the aisle to quickly fill the empty starboard windows for a better view of the majestic naval vessels. Charlie jokingly asked the passengers to stop "rocking the flying boat" and return to their seats for their own protection. Their haphazard movements caused the forty-two-ton aircraft to pitch and roll slightly, which made the pilot's already strenuous job a little more cumbersome.

While the plane continued its slow climb at three hundred feet per minute that Friday, December 5, passengers could see young sailors in their snowy white uniforms on the decks of naval ships waving their caps above their heads at the rising clipper. Pan Am clippers were much larger and had twice the number of engines as

A Boeing B-314 lifting off from the bay. Pan American Airways, *New Horizons*, Vol. 11, No. 7, April 1941, 9; U. Miami PAA.

the US Navy Consolidated PBY Catalina flying boat that sailors were accustomed to seeing, and, for that reason, clipper takeoffs and landings garnered more of the young men's attention and enthusiasm. Some passengers waved back and others just smiled at the sailors' youthful zeal. It wasn't long before those aboard the *Philippine Clipper* lost sight of the young navy souls as they vanished into a sunny haze above Pearl Harbor. Within just forty-eight hours, hundreds of those young men would never be seen alive again.

## CHAPTER 5

# NEW YORK–PAN AM'S HEAD OFFICE

November had been a grueling month for Pan Am's transpacific clippers, as much of 1941 had been. Now December was looking even more hectic. Pan Am only maintained eight flying boats capable of embarking on regularly scheduled flights across the Pacific Ocean. One of those—the *Honolulu Clipper*—was undergoing a major overhaul and wouldn't be ready to fly again until January. Another—the *Hong Kong Clipper*, the smallest of the clipper flying boats—flew solely shuttle flights between Manila and the Portuguese and British colonies of Macau and Hong Kong, respectively. That left only six planes on the West Coast capable of completing flights to Auckland, Manila, and Singapore—and back. It was "the heaviest traffic since [Pan American Airways] was established," reported San Pedro, California's *News-Pilot* on December 1.

The schedules had grown dizzying for the six flying boats and their crews. Yet Pan Am's transoceanic air travel had not always been so hectic. Just five years earlier, it had been nonexistent. Post–World War I had been an age in early aviation history when no one really knew what to do with airplanes. There was no "airline industry," no Civil Aeronautics Board, and no FAA regulations. Pilots treated airplanes as a toy to race or perform tricks at air shows. The pilots were known as "barnstormers" or "birdmen." Pan Am CEO Juan Trippe wasn't interested in airplanes for entertainment. He was an airman in a business suit, who considered airplanes a future means of transportation for freight and passengers. The young Trippe decided that he wanted to provide international air transport exclusively. "I could see that there was less competition abroad than at home," Trippe recalled later. Whereas other US airlines created domestic routes from St. Louis to Cincinnati, for example, Trippe contemplated Rio de Janeiro, London, Hawaii, Hong Kong, Alaska, and New Zealand. "My father saw an opportunity to shrink the world," recalled Charlie Trippe, a son of Pan Am founder and CEO Juan Trippe.

When Juan Trippe first contemplated flying across the Atlantic and Pacific Oceans in the early 1930s, the aircraft technology did not yet exist. With the aid of national aviation hero and Pan Am technical adviser Charles Lindbergh, who'd completed the first solo flight across the Atlantic Ocean in 1927, Trippe pushed aircraft manufacturers to design and build increasingly innovative planes that could fly farther and faster, carrying ever more cargo and passengers. "They don't want a flying boat, they want a miracle," one manufacturer reportedly said. Juan Trippe was relentless in his demands. Eventually the planes were built, and they were magnificent; and the destinations were selected, and they were equally as magnificent, especially in the Pacific—Hawaii, the Philippines, Hong Kong, Singapore, Fiji, New Zealand, and many other exotic isles along the routes—and people who could pay the pricey fares clamored to climb aboard Pan Am's flying boats to visit such mysterious milieus.

"Whether you wish to be gone a week or a year," read an early Pan Am advertisement, "or whether you wish to vagabond as fancy dictates, the luxurious, frequent, and dependable services of Pan American Airways System offer you a new experience in travel."

Despite the cost and the uncertainties of the novel transoceanic air travel, Pan Am's transpacific passenger waiting list exceeded a month and was growing daily. It was no secret why Pan Am's luxurious clippers were in such demand. No other airline in the world flew regularly scheduled passenger flights across the Pacific or Atlantic Oceans—not Eastern, United, American, Northwest, Continental, Braniff, British Overseas, or Howard Hughes's TWA. TWA's name at that time wasn't even Trans World Airlines, but Transcontinental & Western Air. "For total mileage," wrote *Life* magazine in its October 20, 1941 issue, "[Pan Am] is in a class by itself with 90,000 [scheduled route] miles and 311 airports—twice as long as the ten largest domestic airlines put together." No doubt the eighteen-hour overnight luxury trip from San Francisco to Honolulu also enticed travelers who had grown tired of the monotonous five-day and four-night voyage aboard steamships. For others, it may have been the six-day flight aboard a Pan Am clipper to the Orient with stops at luxurious island hotels along the way, rather than being confined aboard an ocean liner battling seasickness during an antiquated three-week sea journey to the Far East.

To meet the rising demand, Pan Am CEO Juan Trippe had ordered six humongous B-314A flying boats (improved from the previous version) from the Boeing Company to add to his inimitable flying enterprise. For the price of those *six* luxury flying boats, Pan Am could have purchased *forty-five* Douglas DC-3 landplanes. However, planes that landed with wheels on the ground were of no use over the Pacific Ocean, because practically none of the islands had runways, at least any open to American commercial traffic. The "super-clippers" had to be designed and constructed to a sufficient size and opulence to carry passengers safely in comfort across the oceans, along with mountains of mailbags and cargo stowed away, and fifteen tons of 100-octane fuel. That's why they were so expensive.

The additional Boeings were delivered to Pan Am in 1941. However, due to the war in Europe, a patriotic Pan Am agreed to cut its fleet and sell three of the B-314As to the British government, which needed them principally for military use. That left Pan Am with only three—the *Anzac* and *Pacific Clippers* assigned to fly the Pacific

Cross-section diagram of a Boeing B-314. *Pan American Air Ways*, Vol. 8, No. 7, August 1937, 5; U. Miami PAA. Cradle of Aviation Museum, Garden City, New York.

Ocean and the *Capetown Clipper* assigned to the Atlantic. Without its full complement of new clippers, Pan Am's existing clippers would have to make up the shortfall.

The rigorous schedule meant pilots, navigators, radio operators, mechanics, stewards, and ground crews often worked weeks without more than a night's rest during that time. It was common for crewmen to miss family gatherings and events, even the births of their children. For example, on his return flight from Singapore, Charlie Relyea's good friend and fellow steward Barney Sawicki was handed a decoded Morse code message on New Year's Day that read: "It's a stewardess . . . her name is Barnette." To provide some temporary relief for the long flights, Pan Am terminated the shuttle flights between San Francisco and Honolulu. In fact, just that very week the *American Clipper* had completed the last shuttle flight between Hawaii and California.

"Trippe's astonishing ability first to perceive what the future may bring and then to cope with it has given rise to a company legend that the globe in his office is actually made of crystal," *Life* magazine reported. Trippe considered reassigning seaplanes from Pan Am's marine base at LaGuardia Field in New York, a base from which seaplanes flew across the Atlantic Ocean. However, with war rampant in Europe, passengers on the European continent clamored for flights to America. Pan Am crews in the Pacific would simply have to make do. At least, that's what Trippe's crystal ball was telling him.

With 1941 coming to a close that December, Pan American Airways was without question the world's largest and finest airline with routes around the world. Pan Am's plans for domination of international air travel within the Western Hemisphere and beyond appeared as if nothing could slow it down.

## CHAPTER 6

# A REGULAR FELLA

A grinning Harry Olson had stepped off the *China Clipper* at Pearl City the day before, December 4, and happily lowered his head to the attractive Hawaiian girls who cheerfully greeted him with red carnation leis. Harry, a middle-aged builder wearing a JC Penney suit and fedora, hadn't caught the *China Clipper* at its Kallang Basin anchorage off the shore of Singapore; that's where the well-to-do and dignitaries like the Soviet Union's new ambassador to the United States, Maxim Litvinov, had boarded. Instead, he'd boarded nearer—at stark and windswept Wake Island—2,500 miles away.

Harry had spent most of 1941 living on the small island of Wake, where he served as the assistant superintendent to 1,145 workers employed by a consortium of firms called Contractors Pacific Naval Air Bases (CPNAB), composed chiefly of Idaho-based Morrison-Knudsen Company employees. CPNAB supplied the men and materials necessary to complete defense contracts proffered by a US government late in its preparation for a possible Japanese attack. However, the lack of "dames," beer, and nightly entertainment proved exceedingly difficult for the workmen on the isolated island. A line from a worker's letter home illustrated the men's feelings: "[I am] usually happy, but out here with little to do I often get disgusted."

Scores of men frequently quit and requested to leave the tiny Pacific isle on the next passing ship. But Harry was a supervisor and earned *tax-free* wages of $400 a month when the average monthly *taxable* wage in the United States was less than $100. He also received two paid vacations each year. Better yet, CPNAB had paid Harry's $300 round-trip fare ($6,000 today) from Wake to Honolulu to begin his second Hawaiian vacation that year, as it did for other members of the CPNAB supervisory staff that alternated their vacations.

So Harry may not have been a wealthy world traveler or a haughty foreign ambassador, but at a time when very few people in the world had ever set foot on the picturesque beach of Waikiki, Harry was spending his second paid vacation there during 1941. When he'd taken the *Philippine Clipper* from Wake to the island paradise on his first vacation months earlier, he described his trip in a letter to his wife, Katherine, as "the nicest vacation I've ever had." It was a "lulu," he wrote. Now he'd returned to Waikiki Beach for another lulu. He had reserved a room in the luxurious Moana Hotel on Waikiki Beach, the hotel he'd stayed in last July, and a hotel that Katherine in frigid Oregon would have surely loved had she been invited. "My window looks out on Waikiki Beach and Diamond Head," Harry wrote Katherine. "The beach and surf is always full of people . . . I saw Loretta Young down at the Royal yesterday. She doesn't look very glamorous in a bathing suit laying [*sic*] in the sand."

Next door to Harry on Waikiki Beach, a government motorcade had just arrived to deposit Ambassador Litvinov and his entourage at the Royal Hawaiian Hotel, where the Bolsheviks quickly disappeared into rooms worthy of champagne socialists. The famous communist's mission was to take up his post in Washington, DC and persuade US President Franklin D. Roosevelt to continue military aid to the Soviets in their fight against Nazi Germany. The Communist ambassador had piqued Harry's curiosity during their shared flight on the *China Clipper*. Harry had composed a letter to his wife aboard the clipper just before landing in Hawaii: "Maxim Litvinoff [*sic*] is stretched out sound asleep across the aisle. Madam Litvinoff [*sic*], an amiable grandmotherly lady . . . finds much to amuse herself about the land of the free. . . . Just now she wanted to know if all Americans chew gum and why. I told her when I found out I would let her know." Most living in the United States had never seen a real communist from the Soviet Union, especially an ambassador from Moscow. Harry may have been disappointed when he learned that the purported hardnosed, godless communist ambassador had attended the Honolulu cinema that evening and watched *Dumbo*—Walt Disney's full-feature animated film about a flying baby elephant.

When Litvinov departed Honolulu the following day for San Francisco on his way to Washington, DC, Harry was just settling into his ten-day vacation. He would miss Christmas with his wife and his two children in Oregon, but he'd send extra money home for their gifts. As soon as his Hawaiian vacation was over, however, he would return to Wake Island in time to spend Christmas with his older son, Ted, whom Harry had gotten a job on the Pacific isle to keep him out of the war in Europe. Although the United States had not yet joined the war against Germany, it had instituted the first peacetime draft in US history, which required men from twenty-one through thirty-five years of age to register for the military draft. Ted had registered, but he was now working on national-defense contracts out in the Pacific, sequestered four thousand miles from the West Coast of the United States. Harry figured that would keep his son far away from the fighting; Ted had figured it that way too.

## CHAPTER 7

# DANGER IN THE VACANT SEA

Dark waves crashed over the bow of the aircraft carrier *Akagi* as the flagship of the Imperial Japanese Navy surged ahead of its steel flotilla that was pitching and rolling into a black, raging storm. The rising and then crashing of the bow against the fathomless depth of the world's largest and most dangerous ocean thundered against the steel hull of each of the massive carriers for all those inside to hear. That, along with the roaring cold winds of the sea, created a typhoon-like scene that struck fear into the bones of even the most seasoned sailor onboard. Many clasped steel cables or lashed themselves to some immovable part of the ship when venturing out onto the decks to prevent themselves from being swept off the five-story-high carriers into the watery darkness. Nonetheless, many were swept overboard.

The armored vessels pounded their way along the water's surface that night with lights doused and radios silenced. The ships could be observed solely by those gripping powerful binoculars while manning the decks of nearby vessels. Only the creamy white crests of the waves and the trailing wakes in the black water were visible on that eighth night of the clandestine voyage, a voyage that had carried the ships loaded with bombers almost three thousand miles eastward toward their unsuspecting target in the Hawaiian Islands. Even garbage was forbidden from being tossed over the side for fear that an American vessel might spot it floating in the water.

The ships cruised at fourteen knots in an impressive formation that stretched for miles. Two battleships headed a long convoy of six aircraft carriers that were flanked by destroyers and cruisers. Earlier that day, three submarines had sailed ahead of the flotilla with their periscopes often breaking the water's surface to provide added protection should a military or commercial ship appear. Orders had been given to sink any ship, even civilian, that might communicate the Japanese fleet's existence and position to Pearl Harbor. Mitsubishi A6M "Zero" fighter planes also zigzagged overhead during daylight hours to complete the protective ring surrounding the task force. After sunset, darkness provided the ships the necessary cover against all dangers above the water; but even the cloak of nightfall could not protect the task force from American submarines loaded with torpedoes that might lurk below—even though none would.

The Empire's plan called for the armada to sail eastward along a route clear of the commercial shipping lanes in an area of the Pacific called the "vacant sea." The Japanese had painstakingly researched the records of the world's shipping companies and learned that for the last ten years there had not been a single merchant ship that sailed along the latitude of 40° north during the winter months. The current violent storm bashing against the hulls of the ships was evidence why.

When Vice Adm. Chuichi Nagumo, who had been placed in command of the fleet, gave the signal, the ships' steam turbines would turn the task force southeastward. The flotilla would continue on that course until it reached a point approximately six hundred miles north of the Hawaiian Islands. There they'd turn once more and head south. At a prearranged point 230 miles north of the tip of Oahu, the carriers would launch their fighters and bombers to attack Pearl Harbor. The circuitous ocean route was believed to be necessary to mitigate the chances of detection. So far, it had worked. The massive task force, armed to inflict death and destruction upon Americans from the air like never seen before, had not been spotted by anything more than a wayward seagull as the Imperial force drew nearer to its target with each nautical mile it left in its wake.

## CHAPTER 8

# ON TO MIDWAY

The *Philippine Clipper* was at last on its way to Singapore early on Friday morning, December 5, unsuspectingly flying into a clandestine oceanic trap. To reach its destination in the Orient, the clipper first had to lay over at Pan Am's marine bases on Midway Atoll, Wake Island, Guam, and then Manila on the island of Luzon in the Philippines. Mac planned to venture no farther than Pan Am's base at Cañacao Bay in Cavite Harbor, twenty miles from Manila. Everyone else would remain on the *Philippine Clipper* heading to Singapore.

The clipper sustained its steady climb—a thousand feet, then two thousand—cruising upward at 130 mph. Mac sniggered at the serious-looking servicemen chewing gum and fiddling with unsightly cotton balls sticking from their ears, hoping to ease the pain of altitude change. It wasn't long before Charlie walked the aisle and retrieved those cotton balls as the seaplane leveled off at eight thousand feet above the ocean. He also adjusted the temperature as the plane's cabins grew colder. "The heating system generates sufficient warmth to heat the average ten room home at zero temperature," a Pan Am brochure boasted.

Charlie talked and laughed as he went, offering a smile and one of his many witticisms. The young bachelor was still bellyaching in good-natured fashion about how Pete Reiser and his Brooklyn Dodgers had lost the World Series just weeks earlier to

Joe DiMaggio and the Yankees, four games to one. Each time he discussed it, he offered a different excuse, always sure to point out that "he was a man of blue—blue eyes, blue Dodgers uniform, and blue Pan Am logo."

Though Charlie hadn't mentioned it, he was also standing inside a plane with an exquisite blue interior. Each Pan Am flying boat was designed with a different color and décor. In fact, Pan Am had commissioned a scientific study to determine what colors were easiest on the eyes during long trips. "Certain colors are conducive to nausea," remarked Howard Ketcham, a color engineer. "Others breed confidence and cheer." Pan Am decided to go with "Pan American Blue," "Miami Sand Beige," and "Skyline Green," in different combinations throughout the eleven compartments of its flying boats.

Charlie characterized the majority of Pan Am's stewards—men, under thirty-five years of age, and of small stature (Charlie was 5'9"), giving rise to the impression that solely "jockey-sized youngsters" were acceptable as stewards. Pan Am did not hire female "stewardesses" at that time. Because Pan Am's clippers flew long distances through isolated territory requiring long hours, it was believed, either chivalrously or chauvinistically, that only men could do the job. "The job has always been considered a little too strenuous for a young woman," a Pan Am periodical stated at the time. Pan Am would hire its first class of stewardesses three years later in 1944, during the war.

Now comfortably seated aboard the *Philippine Clipper* traveling to Midway, Mac couldn't help but overhear Charlie explain, with panache in a slight Brooklyn accent, about the flying boat and how it was the sister ship to the preeminent *China Clipper*. Mac had heard it all before, but every steward told it a bit differently. According to Charlie, both were built by the Glenn L. Martin Company and delivered to Pan Am in 1935. The model was designated the Martin M-130. It was the first time that a commercial airplane had been built according to an airline's specifications.

A Glenn Martin M-130 (the *Philippine Clipper*) in flight. Pan American Airways, *New Horizons*, Vol. 13, No. 3, January 1943, 21; U. Miami PAA. SFOM.

There was a third sister, the *Hawaii Clipper*, which had been christened at Pan Am's marine base in Honolulu with coconut milk rather than champagne. As Charlie carried on with his address, Mac likely remembered how the *Hawaii Clipper* had mysteriously disappeared in 1938 following takeoff from Guam en route to Manila. Six passengers (others had fortunately disembarked at Honolulu) and nine crew members perished over a rough and isolated section of ocean. Despite a naval search, no trace of the plane or its occupants was ever found. The mystery, much like the disappearance of Amelia Earhart the year before, was an international story that found its way into newspapers around the world. Some believed the *Hawaii Clipper* had been hijacked by two Japanese stowaways, either to commandeer the plane so the Japanese government could duplicate it or its engines, or to seize Wah-Sun Choy, a passenger who was reportedly carrying three million dollars in US gold certificates for the Republic of China relief effort (about sixty million dollars today). Many others believed that the pilot had simply been derelict during a violent storm reported in the area. The answer to the mystery wound up deep inside Davy Jones's Locker, where it is still kept secret by the "fiend that presides over all the evil spirits of the deep." The *Hawaii Clipper*'s disappearance constituted the only blemish on Pan Am's impeccable passenger carriage record over the Pacific Ocean as 1941 drew to a close.

It was nearing the time for Charlie to serve breakfast, one that he'd begun preparing prior to the passengers' boarding that morning. Serving food and drink on an unpressurized plane flying through stiff winds and foul weather could be tricky. Yet Pan Am's engineers had not skipped over gravity's effects on food service when designing their floating boats. Everything that stewards placed on tables, from vases of flowers and salt and pepper shakers to plates, cups, and glassware, had heavy vacuum bottoms to prevent spills when passing through bumpy airspace. Even so, accidents weren't entirely preventable. Once when Adm. Chester Nimitz, in his white naval uniform with full regalia, boarded a flight to Pearl Harbor, the Pan Am clipper hit a downdraft just as a steward had poured coffee into the admiral's cup. "This black ball rose out of my coffee cup," the admiral recalled. The ball of coffee floated momentarily in zero gravity till it splashed down on the admiral's starched white uniform. Expecting to be fired, the steward instead witnessed the admiral dying with laughter. "Did you see that black ball?" the admiral asked.

Of course, breakfast would be followed at noon with the three-hour lunch buffet. Charlie wouldn't have to serve dinner, since the passengers would dine at the Pan Am hotel on Midway Atoll after they landed.

Flight time from Honolulu to Midway was nine hours. For the most part, the 1,100-mile trek to the clipper's first night's stop was an easy one, provided the weather remained fair. The stretch of ocean required little navigation, a task that normally would have required the constant attention of the flying boat's navigator and radio operator—Coloradan brothers John and Ted Hrutky.

The undersea highway with its shimmering aqua surrounded by deep midnight blue waters was impossible to miss from the air. The plane's skipper, Capt. Hamilton, assisted by First Officer Moss, simply had to keep the nose of the big clipper pointing northwest above the unmistakable string of islands, atolls, and reefs that are threaded like many-hued gems from Hawaii to Midway. Like the clipper's pilots, Mac had seen nature's string of blue, orange, purple, and yellow coral passing below the *Philippine Clipper* countless times. Still, he couldn't refrain from gazing down at the undersea mountain range with its kaleidoscope of color that extended from Hawaii to the Aleutian Islands of Alaska.

About four hundred miles northwest of Oahu, the *Philippine Clipper* passed over Necker Island. The oldest volcanic rock in the Hawaiian chain, La Perouse Pinnacle was clearly visible, shining to the south like a snow-crested peak. Half an hour later, Mac spotted the crescent-shaped French Frigate Shoals on the port side. He knew their order by heart. At five hundred miles out, the volcanic Gardner Pinnacles interrupted the persistent undulation of ocean waves, trailed a couple hundred miles by the submerged Maro Reef. Mac realized that this reef meant the clipper was fewer than three hours from Midway Atoll.

Even the army and navy servicemen couldn't resist pressing their foreheads against the flying boat's large windows to stare at the peaceful backdrop as the clipper flew on. It was tranquil, much more beautiful than the empty silvery metallic surface of the ocean typically visible from eight thousand feet. The serenity afforded by the colorful ocean vista combined with the relaxing drone of the engines had lulled some to sleep and others very near it until—

"Midway!" Charlie shouted, startling some onboard.

Stretching and yawning, the passengers welcomed the news that they'd soon be landing in Midway's lagoon. It had been a long nine hours. The clipper circled the crystal blue lagoon that lay within the two small coral reefs forming Midway Atoll—Sand Island and Eastern Island. As the plane banked into its turn, those on the clipper observed two steel air beacon radio towers on Sand Island, resembling forest-fire watchtowers, along with a scattering of one-story yellow buildings with red roofs near a line of trees.

The military men were particularly interested in the activity on Eastern Island. US Marines commanded by Col. Harold Shannon with the aid of civilian contractors busily constructed air strips and fortifications where nothing but gnarled trees and shrubs had grown since the formation of the island. Shannon was additionally aided by handsome, twenty-six-year-old 1st Lt. George Cannon, who'd joined the USMC following graduation from the University of Michigan with a degree in mechanical engineering.

Those onboard spotted two-story barracks on Sand Island that clearly weren't military, poking up here and there above the trees. The long-standing station formed part of the Commercial Pacific Cable Company, whose herculean efforts had begun in 1903 to lay and maintain a tar-coated telegraph cable across the bottom of the Pacific Ocean. The cable stretched from America's West Coast to Midway, Guam, and then to Manila, where the company's cable line connected with a competitor's line that ran to Shanghai. President Theodore "Teddy" Roosevelt had sent the inaugural message over the undersea cable from San Francisco that carried his greetings to the governor of the Philippines, William Howard Taft, who would succeed Teddy Roosevelt as president six years later.

The pencil-mustachioed Mac knew every inch of Midway, except for the recent military installations. He'd been in charge of building Pan Am's base on Midway Atoll. When the SS *North Haven* sailed from Pier 22 at the Embarcadero in 1935 and again in 1936, Mac was onboard with the expedition's supervisor, William Grooch, and a construction crew of seventy-four laborers with forty-four technicians. The ship had carried twelve million pounds, enough to fill three hundred railway cars, of everything that would be needed to build and operate Pan Am's island bases, including the Pan Am hotel where he'd soon stay. "A good, capable man, who overcame obstacles ingeniously," said US Navy Lt. Willis Cleaves, who'd accompanied Mac on the SS *North Haven*.

Mac's proven skills had resulted in the entire project and its construction crew being placed under his supervision. Within months, Pan Am had completed identical enterprises on Midway and Wake Island that included a single-story prefabricated hotel, power plant, refrigeration unit, rainwater catchment system, laundry, shops, a landing dock, crew and personnel quarters, and communication facilities. Everything unloaded from the ship had been numbered and labeled to correspond with schematics and instructions on their assembly and placement. Furnishings and appliances were included, from chairs and beds to draperies and inter-room telephones and even coat hangers and ashtrays. Landscaping, incorporating tons of topsoil, along with grass, shade trees, and shrubbery, was beautifully arranged along the walkways and around the hotel on what previously had been hot, barren scrubland. The transformation was miraculous.

As the clipper's passengers continued peering out at the island below them, Capt. Hamilton directed the colossal flying boat toward the lagoon. He gently eased back on the throttles and yoke until the clipper's bow rose five degrees above the horizon on its approach. The plane then commenced a gliding descent—fifty feet, twenty feet, ten, five . . . Its steel-reinforced belly shuddered when it touched water that sprayed high into the air as if trailing a high-powered motorboat racing across the lagoon. The captain quickly brought the plane to a drift with plenty of room to spare before reaching the red flags on buoys that signaled danger near the end of the lagoon.

After mooring to Pan Am's refueling barge that squeezed the seaplane's nose snugly into the barge's rubber V-shaped bow, the ground crew connected a gangway between the edge of the barge's deck and the clipper's port-side sponson so passengers could step out. A white Panair motorboat, the *Midway*, pulled alongside to take on passengers and transport them to a pier at the beach. Passengers stepped aboard the launch as Charlie squirted each with a noxious mist from his Flit gun (a hand-pumped Flit brand insecticide sprayer). Stewards on transpacific flights were required to spray each passenger upon landing to ward off mosquitoes and other island insects. It was a nasty procedure that nearly everyone wrote home about. The launch's cheery skipper then piloted them to the island's white dock built over dazzling white sand, where two waxed and polished General Motors "woodie" station wagons, bearing license plates Midway Island No. 1 and No. 2, awaited.

Once all were ashore, the four passengers who were Pan Am employees set out on foot for the Pan Am compound, where they'd bunk in cottages until their jobs on the island were finished. Conversely, the four servicemen and Mac seated themselves inside the comfortable station wagons with the drivers, who slowly pulled away from the dock. White sand sprayed along the windblown crushed-coral-and-sand road that had been dragged that morning, as the drivers headed for the hotel. The hotel wasn't more than a few hundred yards from the dock, yet it took several minutes to get there. The cause for the delay was the abundance of "gooney birds," an endearing label bestowed upon the hundreds of thousands of Laysan albatrosses that still inhabit the island. Those in the station wagons who'd never visited Midway exclaimed their dismay at the birds' odd behavior, which had contributed to the birds' distinctive nickname. They were so plentiful that Midway inhabitants and clipper passengers could barely walk three paces without stepping around or over one. Hence, the drivers of the station wagons proceeded carefully, honking their horns and shooing the birds out of the road as they went. "The young gooneys would not budge even for a tractor, and we had to send a guard ahead to pick up the youngsters and put them to one side," William Grooch, who'd supervised the building

Pan American Airways Hotel on Midway Atoll with gooney birds. National
Archives and Administration (NARA), San Francisco. U. Miami PAA. SFOM.

of Pan Am bases in the Pacific with Mac during the mid-1930s, recalled. It was no wonder, then, that a sign had been posted along the
road to the hotel amusingly honoring the birds' profuse and wacky
presence: GOONEYVILLE.

The Pan American Airways Hotel, also called the Gooneyville
Lodge, sat along the north central portion of Sand Island. A previous visitor and travel writer, Dorothy Kaucher, described the five-star
hotel designed by the exclusive New York architectural firm Delano
& Aldrich as "a quaint colonial style inn, with substantial pillars and
two wings reaching out like paws, from the pillared center." A sole
kou tree stood nearby. Its leaves fluttered in the sea breeze. Farther

along the beach that curved away from the hotel stood a thicket of stunning lavender scaevola that brightened the bunch grass and coral rock. Carefully placed and watered landscaping around the hotel grounds provided the finishing touch.

Awaiting the guests was Pan Am's port steward, Jack Bramham, who greeted the weary travelers with cool drinks before helping them sign the register that read like a *Who's Who*. Branham's wife, Ruth, who was the hotel matron and only female on the island, had evacuated ten days earlier when Adm. Kimmel ordered all females off the island. She was in Honolulu, awaiting her husband to join her on the *Philippine Clipper*'s return. His replacement had just arrived aboard the clipper.

After guests signed the register, young bellmen clad in starched white pants and jackets carried the guests' luggage and escorted them to their rooms. As was the practice at all Pan Am hotels in the Pacific, Pan Am hired Chamorro men—dark-skinned natives of Guam—to work at its island bases as cooks, waiters, bellmen, and laborers.

Within minutes of the *Philippine Clipper*'s arrival at Midway, a sweet contentment swept over each of the tired visitors on the tranquil island that formed a mere dot in a vast ocean far away from the headaches of civilization. Fresh flowers sat atop each room's dresser, and a radio tuned to the clearest station played music softly. Everyone was given plenty of time to rest and freshen up before the mellifluous dinner gong sounded, calling Pan Am employees and guests to assemble in the spacious dining room. The servicemen were seated at round dining tables in full uniform, with Mac donning a blazer. Wood-bladed fans twirled incessantly overhead to circulate the sand-baked air around the room above them. Young Guamanian men, dressed in white pants and jackets with navy bow ties, served the small dining group a cornucopia of repasts, comparable to that served in the air, which bolstered those tired from the long flight.

After dinner, the passengers moved out onto the screened veranda and sat in rattan chairs, where they sipped their drinks and smoked while perusing the *Gooney Gazette*, Midway's single-page newspaper, before retiring for the night. Mac continued his smoke as the warm breeze filtered across the veranda, wafted by the clicking fans. Mac's career could not have been going better during 1941. He was making more than $5,000 per year ($100,000 today), not including Pacific Island perks and an impressive expense account, when many people were still struggling to recover from the Great Depression. Pan Am was a great company to work for, and he, like many at Pan Am, felt a part of something big, innovative, and exciting. Telling someone in 1941 that you worked for Pan American Airways was always impressive, akin to saying you worked for NASA during the 1960s or perhaps one of the private aerospace companies today.

But 1941 had also delivered Mac the deepest sorrow. His wife of many years, Hazle, who'd loved the arts and her husband deeply, had died of cancer at home in Alameda just five months earlier on July 4. Her death was devastating, but Mac had little time to grieve with his golden-haired eleven-year-old daughter, Doreen, at home and an international career that carried him far away from her for weeks and even months at a time. Doreen was forced to rotate stays between aunts in California. Even as a child, she sensed that she had simply become a burden to be shared equitably as she was passed among the family. She missed her mother terribly, along with the stable home life she'd known before. Doreen wrote her father letters, and he did the same to her, buttressed by a periodic telegram or telephone call and a visit now and then. The separation was heartrending for both, especially for Doreen. That's why Mac wanted to complete his work in Manila as quickly as possible, so he could spend Christmas with his little girl in Alameda, just as he'd promised her.

Mac finished his scotch and drew the last puff of his cigarette before leaving the terrace. He ambled through the lobby and down the left wing's hallway of Pan Am's hotel. The walls, the ceiling, the carpet on the floor—those things that go unnoticed when one is tired—led to the door of room #12, which Mac closed behind him as he entered. It wasn't long before the light in his room went dark. Early the next morning, he'd be on his way to Wake Island, and then to Guam, and finally to Manila. His journey would take three more days.

Within minutes, the sun set, showering a persimmon-colored tint across the ocean's face before being replaced by the milky glow of a full moon. And that's how December 5 drew to a close for Mac and the other *Philippine Clipper* passengers—with gorgeous serenity, blissfully unaware of the horror that was approaching.

## CHAPTER 9

# YAMAMOTO'S PLAN

Almost a year earlier, on January 7, 1941, Adm. Isoroku Yamamoto, commander in chief of Japan's Combined Fleet, sat in his cabin aboard the battleship *Nagato* anchored at the Japanese naval base at Hashirajima Island in Hiroshima Bay. His morning's self-appointed task: set down on paper a bold military plan to knock the United States Navy out of the Pacific Ocean for up to a year, or perhaps for good.

Japan had increasingly skirmished with the Republic of China (then a nationalist-controlled government) for a decade, and had been at all-out war with that country since 1937 as part of Japan's imperialist policy to expand its influence and control in Asia. In late 1940 after Nazi Germany's conquest of France, Japanese troops moved into French Indochina in preparation for an assault on Hong Kong and Singapore, the Philippine Islands, and the Netherlands East Indies (now Indonesia), which plan Japan had labeled the Southern Operation.

Japan, which is composed of small volcanic islands that collectively are half the size of Texas, and which was then populated with sixty-one million people, sought to secure subservient labor and a largesse of raw materials that included oil, coal, wood, and metallic ores. Japan's military machine believed that the Southern Operation would accomplish that goal. Moreover, the Southern Operation would expel antithetical Europeans such as the British, French, and

Dutch, who Japan believed had intruded into its hemisphere through colonization and post–World War I treaties. The Japanese called the situation *Taiheiyo-no-gan* (Cancer of the Pacific). France and the Netherlands had already surrendered to Japan's ally, Nazi Germany, and with the British fully immersed in the war in Europe, Japan believed that only one country genuinely had the potential to stand in its way—the United States of America, the worst malignancy of all.

Since Japan's invasion of China, the United States had imposed a series of economic embargoes that had grown increasingly severe. The latest—the embargo of much-needed petroleum and scrap metal, coupled with the transfer of the formidable US Pacific Fleet from San Pedro Bay in California to Pearl Harbor in the Hawaiian Islands—had drawn Japan and the United States closer to war. Yamamoto realized that once initiated, the Southern Operation would require a huge amount of fuel and would be in danger of the US naval attack that was sure to come. A plan had to be devised to obtain petroleum and other vital resources while neutralizing any military threat from America. That's what Yamamoto was contemplating at his naval desk that day.

Yamamoto loved the Empire of Japan and believed that the Japanese people were superior to their Asian neighbors. Nevertheless, he had voiced his disagreement with the Empire's decision to go to war with China and was vehemently averse to the possibility of war with the United States. His cautious attitude had made him so unpopular among the nationalists that they regularly threatened him with assassination. Ironically, as Yamamoto protected himself from assassination by his countrymen for not being sufficiently belligerent, he was developing secret plans to attack Japan's strongest threat—America—in what would be called Operation Hawaii (later changed to Operation Z).

Writing in his native language, Yamamoto's right hand moved in quick strokes as the columns of script moved from right to left across the page. The five-foot, three-inch naval officer had spent his youth in Japanese naval academies and aboard Imperial ships. He'd also visited

Adm. Isoroku Yamamoto. US Navy, Naval History and Heritage Command.

the United States, where he attended Harvard University and traveled extensively as a naval attaché posted in Washington, DC. He understood American culture and its military production capabilities but held little respect for American military leaders, whom he viewed as slothful, lighthearted drinkers and golfers. Japan's best chance of keeping the United States caged for the duration of the Southern Operation, Yamamoto believed, was not a defensive operation that he calculated would ultimately fail, but a preemptive strike so devastating that America's morale would "sink to the extent that it could not be recovered." The United States would then be forced to negotiate a treaty to cease interfering with Japan's conquests in China and Southeast Asia.

Renowned as an insatiable gambler, the Japanese admiral's strategy promised a great reward but at an enormous risk. A surprise attack against the US Pacific Fleet anchored at Pearl Harbor in Oahu,

Hawaii, could be, as Yamamoto described, "so difficult and so dangerous that we must be prepared to risk complete annihilation." If detected before striking, or, worse, if it were to fall prey to a preconceived American trap, the entire Japanese task force could find itself at the mercy of the Pacific Fleet and US bombers.

To enhance his chances of success, Yamamoto requested the aid of the Imperial Navy's brilliant and cunning airman, Cmdr. Minoru Genda, known as "Mad Gen," to develop the tactics of the air strike. Genda was an airman with unmatched foresight who believed that modern warfare on the oceans would be determined by the airplane, not the outdated battleship that had ruled the waters during World War I. Although Mad Gen recommended a full-blown invasion of the Hawaiian Islands, Yamamoto preferred a limited attack on the US Pacific Fleet.

The plan settled on by Yamamoto called for a task force of all available Japanese aircraft carriers, supported by an armada of battleships, heavy and light cruisers, and submarines, to trek secretly across 3,500 miles of open ocean to attack and destroy all US aircraft carriers, battleships, and land-based planes stationed at Pearl Harbor and nearby Hawaiian bases. The audacious plan also called for a coordinated attack on US bases at Midway Atoll, Wake Island, Guam, and the Philippines, as well as British, Canadian, and Australian forces at Malaya, Borneo, Singapore, and Hong Kong. The independent country of Thailand would also be attacked.

The success of the massive air and naval strike depended on total secrecy. Yet, two weeks after Yamamoto first put ink to paper, the US Ambassador to Japan, Joseph Grew, learned through unofficial sources that not only was Japan preparing for its Southern Operation, it was also planning an all-out attack on Pearl Harbor. Ambassador Grew's concern passed from the Department of State to the Department of the Navy, where it landed in the hands of Chief of Naval Operations Adm. Harold Stark. Stark telegraphed Adm. Husband E. Kimmel, who was commander in chief not only of the US Pacific Fleet based at Pearl Harbor but the overall US Fleet that included the US Pacific, Atlantic, and Asiatic fleets. Stark's telegram relayed Ambassador Grew's concern, but with the addition of a blatant dismissal: "The Division of Naval Intelligence places no credence in these rumors. Furthermore, based on known data regarding the present disposition and employment of Japanese naval and army forces, no move against Pearl Harbor appears imminent or planned for in the forseeable [sic] future." Nothing further was done.

American political and military leaders expected that war with Japan was inevitable unless diplomats from both countries, particularly US Secretary of State Cordell Hull and Japanese special envoy Saburō Kurusu, could reach a satisfactory agreement. Most Americans were against joining the war in Europe and fighting Germans again, giving little thought to Japan initially. Despite the fall of France and the merciless bombing of London by Nazi Germany, many Americans joined isolationist groups, like the America First Committee, and ran isolationist candidates for office who pledged to keep the United States out of another foreign war.

As the month of December 1941 began, however, isolationists recognized that rather than the Germans, it might be a Japanese attack, on US bases in the Philippines, that could draw the United States into a world war again. The only hope for the isolationists was that in the event of a diplomatic stalemate, Japan would postpone any aggressive action against the United States until the war's outcome in Europe became clear; or, in any case, Japan would limit its attacks to European interests in the Pacific or to faraway American bases deemed expendable by Washington.

Few, if any, considered the US Pacific Fleet at Pearl Harbor a potential target. Other than those in Hawaii and the families of servicemen stationed there, most Americans had never heard of Pearl Harbor. Although army and navy brass understood that an attack on Hawaii was possible, it seemed highly improbable, especially while the formidable US Pacific Fleet lay anchored at Pearl Harbor. "If there were ever men and a fleet ready for any emergency, it's Uncle Sam's fighting ships," crowed the *Honolulu Advertiser* in 1941. Even more foolishly, much of the US military and many American people viewed the Japanese as short, buck-toothed fools who couldn't see a target through their thick eyeglasses—at least that was the pervasive derogatory stereotype. They were worried about Adolf Hitler and his Blitzkrieg, not the obscure island of Japan on the other side of the largest ocean on the planet.

As the American people returned to work on Monday, December 1, following a long Thanksgiving holiday, none could have imagined that Yamamoto's massive attack plan against the United States was already in motion. The Japanese admiral's high-stakes gamble was about to pay off.

## CHAPTER 10

# THREE OTHER CLIPPERS IN THE PACIFIC

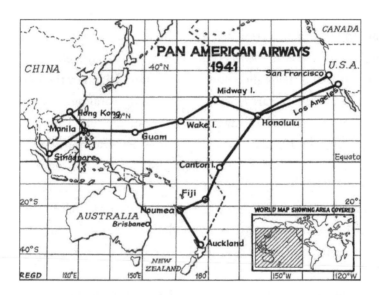

Map of the routes to Hawaii, the Antipodes, and the Orient. Pan American Airways System, "Map of Company's Pacific Ocean Routes,"1940, 1; U. Miami PAA.

The *Philippine Clipper* wasn't the only Pan Am flying boat carrying passengers across the Pacific Ocean that first week of December 1941. The *Pacific Clipper* had taken off from Pearl City for Auckland, New Zealand, the day before. The *Anzac Clipper* would fly from Treasure Island for Singapore on December 5, and the *Hong Kong Clipper* would prepare to take off from Manila for Hong Kong a day later.

# PACIFIC CLIPPER

On Friday, December 5, the *Pacific Clipper* with Capt. Robert Ford at the helm was a day into its 5,116-mile journey over the South Pacific to Auckland. So far, the flight's special Antipodes cocktail—a concoction of gin, orange juice, Curaçao, and cracked ice, shaken—had made the flight more enjoyable for those who'd partaken.

The twice-monthly Antipodes route was Pan Am's newest, having opened the year before. Because of the heavy payload to be carried over such a great distance, the clipper would make three stops before reaching Auckland. The first of the layovers had been Canton Island the night before (now Kanton Island in the Republic of Kiribati), a narrow strip of low-lying coral surrounding a pear-shaped lagoon halfway between Hawaii and Fiji. Under Mac's supervision in 1939, Pan Am had constructed a marine base on the island that included a lush single-story twenty-four-room hotel that was soon to be expanded. The tiny isle had become newsworthy four years earlier when Amelia Earhart and her navigator, former Pan Am navigator Fred Noonan, mysteriously disappeared while trying to land at nearby Howland Island on their around-the-world flight.

Following a night's stay at the Pan Am hotel, the passengers aboard the *Pacific Clipper* departed Canton Island and were about to complete a smooth and uneventful 1,250-mile flight to the next island stopover—Fiji. The eight-and-a-half-hour flight had crossed both west of the International Date Line and south of the equator, providing an exceptional experience for those onboard. The clipper landed at Pan Am's marine base in Suva Harbor on Saturday, December 6, 1941 (December 5, Hawaiian time). Pan Am had added Fiji to the route the month before in order to lessen fuel load and increase payload, effectively adopting a timetable of shorter hops rather than longer ones.

A Boeing B-314 (the *Pacific Clipper*) during takeoff. U. Miami PAA.

Exuberant Fijians welcomed the clipper with Fiji's governor, Sir Harry Luke, aboard. Having boarded at Canton Island, the Fijian governor had requested permission to join the pilots on the bridge to view his province from the air. "As we neared Suva," Sir Harry wrote, "I asked the captain to circle over our leper island, Makongai, which I thought would interest the passengers and knew would delight the patients."

Fiji is the quintessential tropical destination. "The colors are truly kaleidoscopic," read a Pan Am periodical, "ranging from the deep blue and white foam of the sea to the lush tropic green of the jungle, splashed with brilliant red tulip trees and the pastel shades of hibiscus, and marked by frequent waterfalls tumbling down the mountain slopes." Pan Am public relations director William Van Dusen described Fiji as "the place Adam and Eve got chased out of."

The clipper passengers checked into Suva's Grand Pacific Hotel (or G.P.H., as it was often called). The G.P.H. was not only the finest accommodation on the island but one of the finest luxury hotels in the South Pacific. Built in 1914 by the Union Steamship Company to accommodate its passengers during stopovers, the hotel had been uniquely designed to resemble a luxury cruise liner inside and out, so that passengers would feel as if they'd never gone ashore. The inimitable hotel had welcomed not merely the wealthy and dignitaries but British royalty, who would include Queen Elizabeth II a decade later. American author James Michener described the splendid lodging as "One of the memorable hotels of the world, not majestic and not particularly spacious, but a haven to all who crossed the Pacific on tourist ships or who now came by airplane."

Home for nearly all of the *Pacific Clipper*'s passengers staying at the G.P.H. was now a smidgeon under 1,500 miles away. Newly knighted Sir John Madsen and Australian magazine editor Alice Jackson had already flown 25,000 miles from Australia to London and back and, like the other passengers, were anxious to arrive at Auckland. The clipper could have reached their destination in a single hop from Fiji; but because of Pan Am's shorter hop timetable, the clipper would instead take off the following day for New Caledonia, providing passengers with another night's respite before ultimately landing in Auckland on Monday, December 8 (December 7, Hawaiian time). Once in Auckland, it would be a short flight over the Tasman Sea to Australia.

Though so far only German vessels had struck in minor skirmishes in the Coral and Tasman Seas, those living in the Antipodes were about to sense a real fear of invasion—not from the Germans, but from the Imperial Japanese Navy.

# ANZAC CLIPPER

At 4:18 p.m., three minutes after the scheduled takeoff time, Capt. H. Lanier Turner skippered the *Anzac Clipper* from its marine port in Treasure Island toward Hawaii. The clipper was due to land in Pearl City around 6:30 the next morning, Saturday, December 6, just after sunrise, on its way to Singapore. Named after the acronym for the World War I combined military group—Australian and New Zealand Army Corps—the *Anzac Clipper* was the newest of Pan Am's whopping Boeings equipped with the finest amenities.

Unlike the military officers with whom Mac was sharing cabin space on the latest *Philippine Clipper* flight and those aboard the *Pacific Clipper* who'd had an audience with the king and queen of the United Kingdom, the passengers aboard the *Anzac Clipper* represented an ordinary sampling of 1941 wealth. There were young people like Joyce Granner and her friend Bernice LaMarr, both single women in their twenties living in Honolulu, and professionals like Dr. V. G. Clark, a thirty-year-old female osteopathic physician practicing in Honolulu, as well as businessman Randolph Crossley, the son-in-law of the enormously successful George Pepperdine, who'd started Western Auto Supply Company and eventually founded Pepperdine University in Malibu, California.

The *Anzac Clipper*'s sole VIP was Galon U Saw, the prime minister of Burma (now Myanmar). U Saw (U was a title of honor in Burma at that time) had visited London in November to meet with British Prime Minister Winston Churchill in an unsuccessful attempt to obtain self-governing British Dominion status for Burma comparable to that of Canada, Australia, and New Zealand. Disappointed, the Burmese prime minister met with President Roosevelt to request the American president to intervene with Churchill on his behalf, but Roosevelt declined. U Saw was now traveling back home with an alternative and more sinister plan up his sleeve.

It was nearing 8:15 p.m. PT on December 5, just four hours into the flight. The stewards began preparing berths and turning down the beds for the passengers. It was then that the captain made a surprise announcement on the PA system—due to mechanical trouble, the *Anzac Clipper* would be returning to Treasure Island.

The stewards heard the groans of disappointment rise among those onboard. The captain apologized, but assured everyone that the plane would be repaired and ready to depart San Francisco at the same scheduled time the following day. A catwalk in the plane's broad wings had allowed the flight engineer to attempt to repair the engine in flight, but the clipper's troubled engine required more comprehensive repair. Though not advisable, a Boeing B-314A like the *Anzac Clipper* was designed to fly with three of its four engines inoperable. Rarely if ever did a pilot tempt the fourth engine.

More often than liked, Pan Am clippers turned around during the course of their flights. Most passengers understood that scheduled takeoff and landing times were flexible, to take into account various unforeseen events. "And we were all prepared for it," Pan Am crew member John Cooke Jr. (referred to simply as John Cooke hereafter) recalled, "and it happened frequently, and the passengers didn't seem to mind." The usual cause was extremely bad weather like a typhoon or intense winds, since the seaplanes were not pressurized and could not always fly above a storm (the technology for pressurized planes had just been developed). An airplane's ground speed can be reduced to a standstill against strong winds, while expending precious fuel. Other times, it was oil leaks or more serious mechanical issues. Any decision to turn around, however, had to be made before the flight reached its point of no return, which is the location during a flight at which the destination is as close to the plane's current position as is its point of origin. Pilots call it the "splash point." The longest Pan Am clipper flight that ever returned was one on the *China Clipper* that turned back halfway from the West Coast to Hawaii—an eighteen-hour round-trip flight that ended where it had begun.

For the passengers of the *Anzac Clipper*, making a round-trip flight of eight hours and returning to their point of origin, Treasure Island, was obviously frustrating. Yet, for those flying on to Singapore, they'd reach their destination within a week, which was still much faster than the three to four weeks that it would take by ship. They'd simply try again Saturday afternoon, December 6, perhaps after spending time at the Embarcadero where they could shop and have some lighthearted fun, at least for one more day.

# HONG KONG CLIPPER

The Crown colony of Hong Kong, one of the supremely beautiful ports in the entire world, lay in the Far East; it was an exotic destination for the *Hong Kong Clipper*. Meaning "fragrant harbor" from its early days as an exporter of incense, Hong Kong actually embraces several small, closely grouped islands but principally Hong Kong Island and the opposite peninsula of Kowloon, with a larger area extending twenty miles behind Kowloon called the New Territories. The British Empire had appropriated Hong Kong and then Kowloon following its victories in the First and Second Opium Wars in the mid-1800s. In 1898, Britain entered into a ninety-nine-year lease for the New Territories, giving it control of Hong Kong until 1997, when it would revert to China.

Because of Britain's colonization, Pan Am's patrons could travel to a far eastern country where its inhabitants spoke English in addition to native Chinese dialects. "The dream of aviators, businessmen and travelers for many years has been realized," read Hong Kong's *South China Morning Post* when the *Philippine Clipper* landed in Hong Kong for the first time in 1936. Ernest Hemingway had experienced that dream when he flew aboard the *California Clipper* in February 1941 with his newest wife, the novelist and journalist Martha Gellhorn, for a three-month stay.

With the addition of marine bases in Hong Kong and then Singapore that Mac had helped to construct, Pan Am solidified its position as the foremost international air carrier in the world. Its fleet of 162 sea and land planes offered regularly scheduled flights that during 1941 had carried 375,000 passengers over 227.5 million passenger miles across 62 countries and colonies. It also had transported 11.8 million pounds of freight that year. From thousands of baby chicks to a single panda bear and everything in between, if it could be carried on a plane, Pan Am transported it. No other airline even came close.

But Pan Am was strictly an international carrier; it did not possess any US domestic routes. It did, however, contract with United Air Lines (now United Airlines) and Transcontinental & Western Air (TWA) to provide carrier service across the United States. Pan Am also co-owned the China National Aviation Corporation (CNAC) with the Chinese government that connected with Pan Am's route at Hong Kong (China would not grant Pan Am landing rights except through CNAC). From Hong Kong, passengers could board CNAC planes to Shanghai and Peiping (Beijing) and to additional stops along the Yangtze River. As a result, Pan Am could transport people to the Orient in record time in 1941. For example, a couple could take a United Air Lines flight from New York City to San Francisco under contract with Pan Am, then take off from Treasure Island on a Pan Am clipper and be riding along in rickshaws in Hong Kong sipping gimlets merely seven days after having left New York. Moreover, that same couple could transfer to a CNAC plane in Hong Kong, co-owned by Pan Am, and fly inland where they could stand in awe of the Great Wall of China. Pan Am had indeed shrunk the world.

On the morning of Sunday, December 7 (Saturday, December 6 in Hawaii), twenty-four passengers boarded the *Hong Kong Clipper* at its marine base in the Philippines and took off for Hong Kong. Inasmuch as Manila Bay's waters were too rough for safe landings, Pan Am had leased and placed Mac in charge of renovating an old US Marine Corps flying-boat base eight miles south of Manila at Cañacao Bay in Cavite Harbor.

The *Hong Kong Clipper*, affectionately nicknamed Myrtle, was

A Sikorsky S-42 (the *Hong Kong Clipper*) taking off. U. Miami PAA.

a Sikorsky S-42B and had been an amazing flying boat when first delivered to Pan Am in 1935. But because the S-42 could fly no farther than 1,200 miles nonstop, it never had the fuel capacity to fly passengers great distances across the Pacific. By 1941, the Sikorsky S-42 had been surpassed in luxury and technology by the Glenn Martin M-130 flying boat that included the *China* and *Philippine Clippers*, and by the Boeing B-314A, like the *Pacific* and *Anzac Clippers*. Nonetheless, the *Hong Kong Clipper* was still among the supremely luxurious planes in the air or on the sea.

The shuttle flight between Manila and Hong Kong was a very comfortable and profitable one for Pan Am. What had taken travelers a day and a half aboard a ship, the *Hong Kong Clipper* slashed to five and a half hours. In the business world, time is money; and in the case of travel by clipper, it took a lot of money to save time.

For the speedy seven-hundred-mile trip between Manila and Hong Kong (comparable in distance to flying from Chicago to New York) in the comfortable *Hong Kong Clipper*, passengers paid $208 one-way or $374.40 round-trip ($6,500 today). For that price, the shuttle passengers consisted principally of local royalty, government officials, and businessmen such as importers, financiers, and industrialists. Among the twenty-four passengers aboard Pan Am's *Hong Kong Clipper* on December 7 were Manila and Hong Kong businessmen, eight American missionaries, and Joseph Alsop Jr., a thirty-one-year-old American journalist and syndicated newspaper columnist.

At 4:00 p.m. that Sunday, December 7, Hong Kong time, Capt. Fred Ralph skippered the *Hong Kong Clipper* to a perfect landing in Victoria Harbor, avoiding collisions with the myriad sampans and junks sailing on Kowloon Bay. The clipper taxied to Pan Am's marine base beside a British aerodrome at Kai Tak Airport on the Kowloon side of the harbor. Once passengers cleared customs and immigration, most hopped in awaiting coaches that traveled the ten-minute route to the Peninsula Hotel on Kowloon Peninsula's point. They could sip a cocktail on the terrace and enjoy the gorgeous views of the bay and the ridge of mountains that surrounds Hong Kong.

The travelers who'd just landed aboard the *Hong Kong Clipper* would not be returning to Manila on Monday's flight, but twenty-seven other passengers would. They had early wakeup calls scheduled for the next morning, December 8, Hong Kong time. Among them was Jan Henrik "Hank" Marsman, a forty-nine-year-old Dutch-born millionaire, who'd traveled to Hong Kong from the United States to inspect his gold-mining and construction empires as well as various other business interests in the Orient. He'd intended to fly back home to San Francisco earlier, but was called to Java and Hong Kong on business. Like Mac, Marsman had an eleven-year-old daughter, Anne, expecting him home for Christmas. His wife, Mary, also eagerly awaited his return.

The *Philippine Clipper* flying over Macau on its way to Hong Kong. U. Miami PAA.

The *Hong Kong Clipper* was scheduled to depart Kai Tak Airport at 9:00 a.m., Monday, December 8, which was Sunday, December 7, Hawaiian time—but what is scheduled does not always take off.

## CHAPTER 11

# NEXT HOP—WAKE ISLAND

Mac looked down at the atoll vanishing from his window as Capt. John Hamilton steered the *Philippine Clipper* up and away from Midway's lagoon. After just a single night's layover at Midway, the captain and his seven-man crew coaxed the silver-lacquered big bird toward scattered clouds as it set off for Wake Island on the way to its ultimate destination of Singapore. Photographs were forbidden as dawn illuminated the vanishing Midway Atoll, though Gen. Claire Lee Chennault once stated that the proscription was unnecessary on any of Pan Am's Pacific island hops: "Actually there was little to see except gooney birds on Midway, sooty terns on Wake Island, and grass shacks on Guam." Civilian defense contractors with supervisor Harry Olson on Wake were now laboring intensely to change that poor state of military readiness on the Pacific islands.

Seated in the *Philippine Clipper* with Mac were Maj. Thomas Harper; Sgt. Henry Willcox; 2nd Lt. Albert "Ajax" Baumler, a young fighter pilot headed to China to fight with Gen. Chennault; and Lt. Col. John Tamraz of the US Army Medical Corps, who was the second-highest-ranking medical officer in the China-Burma-India theater. The four Pan Am employees who'd taken off from Honolulu had stayed behind at Midway, where an additional passenger, Herman Hevenor, had boarded. Hevenor was a fifty-five-year-old examiner with the US Bureau of Budget in Washington, DC. He'd been assigned the unpopular task of inspecting military construction on

Wake and other Pacific islands, as well as reviewing contractors' account books for errors or fraud.

On this early morning leg of the flight to Wake Island, conversations promptly gave way to naps and reading following Charlie's deliciously prepared breakfast. Watching the vast ocean pass below, Mac must have mused about how six years earlier he'd arrived on the bleak coral island of Wake with his boss, William Grooch. After the completion of their work at Midway Atoll, Pan Am had sent them to oversee the construction of essentially identical facilities on Wake. They'd followed the same route there, only by ship.

Any thought of his buddy Grooch, however, had to conjure up the memory of Grooch's wife, Belle. From what has been called a "tragedy of homesickness" and "temporary insanity," Belle Grooch jumped off the roof of the eight-story Washington Apartments with her two young sons, William and Thomas. She fell ninety feet with "one under each arm" in the French Concession of Shanghai where Grooch was then serving as Pan Am's operations manager in 1934 before the Japanese invasion. A month afterward, Belle's father left a note in his New York apartment, "I can stand the pain no longer," before firing a bullet into his wife's left temple and then sticking the revolver in his own mouth. Inconsolably grief-stricken, William Grooch had considered suicide and required a constant guard for weeks. He would survive the supreme tragedy, only to die in a plane crash over South America five years later.

As Mac reflected on old times, good and bad, the *Philippine Clipper*'s engines droned on, drawing the flying boat closer to the flyspeck of an island peeking through the surface of the planet's largest ocean. The most challenging of the bases to locate along the forbidding Pacific route, Mac's former boss William Grooch once described Wake Island as "shrub trees, brush and jumbled masses of rock" that was the "only spot of land within a radius of twelve hundred miles." It was a fairly accurate description.

Despite the fact that Wake Island had been equipped with the latest land-based direction finder—the Leuteritz long-range DF—it wasn't always reliable. Precise navigation required intelligent and meticulous Second Officer John Hrutky to remain at his station on the bridge reviewing charts on a seven-foot-long table opposite a panel jam-packed with sensitive instruments. From time to time, he manned one of the two drift sight stations where he might drop bomb-shaped ceramic flasks filled with aluminum or bronze powder onto the ocean's surface. He'd then observe the silvery splotch on the ocean with a pelorus (similar to a compass without magnetic needles and having two sight vanes) to determine the plane's drift from prevailing winds. Other times, Hrutky climbed up to the plane's celestial observation dome at the wing's top center to use an octant to calculate the plane's location relative to celestial bodies, much as captains of clipper sailing ships had used sextants a century earlier. In storms or thick cloud cover, John Hrutky was relegated to simply using dead reckoning. Second Radio Officer Ted Hrutky also completed radio checks with the nearest Pan Am marine base every half hour and, when fortunate, with passing ships to share their nautical bearings.

In the early days of transoceanic flights, such constant checking and rechecking by the navigator and radio operator were critical to the success and safety of the voyage. One degree off could mean the plane would miss its next island stop by miles with disastrous consequences, which is likely what happened to Amelia Earhart and her navigator Fred Noonan. "How the captain could find those tiny islands down there in the vast Pacific was a mystery to me," wrote Catherine Cotterman Hoskins, who'd traveled aboard flying boats in her youth. Despite such difficulties, Pan Am clippers always hit their mark.

Regardless of its size, Wake Island had turned out to be Pan Am's transpacific salvation. The distance over water between Midway and Guam is wider than the continental United States, more than a Pan Am flying boat could safely reach at the time, taking into account fuel requirements and potentially strong headwinds. Pan Am CEO Juan Trippe needed another island or atoll as a stopover point. He'd checked with the US Navy, ship companies, and even old mariners, but the answer was the same—there's nothing out there but thousands of nautical miles of salt water. Some suggested anchoring floating airports called "seadromes," while others proposed planes landing on the ocean, being hoisted aboard a ship, refueled, and then catapulted into the air. Eventually, Pan Am received the sensible answer it had been looking for from old ship logs and oceanic charts in the New York Public Library—Wake Island, a small volcanic island claimed by the United States in 1899 around the time that the US annexed the Hawaiian Islands.

The horseshoe-shaped island was extremely small—two and a half square miles—but charts showed a calm lagoon that lay within a twelve-foot rise of sand and coral. After surveys revealed that aerial island hopping was feasible, Pan Am acquired leases from the US Navy for marine bases at Pearl Harbor, Midway, Wake, and Guam. President Franklin Roosevelt even signed the executive order for Wake Island himself.

Roosevelt and the US Navy recognized the military value of having an American commercial airline blaze the trail from the United States to China. The United States was a party with Japan to the Washington Naval Treaty, which had forbidden US military development of its possessions west of the Hawaiian Islands. It was fairly clear to many that Pan Am and the US Navy were in cahoots, and Japan filed a formal protest; but no action was taken. "Pan American . . . also functions even more importantly as a branch of the defense effort," *Life* magazine wrote in 1941. "It does this so effectively that sometimes it has seemed that the rest of the defense effort, still largely composed of creaks and groans in Washington, should become an arm of Pan American."

Now, six years after Wake Island had become a Pan Am marine base, Mac, who'd been a part of Pan Am's island-hopping plan from the beginning, continued his voyage aboard the *Philippine Clipper* as it crossed the International Date Line 140 miles west of Midway. Suddenly, today became tomorrow—Saturday, December 6, 1941 became Sunday, December 7. East of the imaginary timeline, however, it remained Saturday, December 6 in Midway, Hawaii, and the continental United States. "Traveling on the Flying Clippers on the serial sky road which connects Midway and Wake has provided some people with two Christmases, some with two birthdays, or two New Year's celebrations in immediately succeeding twenty-four-hour periods," read a Pan Am travel magazine.

To memorialize the occasion, Charlie, the lone steward, handed passengers a gold-and-blue certificate filled out with each of their names and the clipper's name, signed and dated by Capt. Hamilton. The ostentatious certificate, entitled DOMAIN OF PHOEBUS APOLLO, had been designed with the idea to entertain well-to-do tourists on vacation rather than the clipper's current passengers—a Pan Am employee, four military officers, and a US budget agent. (A similar certificate with "Jupiter Rex" mimicking the King Neptune ritual aboard ocean liners was handed out when crossing the equator.) The Phoebus Apollo certificate read in part: "Know All Peoples That [Frank McKenzie], once eastbound and time-laden, is now declared a subject of the Realm of the Sun and Heavens. . . . That with the speed of Our Flaming Chariot this subject did fly the skies over the International Date Line. . . . That . . . the Today of mortals at once becomes Yesterday and all is confusion . . ." Mac had likely collected a small stack of these certificates through the years, which he may have passed along to his young daughter, Doreen, back home in California.

With the farcical certificate came an even more foolish ceremony where Charlie donned a frilly hat and performed a brief dance ritual before placing a paper crown atop the head of the serious-looking

A "Domain of Phoebus Apollo" certificate belonging to Charlie Relyea. Gary Relyea collection.

2nd Lt. Ajax Baumler, the youngest of those onboard, who would go on to fight in four wars and become an ace fighter pilot. Mac and the others laughed, and so did the battle-hardened Baumler. There was no better person to pull off the gag than Charlie, a consummate jokester. Like most things he attempted, Charlie put every bit of energy he had into the part. The ritual may have been silly, but it broke the monotony of a long flight. Wake Island still lay seven hours away.

## CHAPTER 12

# FINAL PREPARATIONS FOR X DAY

The day to strike Pearl Harbor, called X Day by Japanese military planners, had been set as December 7, Hawaiian time. That's why the Japanese attack group's main task force was relentlessly advancing day and night through storms and constant danger toward Oahu. December 7 would be a Sunday morning. Sunday was chosen because the US Pacific Fleet typically returned to Pearl Harbor on weekends after conducting exercises in the Pacific during the week. Sunday also was a day of rest for the thousands of young sailors and Marines aboard the ninety-six warships moored in the harbor.

The other attacks planned across the British, Dutch, and American-held territory in the Pacific Ocean—Singapore, Hong Kong, Borneo, Malaya, Thailand, Netherlands East Indies, the Philippines, Guam, Wake Island, and Midway Atoll—would be coordinated to occur in conjunction with X Day, after the attack on Pearl Harbor had begun.

Unaware of their objective when leaving Japan, Japanese pilots and crews now proudly sat erect in the briefing room of each aircraft carrier knowing that they were on their way to Pearl Harbor, attentively receiving additional instruction from flight commanders. Each bombing group, whether torpedo, dive-bombing, or low-level and high-level bombing, attended separate sessions. The instructor drew arrows on a blackboard with chalk to demonstrate the correct bombing path of each group of aerial bombers. A large model of

Pearl Harbor also rested on a table with toy-sized battleships and carriers at the locations where they were expected to be moored, based on intelligence coming from Japanese spies in Honolulu.

Pilots and bombardiers also shouted out the names of ships shown to them in photographs or in silhouettes on white flashcards. It would have been strange to hear the names of American states shouted aboard a Japanese aircraft carrier—California, Oklahoma, Maryland, West Virginia, Tennessee, Pennsylvania, Arizona, and Nevada, representing the eight battleships that hopefully would be moored in Pearl Harbor at the time of attack. Other ships were identified and their names shouted, including those that might return to harbor after their carrier escort missions were completed. Though they'd studied for weeks, the instruction continued, if for no other reason than to keep the pilots' minds occupied and sharp.

"Young boys of the flying crews were boiling over with fighting spirit," remembered Cmdr. Mitsuo Fuchida aboard the task force flagship, *Akagi*. "Hard nights and days of training had been followed by hasty preparations, and now the sortie, which meant that they were [soon] going to war."

## CHAPTER 13

# BOAT DAY

Harry Olson, the middle-aged Wake Island construction supervisor, stepped out of the Moana Hotel and gestured for a cab. A valet relayed Harry's signal and rushed to open the car door. "Honolulu Harbor" was the instruction. Harry wanted to witness one of Hawaii's traditions that he'd heard so much about at the hotel while vacationing at Waikiki. Friday, December 5, was "Boat Day," and the SS *Lurline*, the flagship of the Matson Navigation Company, rested moored and anchored at Pier 11, ready for its noon departure to San Francisco.

As the taxi rounded the corner on Ala Moana Boulevard, Harry not only could see the commotion, he could hear it. Harry, looking snappy in pressed khakis and a white dress shirt, jumped out of the cab onto the sidewalk, anxious to join the fun. He was instantly waylaid by men and women lining the block, selling their colorful and fragrant leis. Harry brushed past their makeshift tables and quickened his step, putting the indistinct banter of those hawking their goods behind him. Nearing the Aloha Tower, he could see portions of a large white ship between the buildings along the harbor. When he reached the dock marked Pier 11, he understood what was causing the uproar. Hundreds of men, women, and children stood rambunctiously waving and shouting at a legion of passengers lining two levels of railings on a grand white steamship. Above the ship's top row of portholes, a mob of seafarers stood shoulder to shoulder, enthusiastically returning the landlubbers' attention, taking care not to fall overboard while doing so.

"Boat day in Hawaii is famous the world over," syndicated columnist Ernie Pyle wrote. "I believe nobody can be quite sane when he sails from Hawaii. Everything forbids sanity. The shouting, the flowers, the band, the streamers, sunshine, palms, dark faces, colorful clothes, and the weeping and the goodbyes."

On the opposite end of the gangway, the SS *Lurline* rose like a long iceberg from the tropical harbor. Sleek and shiny and completely white, she was a beaut. Two of Harry's fellow assistant superintendents, Herman Echols and Bill Puccetti, had already walked up the lone gangway and boarded. Unlike Harry, who preferred spending his December boondoggle basking alone in Hawaii's sun, his two coworkers planned to visit their families on the mainland for Christmas. Harry had not yet spotted his colleagues amid the pandemonium, and no wonder—the *Lurline* was carrying 765 passengers that Friday, and more than 7,000 sacks of packages and 350 letter pouches. It was a record for any Matson ship. Christmas was right around the corner, and folks wanted to return to the mainland to spend it with families. Economic times were good, the best since 1929 when the Great Depression had begun. Consequently, the 1941 holiday season was shaping up to be a spirited one.

Harry leaned against a concrete pillar along the pier to watch the friendly chaos. He observed people crying and others cheerfully waving their hands, handkerchiefs, and hats, shouting "bon voyage" and "aloha." A band played Hawaiian music, and a group sang folksy songs into a microphone. Tall native men with bronze faces wearing gold-colored Hawaiian headdresses and cloaks strolled about as hula dancers swayed their hips, with their arms and hands undulating through the air.

It wasn't long before two long thundering blasts of the steamship's horn triggered a momentary hush over the mob, startling many of them. Everyone knew what that sound meant—it was time

Boat Day in Honolulu. Everett Collection Historical/Alamy stock photo.

for the SS *Lurline* to shove off. Native boys permitted on the ocean liner also knew it was their cue to dive off the deck. With change collected from passengers to watch their high dives, the boys hit the water's surface as smoothly as arrows shot from the ship and resurfaced with enthusiastic waves and shouts of aloha.

Outrigger canoes and speedboats crisscrossed the harbor as a tugboat nudged the big ship's stern and pushed it slowly from its berth. As the gap between the pier and the ship widened, passengers watched the colored paper streamers snap and drift downward into the churning water. Some tossed their leis into the breeze, watching them drop into the stirring wake of the slow-moving ocean liner. Many of the pier's onlookers sauntered away as the *Lurline* departed, but Harry waited as the ocean liner made its way farther along the coast toward Diamond Head. He could still see the steamship's passengers frantically waving as black smoke belched from one of the ship's twin stacks. Before long, the ship and its commotion disappeared into a crinkling haze along the horizon.

———

Earlier that December 5 morning, another ship had departed Honolulu, though not as part of Boat Day. The USS *Lexington*, the lone aircraft carrier of the US Pacific Fleet that was still anchored at Pearl Harbor that morning, sailed out of the harbor at 8:10 a.m., escorted by the three heavy cruisers and five destroyers comprising Task Force 12. Their mission was to deliver fighter planes to the small naval base at Midway Atoll. Harry hadn't seen the *Lexington* sail out of the harbor, but Oregon state senator Douglas McKay had. Like Harry, he was staying at the Moana Hotel. Senator McKay had arrived on the SS *Lurline* to watch a team from his state play in the upcoming Shriners college football game in Honolulu. Lounging in his room that morning, the senator shared his island experience in a brief letter to his wife: "The clipper leaves at noon so will make a short report [The *China Clipper* would carry his letter to the mainland]. This is a great place—I'm sitting beside an open window overlooking the beach and I can see the fleet putting out to sea. . . . The boat [SS *Lurline*] leaves today at noon too & we will leave on her next trip. . . . If I feel too lonesome I'll phone you—costs $7.50 [$147.50 today] which seems like an extravagance."

The day before, the US aircraft carrier *Enterprise* and its supporting ships of Task Force 8 had delivered USMC Squadron VMF-211 Grumman Wildcat fighter planes to Wake Island and then begun its return voyage to Pearl Harbor. It was due to arrive back at Pearl on December 6, but bad weather and mishaps had slowed its return by more than a day. Another carrier, the USS *Saratoga*, had undergone an overhaul at the navy yard in Bremerton, Washington, and on December 6 was sailing for San Diego to embark its air group before leaving for Pearl Harbor, a harbor which now found itself for the time being without any aircraft carriers to moor.

The Oregon senator wasn't the only person who observed the *Lexington* put out to sea that Friday morning. A young diplomatic clerk in the Japanese Consulate in Honolulu—Takeo Yoshikawa—stood on a hill with binoculars and a pad and pen. Like the senator, the Japanese spy wasted little time writing his letter, though his was in the form of a cable to Tokyo that was quickly relayed to the Japanese task force steaming toward the Hawaiian Islands. It seemed that Friday, December 5, had been a marvelous "Boat Day" for everyone.

## CHAPTER 14

# WAKE ISLAND

John Cooke waved from the dock to the *Philippine Clipper* as it circled over Wake Island's lagoon after a flight of nine hours from Midway. Pan Am flying boat pilots frequently circled before landing—not only to inspect the lagoon but to "give those watching from below a thrill," Pan Am captains recalled.

Cooke was Wake's airport manager. He'd been in radio contact with the clipper since it approached within range of Wake's radio shack. Because radio audio signals could traverse the ocean no more than a few miles, especially when interfered with by storms or other atmospheric disturbances, the clipper's radio officers used Morse code during most of the flight. A clipboard for messages lay beside the transmitter key and headset on the radio officer's table. It was always reassuring to hear a scratchy voice emerge over the headphones after hours of quiet, informing the radio officer that the clipper was nearing its destination, just as Cooke had done minutes earlier.

After signing off, Cooke hurried from the radio shack along a path of crushed coral and sand. He reached the dock in time to see the landing and to welcome those disembarking. Cooke wasn't alone. The island's chief engineer and assistant, the chief mechanic, and the doctor stood with Cooke on the long dock stretching out into the turquoise lagoon. It was standard Pan Am procedure. White-uniformed Pan Am ground crew members, some with white caps, others with tanned bare heads,

The long dock at Wake Island. NARA, San Francisco; SFOM.

stood ready to toss the bow lines, tether the plane to the dock, and unload the passengers and mail. Unlike Midway, which used a landing barge on which to unload passengers and mail, Pan Am's marine base at Wake Island featured an impressive wood-and-concrete pier with whitewashed railing that stretched three hundred feet into the lagoon and another hundred feet or so onto the beach.

"This ecstasy of greeting a flying clipper out of space to one of the tiny island landfalls of the trans-Pacific air route . . . was like no other experience in a lifetime," wrote former passenger Dorothy Kaucher.

Maj. James Devereux, who commanded the Marines on the island, described a somewhat different joy upon a clipper's landing: "These arrivals were the Wake Island version of a gala event, especially for any junior officer fortunate enough to be off duty on the infrequent occasions when the passengers included a personable young woman."

John Cooke's wife, Isyl, and his two young sons, Bleecker and Phillip, normally would have been with Cooke on the dock that day, but they'd been evacuated to Honolulu three weeks earlier as Japanese aggression heated up in French Indochina. "I would walk down the dock to greet the clippers when they would arrive on Wake and follow passengers back without talking," Phillip Cooke remembered eighty years later. "That made my father decide to nickname me Harpo after Harpo Marx." (Harpo, part of the Marx Brothers comedy group, never spoke during his performances.)

Once the *Philippine Clipper* was securely moored and its engines shut down, Capt. Hamilton stepped onto the pontoon landing, followed by his crew. Mac and the four military officers, along with the US budget examiner, also disembarked, stooping as they exited through the hatch. Unlike Mac, who knew every grain of sand on the island just as he did at Midway, it was Hevenor's first time at Wake. The bookish Hevenor stretched and looked across the lagoon from the dock. He was greeted with the aroma of the sea and sand, mixed with the sparse island shrubs and flora, as he fretfully scanned the lagoon for sharks.

"Wake sits on top of a single mountain peak . . . volcanic, and is one of the loneliest spots on earth," recalled Jack Wahle, a Pan Am flight engineer and pilot. "It is surrounded by open ocean for more than a thousand miles in any direction."

Some visitors believed the island to be an ecological oddity. "Wake Island is a queer place," wrote a civilian contractor who'd worked on the island. "Rocks float, wood sinks, fish fly, and . . . birds run."

But many saw its beauty, like construction supervisor Harry Olson: "The beach is dazzling white in the sunlight and one cannot stand it without dark glasses. . . . The sea water is the most heavenly shade of blue you can imagine. I stand and gaze into it for hours enchanted by the shifting play of colors."

Pan Am crew members standing under Wake Island sign on dock. *Flying the Oceans: A Pilot's Story of Pan Am 1935–1955*, 1978.

After a few words of welcome, Cooke escorted Hevenor, Mac, and the others along the pier toward the hotel. Soon they passed beneath a white sign with black lettering—Wake Island—displaying latitude and longitude as well as the great distances to Midway and Guam. It was conspicuously posted above the walkway and served as a novelty for visiting passengers, who often requested that their picture be snapped underneath it.

Just beyond the sign stood a red-roofed pergola, and beyond that rested a large rusty anchor leaning atop a sandy foundation. The eye-catching anchor belonged to the German sailing ship *Libelle* that wrecked on the island in 1866. Mac remembered the anchor

Pan Am hotel and compound on Wake Island. NARA, San Francisco.

well. He and his men discovered it, buried deeply in the sand, while clearing the beach for Pan Am's base in 1935. Its placement at the end of the dock added to the base's ambience and initiated a conversation about its origin for those arriving for the first time.

Wake Island is actually three islets—Wilkes, Peale, and Wake Islands—connected in the shape of a horseshoe, all named after eighteenth- and nineteenth-century seafarers. The Pan American Airways Hotel and its complex of offices, quarters, and supporting facilities called PAAville were built on Peale Island, whereas the recent construction of the US Marine base was centered primarily on Wilkes Island. The largest islet, Wake Island, whose name also encompasses all three islets, was scarcely used at that time but would eventually be graded for runways during the upcoming war in the Pacific.

Though station wagons waited, all those from the arriving seaplane elected to walk the short distance to the hotel. The dutiful Guamanian men followed behind in their white uniforms, pulling luggage carriers along the concrete sidewalk. Soon they approached a large circular fountain pool and a flagpole on which fluttered the American flag above a blue-and-white Pan Am flag. Beyond the fountain stood Godfrey Free, the steward of Pan American Airways Hotel. His wife, Peggy, who was the hotel matron and would have joined him, had traveled to San Francisco the week before. Godfrey greeted everyone with a hardy "Hello! Welcome!" and invited them in for something all visitors desired on this scorching-hot Pacific isle—ice-cold drinks.

As the others stepped inside, Capt. Hamilton, Mac, and Charlie stopped on the porch to hobnob with Godfrey. They'd gotten to know each other well from their previous layovers on the island and elsewhere. Charlie sometimes stayed with the Frees at their home in California. Almost forty, the college-educated Godfrey had been born in England before immigrating to the United States, where he'd worked as a steward on steamships off the West Coast much the same as Charlie had done. The four men spoke routinely, filling the tiny island's warm breeze with their accents—Arkansan, Scottish, Brooklynite, and British. After finishing with pleasantries, Hamilton and Mac walked inside and into the lobby. As fellow stewards, Charlie and Godfrey went into the hotel's kitchen. They had plenty to talk about, particularly the availability of various foodstuffs for the flight the next morning.

Hamilton hurried to his room and changed. The six-foot, 175-pound athletic Pan Am captain wanted to play a quick game of tennis on Wake's green cement court before dinner. He'd arrived too late to fish. Wake Island was renowned for its fishing. With close to fifty species of fish and innumerable subspecies surrounding the small island, Wake was literally a fisherman's paradise. After tennis,

Hamilton took a dip in the constant eighty-three-degree saltwater pool blasted out of coral that was "guaranteed to be free of sharks."

Mac also didn't loiter in the lobby for long. He walked down the hallway of the hotel's left wing before stepping through the ivory-colored, shuttered door into his room. He'd seen the rooms innumerable times and took little notice, especially since he'd just left a similar hotel on Midway. Unlike Mac, whose eyes rarely noticed anything inside the hotel but potential problems, visiting passengers thought the hotel and its forty-five rooms were luxurious. "[A young Chamorro man] bowed solemnly and ushered me into the company of a model *Better Homes and Gardens* collection of gently fluttering curtains, . . . electric fan . . . a Simmons mattressed bed, a clear and beautiful mirror, a vase of pinched verbenas," wrote Dorothy Kaucher, who'd visited the island on her way to Hong Kong.

The weary Pan Am contractor headed straight for the shower, where the water was splendidly hot. The hotel's water was heated outdoors in coiled copper pipes under dark glass that soaked up the Pacific sunshine. The fresh water emerged from a large cistern that collected thousands of gallons of island rain. The inn also provided coconut soap in each shower, which, according to a Pan Am brochure, "smelled as clean as the trade winds," though it is doubtful that Mac noticed.

A small typewritten card with his name, room number, and the following message had been placed on the desk in Mac's room, as it had at Midway. Similar cards were placed in the other passengers' rooms:

The *Philippine Clipper* will depart at 6:30 A.M. tomorrow from the float. You will be called at 5:45 A.M. and your breakfast will be ready immediately upon your appearance in the lobby. Will you kindly have your baggage ready to dispatch to the plane at 6:15 A.M. We desire to make your short stay at Wake a comfortable and enjoyable one. WAKE ISLAND PACIFIC OCEAN December 7, 1941.

Pan American Airways Hotel dining room on Wake. U. Miami PAA

After changing clothes, Mac joined the others in the dining room, where tables were immaculately set with fine china and real silverware. Wake Island is five thousand miles from the US mainland, yet the inn's restaurant rivaled many in San Francisco. "It was fantastic that I had just eaten a four-course dinner in a dining room with streamline blue, steel furniture that would look well in a penthouse on Park Avenue," wrote Dorothy Kaucher.

Following dinner, the men strolled through the lobby where the polished woodgrain RCA 14-tube radio set played. They made their way past the inn's front desk onto the screened porch, just as they had at Midway. Because the two islands' amenities were virtually identical, some passengers likely experienced a bit of *déjà vu*, except that the sound of the booming surf dwarfed that on Midway. It was so loud that the island's naval base commander once commented: "Everywhere there was sound, the constant roar of the surf breaking against the narrow reef that encircled the atoll . . . so loud that neither whistles nor sirens could be heard at any great distance."

Taking their places in wicker chairs, the men pulled out their favorite tobacco and shared their smokes and sipped their drinks as soothing island music seeped in from the lobby. Hamilton shared a black-and-white picture of his wife, Geraldine, holding his baby girl, Michelle, a photo that he carried in his wallet. Mac would similarly withdraw a black-and-white photo of Doreen that would be passed around the room.

The discussion quickly moved to the news in the typed one-page radio bulletin, *Wake Wig Wag*. That's when Herman Hevenor chimed in. Carrying the title Principal Budget Examiner, Hevenor told everyone what he'd seen and heard at the islands he'd visited. Since arriving in Honolulu on November 12, Hevenor had island-hopped aboard military ships, visiting Johnston and Palmyra Islands and returning to Honolulu, striking out again to Midway Atoll, where he'd boarded the *Philippine Clipper* on December 6 to Wake. Everywhere he went, there was talk of the Japanese in French Indochina and rumors of preparations for an attack on the Netherlands East Indies and perhaps even the Philippines.

That concerned Engineering Officer Ed Barnett, a member of the *Philippine Clipper*'s nine-man crew. Smoking his Chesterfields, the tall, thin Pan Am engineer wasn't one for shooting the breeze; but with Japanese aggression growing in that part of the world, he expressed concern for his wife's safety in Manila. When not living with his in-laws in Berkeley, California, near Pan Am's Pacific base at Treasure Island, Ed lived with his wife of four years, Cecile, in the Philippines. She'd recently had an opportunity to leave the Philippines and return to California but chose to stay near the Pan Am base in Cavite where she and Ed had lived since July 1940, having arrived on the *Philippine Clipper*, no less. She enjoyed "being where the action is." Besides, most of her friends lived there, and they were staying. Ed explained that his twenty-five-year-old wife had recently become a civil servant and gotten a job with the US Navy, believing that working for the Navy would cloak her with military protection should trouble arise. Even more, Ed's brother George was in the US Army stationed near Manila.

The others sitting on the terrace with Ed agreed that there was cause for concern but believed that any Japanese attack on the Philippines would be repelled by the considerable US military presence there, particularly with nearby Corregidor under the command of Lt. Gen. Douglas MacArthur, commanding general of the US Army Forces in the Far East. Ajax Baumler echoed the group's confidence in the US military's capabilities in the Philippines, an opinion that carried considerable weight with Ed. The young second lieutenant had piloted fighter planes with the Spanish Loyalists during the Spanish Civil War, and had shared drinks with Ernest Hemingway in Madrid. He was on his way to Kunming, China, to join Gen. Claire Chennault's squadron of Flying Tigers fighting the Japanese in China. Ajax would soon earn the distinction of being the first pilot to shoot down planes from each of the three Axis Powers—Germany, Italy, and Japan—on his way to becoming an ace fighter pilot. Ajax's opinion should have eased Ed's fears—but it didn't.

Capt. Hamilton also joined in, sharing some of the discussion he'd had with the island commanders before dinner. Hamilton had gained permission to visit Wake Island's naval base on Wilkes by boat, where he'd met with the base's new commander, Winfield Scott Cunningham, and US Marine Maj. James Devereux, who'd been placed in charge of the First Marine Defense Battalion's detachment. Capt. Hamilton's conversation was welcomed by the military commanders. Hamilton had flown for the US Navy prior to joining Pan Am, and he knew a great deal about military operations in the Pacific. Besides being a Pan Am captain, Hamilton was a lieutenant in the US Naval Air Reserve and had served under Cunningham at Oakland. The three discussed Wake's defense readiness and general concerns about Japanese aggression in China and Southeast Asia.

With the evening growing late, the chitchat eventually broke up. Stubbing out their cigarettes in Pan Am logoed ashtrays, the men ventured back inside the hotel to retire for the night, except Mac, who headed toward the dock where the *Philippine Clipper* was anchored. He strolled along the lighted pier that stretched far out into the lagoon, seemingly without end. He paused long enough to watch two white-coated Guamanian boys near the beach lower the American flag from the top of a tall mast. One youngster worked the ropes slowly as the other boy saluted.

Mac joined the salute from the dock. He then turned to gaze at the sunset stretching long across the water with its pastel shades of gold, orange, and purple. The beach was empty. The wicker beach chairs and umbrellas, as well as the beach golf flags, had been stowed away for the night. Mac did spot, however, three colored glass balls about the size of basketballs that had washed ashore and glimmered in the moonlight. It wasn't the first time he'd seen them. They frequently washed up on the beach. Fishermen in Japan used the glass balls as floats for their nets in a country where cork was scarce. They'd apparently broken loose and floated two thousand miles to find a resting place on Wake's beaches. Visitors to the island often collected the red, yellow, white, and orange balls made of blown glass.

Alone in that setting with the surf thundering against the island's shores, Mac spotted some initials carved into a plank beneath a light on the pier—WJM. They were difficult to see, but Mac had known where to find them. His mind sprang back as it often did to his early days on Wake Island with his friend and former boss William Grooch and all the others, including one man whose feats of physical prowess on Wake stood out from the rest—the man who'd carved those initials—William J. "Bill" Mullahey. The young Mullahey had been somewhat of a living legend during his early Pan Am days. Growing up in Honolulu, he'd spent his youth surfing and canoeing as a member of Honolulu's Outrigger Canoe Club, and later he organized the Waikiki Beach Patrol. It was on Waikiki Beach that the Columbia University-educated Mullahey first met William Grooch, head of Pan Am's *North Haven* expedition team, along with other top expedition members that included Mac. "They proposed that I join the expedition and go with them to Midway and Wake and Guam. . . . So, [I] went down to the ship SS *North Haven* and I had my longboard and my spears and my goggles and an old Bell and Howell 16 mm camera," Mullahey recalled, "and that's how I started out with Pan American's first expedition."

It was at Wake Island that the future Pan Am career man gained his nickname "Mr. Pacific." In spite of the fact that Pan Am had invested millions in planes, hangars, bases, and personnel, it didn't purchase any dredging equipment to clear coral heads from Wake's lagoon so the clippers could land safely. Instead, Mullahey, who could swim like a fish but had never handled dynamite, became Pan Am's underwater demolition expert (SCUBA gear had not yet been invented). He completed hundreds of dives handling dynamite under dangerous conditions, clearing out the lagoon for Pan Am's clippers. Evocative of a mythical god of the sea, only with goggles, Mr. Pacific fought off sharks and eels with his homemade harpoon, along with a cane and rubber band sling with metal rods fashioned as arrows. It wasn't long before he became the talk of the island. "The dock crew was intrigued beyond words at his performance under water," William Grooch wrote.

Yet, on the night of December 7 west of the International Date Line, it all seemed so long ago. Grooch was dead and Mullahey was the airport manager at Auckland, where he'd traded his spears for a desk and a few extra pounds.

The tiny flat island that possessed a horizon of nothing but thousands of miles of ocean had traded its sun for a sparkling starlit sky as Mac had mused . . . and now yawned. He decided that it was time to return to the hotel and get some sleep like the others. By morning, he'd be on his way to Guam. The *Philippine Clipper* was scheduled to take off at seven o'clock and land on the afternoon of December 8 (December 7 in Hawaii) at the old US Marine Corps seaplane base in Guam's Apra Harbor, where he'd stay at Pan Am's Skyways Inn. But Mac knew that once his work was done in Manila and he was traveling home to be with his daughter, he'd have another chance to see wondrous Wake Island again. He had constructed a marvelous Pan Am compound upon it and had nurtured its development, and now he was its occasional overseer. He was so fond of the Pan Am base that he frequently referred to it as his "baby."

What Mac didn't know was that the Imperial Japanese Navy was drawing nearer to his baby on that same beautiful starlit night that he was so admiring. The wonder of Wake Island—its brilliant white beaches, sparkling deep blue water, tranquil isolation, and delightful hotel—would soon become an isle of deserted castaways facing a savagely cruel onslaught meted out by the Empire of Japan.

## CHAPTER 15

# PREPARATION FOR ISLAND INVASIONS

With the sunrise came another beautiful day in Guam. The streets were already bustling on December 7 as shop owners raised bamboo blinds and set their fresh fish and produce in crates outside their tin-roofed stores. One of those busy that morning was a Guamanian proprietor at Sumay named Felix Torres. The Torres family was one of the more prominent Chamorro families on Guam. Over the last two years, Charlie and Felix had become fast friends. Each time the clippers stopped at Guam for a layover with Charlie aboard, Charlie visited Felix to pick up provisions for the next leg of the clipper flight. The two would shoot the breeze and share jokes and Camel cigarettes, perhaps more than they transacted business. The last time Charlie had seen his friend, Felix had introduced his shy wife and rambunctious eighteen-month-old son. Charlie held the little tyke and was happy for his friend and new father. He wanted a family too, and was always on the lookout for that special girl. But for now he'd satisfy himself with seeing his Guamanian friend and his family the following day when the *Philippine Clipper* landed at Guam.

The Japanese troop transport *Asama Maru* lay anchored at Saipan in the Mariana Islands as 2,900 soldiers embarked. Cranes with chain slings and lift-boards hoisted almost six million pounds of ammunition and cargo aboard. All were believed to be needed for the invasion of Guam. Nearby, Japanese fighter planes underwent fueling and last-minute checks. The planes would lead the attack.

Four heavy cruisers of the Imperial Japanese Navy's Sixth Cruiser Division, with three destroyers, advanced from the harbor at Haha-jima with six thousand infantry aboard, ten times the number of US Marines and sailors defending Guam. The disproportionate Japanese force had been deployed based on faulty Japanese intelligence that greatly miscalculated US military defenses on Guam. They now sped across the Philippine Sea in order to unite with gunboats, minesweepers, and submarine chasers launched from Saipan. Together they would provide cover fire when the thousands of infantry hit the beaches of the small, meagerly defended Pacific island of Guam.

―――――――――

The people of the United States were not pleased with the current state of peace negotiations with Japan in Washington. For the last two weeks, American newspapers had tracked the daily progress or lack thereof between US Secretary of State Cordell Hull and Japanese Ambassador Admiral Kichisaburō Nomura and special envoy Saburō Kurusu. While Americans remained hopeful of at least a temporary peace, it appeared that the Empire of Japan was not in favor of peace at all. American newspapers, with bold headlines, included and editorialized a recent speech in Tokyo made by Japanese Prime Minister Hideki Tōjō in which Tōjō had remarked that the United States and Great Britain must be purged from East Asia. Many Americans took the speech as evidence that a belligerent Gen. Tōjō had wanted war all along, and the negotiations were simply a ruse to stall until Japan strategically placed its military.

President Roosevelt cut short his Thanksgiving holiday in Warm Springs, Georgia, and returned to Washington. He directed Secretary of State Hull to call a meeting with the Japanese ambassador and the special envoy to obtain the answers to two questions. First, the president wanted to know why Japanese forces were continuing their rapid buildup in French Indochina when it appeared no reason existed other than to launch forces against China, the Netherlands East Indies, or even the Philippines. Ambassador Nomura and Kurusu responded at a meeting with Hull on December 5 that the buildup was defensive in nature and necessary to curb Chinese aggression. When pressed, the ambassador acknowledged that sometimes offensive military movements are the best defense.

Hull then inquired about Gen. Tōjō's recent remarks about purging the United States and Britain from the East. The Secretary told Nomura and Kurusu that the "malignant campaign" only served to confuse the peace process and "created an atmosphere not conducive to peace." Hull pointed out that unlike in the United States, Japan not only controlled its press, but used it as a propaganda tool. Kurusu's reply was simply to criticize the American press that had often maligned him.

After much back-and-forth between the diplomats, Kurusu muttered, "This isn't getting us anywhere," and the Japanese ambassador and envoy took their leave, apologizing for taking up so much of Secretary Hull's time. The meeting was representative of previous negotiations—cordial accusations without any resolution. Hull made one thing clear to Kurusu, however, as the Japanese diplomats departed: "We [the United States] aren't looking for trouble, but at the same time we are not running away from menaces."

The following day, December 6, Kurusu sat with Nomura inside the Japanese embassy, waiting for a coded fourteen-point response from Tokyo to President Roosevelt's last edict made on November 26. Roosevelt was resolute that the United States would resume trade with Japan only if Japan withdrew all of its military forces from China and French Indochina. Kurusu believed he had failed at his appointed mission. He realized that Gen. Tōjō would never agree to Roosevelt's stipulations. Nonetheless, he had one last task before returning to Japan—to deliver Tōjō's response to Secretary of State Hull. So he continued to wait till the coded message from Tokyo arrived.

Unbeknownst to the Japanese diplomats, President Roosevelt had already received the Tokyo message at 9:30 on the night of December 6. The PURPLE diplomatic message had been decoded by the US Navy's MAGIC analogue machine. Though its last part had not yet been received and decoded, Japan's intent to sever negotiations was clear. Roosevelt read the message and then looked at his friend and closest advisor, Harry Hopkins, and said: "This means war."

The president commenced studying a map of the Malay Peninsula and the South China Sea, making notations where a Japanese fleet had most recently been spotted. It appeared to the president and his advisors that the Japanese were heading for Thailand or British Malaya to attack. The men didn't realize that the Imperial Japanese Navy had ships steaming toward targets all over the Pacific, particularly Pearl Harbor.

At some point during the night, Hopkins suggested to the president that the United States should launch a preemptive strike against Japan. Roosevelt reportedly replied, "No, we can't do that. We are a democracy and a peaceful people." So Roosevelt waited.

And so did Kurusu. He waited even though Roosevelt already knew that peace negotiations were being terminated and that Japan likely would strike in Southeast Asia. And he waited even though Japanese air, sea, and ground forces in China, the China Sea, and the Marshall and Mariana islands continued their preparations for a widespread and coordinated attack on several American, British, and Dutch islands in the Pacific. And he also waited as the Japanese attack group's main task force split the Pacific Ocean's surface, steaming speedily ahead for Pearl Harbor.

But Roosevelt and Kurusu would not have to wait much longer.

## CHAPTER 16

# THE *PACIFIC* AND *ANZAC* CLIPPERS

Just as the *Philippine Clipper* had taken off from Midway Atoll on to its next scheduled stop at Wake Island, the *Pacific* and *Anzac Clippers* took off, heading for their next stops at New Caledonia and Honolulu. It was December 6 in Hawaii and a day later west of the International Date Line, and the powerful engines spun the Pan Am clippers' propellers faster, drawing those onboard ever closer to infamy.

## PACIFIC CLIPPER

After a wonderful breakfast in Fiji's Grand Pacific Hotel on December 7, the *Pacific Clipper*'s crew boarded a sleek blue-and-silver Bedford coach that carried them to the breezy dock at Suva Harbor. Gannets and gulls lined the railings amid the sharp aroma of idle ocean water. The crew members exited and were greeted by Pan Am's airport manager, Charles Ruegg. After the morning briefing in the company's stale dispatch office, the crew caught the launch out to the barge where the *Pacific Clipper* was moored and commenced their preflight procedures—altimeter set, fuel gauges checked, master power switch on, ignition switches on, advance throttles . . . Following the loading of passengers, the clipper lifted off under clear skies for Nouméa, the capital and largest city of the French colony of New Caledonia, the last layover before reaching Auckland. With a land mass the size of New Jersey and a population of twelve thousand in its capital city, New Caledonia was Pan Am's largest destination in the South Pacific, outside of New Zealand.

With fewer than 825 miles to travel, the *Pacific Clipper* landed in Moselle Bay at Nouméa early that Sunday afternoon after only six hours and fifteen minutes in the air—a short flight for a big transoceanic clipper. With time to spare, everyone savored the beautiful weather and Pan Am's hospitality.

"Spent most of the afternoon sun bathing on the deck of the yacht, drinking beer and swapping stories with the Limey's [*sic*] and Aussies," Fourth Officer John Steers recalled.

The yacht referred to was actually Pan Am's "hotel" for its passengers and crew. Pan Am had not yet sent Mac to oversee the completion of passenger accommodations in Nouméa, which an Australian newspaper had described as "an old-fashioned shabby town . . . in which the average Australian would not care to live." Without any local accommodations of acceptable opulence at the one-time penal colony, Pan Am purchased a yacht that it christened the MV *Southern Seas*.

Anchored a half mile from the village of Nouméa, the sparkling yacht showcased twenty luxurious staterooms that afforded the utmost of comfort for forty passengers, with solid teakwood panels, railing, and decks, all polished to a sleek shine, and a fine dining room that flaunted a top chef. Its single white funnel brandished an illuminated blue P.A.A. emblem. *The Courier-Mail* of Brisbane, Australia, described the MV *Southern Seas* as a "dazzling white motor yacht, 200 feet long, the embodiment of smartness and comfort. . . . [I]ngenuity would be needed to discover comforts which might be added. From commander to boot cleaner, all help passengers in luxury surroundings feel like millionaires for a night."

And that was indeed a good thing, since many of Pan Am's passengers were already millionaires and most likely enjoyed being

Captain Harry Lanier Turner. Pan American Airways, "Meet Your Captain," brochure; U. Miami PAA.

treated that way. For on that December 7 west of the International Date Line, things like slightly chilled champagne and cold beads of caviar, along with creased linens and soft slippers, were still of the utmost importance to those onboard the *Pacific Clipper*.

## ANZAC CLIPPER

Lanier Turner, captain of Pan Am's *Anzac Clipper*, leaned back in an auditorium chair beside his wife and young daughter, listening to a piano recital in Oakland. Smartly dressed in his starched white shirt and navy Pan Am uniform with his cap neatly placed on his lap, the flying boat's pilot anxiously waited for his older daughter to take the stage. "I had wanted to drop in and hear at least the first few notes," Turner recalled, "so I telephoned dispatch at Treasure Island and got permission."

At Pan Am's terminal on Treasure Island, the black departure board in white lettering read:

## Trans-Pacific Crossing Anzac Clipper
## Captain Turner Departing Treasure Island 5:00 P.M.

Despite what was plainly written, five o'clock had come and gone without the clipper's captain appearing. The plane had already missed its scheduled landing in Hawaii the day before when the crew discovered mechanical problems and was forced to fly back to San Francisco. Pan Am's ace mechanics had worked during the night and into the morning. They'd repaired the big seaplane and had it ready to fly, but now its chief pilot was absent.

The Pan Am ticketing agent told anyone who asked that the plane's captain was running late but would arrive soon, an explanation that was satisfactory to most. Passengers tended to be more patient in those days. Also, captains of airplanes, like those of ships, tended to be beyond reproach and their decisions generally were sacrosanct. And most everyone flying understood that scheduled takeoff and landing times had to be flexible to take into account bad weather, mechanical problems, and other unforeseen events, although a delay due to a captain's attendance at his daughter's piano recital may have been a first. The cause of the captain's delay certainly was not shared with the passengers, especially at the ticket prices they were paying.

The clipper's captain was doing his best to drive to Treasure Island's terminal, but five o'clock traffic was vexing even on a Saturday. At last, he arrived and wisely avoided the passenger lounge, walking straight into an office where he joined his crew for the preflight briefing. Before long, the sound of the first bell rang out. The Pan Am crew marched out to the flying boat and, despite being behind schedule, commenced their time-consuming preflight checks. "Start number one," the captain instructed the first engineer, who

A Boeing B-314 (the *Anzac Clipper*) anchored in a California lake. Museums of Lake County.

acknowledged, as he started each engine one by one. With the four engines cranked and their RPMs revving up and down, the long, shining propellers spun so fast that their appearance transformed into four glittering circles. At that moment, the sound of two bells rang out. It was time for the passengers to board—again.

The *Anzac Clipper* and its seventeen passengers and eleven members of its double crew finally lifted off from Treasure Island on Saturday, December 6. It was a light load, but additional passengers would be boarding in Honolulu on Sunday, December 7, for the trip to Manila, Hong Kong, and Singapore. The time at takeoff was 5:40 p.m., forty minutes after their scheduled departure time.

Dining aboard a Boeing B-314. U. Miami.

During the early days of commercial aviation, when planes weren't pressurized, cruised under 200 mph, and experienced frequent mechanical problems, captains of transoceanic flying boats didn't try to make up lost time. They would simply land when they landed.

Not long after takeoff, darkness began cloaking the departure city of San Francisco, but the sun hadn't fully set as the travelers watched from their windows high above the Pacific Ocean's surface. With eighteen hours of flight time ahead of them, many realized that a night flight on a clipper was actually desirable. For example, a flight to Honolulu typically took off just before dark, and following a four-course dinner, passengers could retire to their berths. The next morning, they'd awaken, eat a delicious breakfast, and prepare for landing in beautiful Hawaii. That way, the flight of eighteen hours seemed much shorter.

And that's just what the passengers aboard the *Anzac Clipper* commenced doing. As the hours passed and so did a marvelous dinner, the evening grew late. With the chatter turning to yawns, thoughts turned to preparing for sleep. With just three women on the plane, using the "lady's powder room" was a cinch. Located near the stern of the plane, the women's restroom was large, containing two cushioned stools for women to sit in front of separate vanities. On the opposite side of the restroom were two sinks with hot and cold running water. A toilet sat in an enclosed compartment within the restroom. For the male passengers, there was the "gentleman's retiring room" near the bow that contained two urinals, a toilet, a sink, and a mirror, with three smaller restrooms in convenient locations.

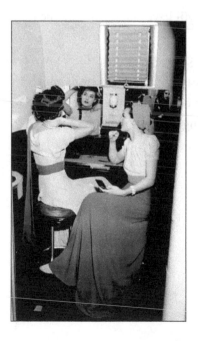

Two passengers in the "lady's powder room." U. Miami PAA.

As the passengers prepared for bed, the stewards erected the large navy-colored berths, converting seating into comfortable beds with zippered curtains appointed with blankets and sheets of the finest material, along with plump pillows that were the softest on the market. The berths were identified by gray numbers embroidered inside a circle containing the Pan Am logo. Once inside, each passenger could push a call button, summoning a steward with a cool glass of water or perhaps milk and a midnight snack to their berth that was equipped with its own lighting.

One passenger, Edward Randolph "Ran" Lacy, a twenty-three-year-old TVA engineer on his way to Burma to fight malaria, captured the night's mood aboard the *Anzac Clipper* in his diary:

As the moon shines across the waters lighting a sea of diamonds and pearls, our thoughts automatically turned to things we left behind, to our families and sweethearts, and wondering of changes that will have taken place by the time we return home.

Little did Lacy know that the clipper was headed into a raging storm, not of nature, but of man, from which it would be difficult to survive; and should he be fortunate enough to survive, he could still end up wasting away for years in a prison camp. Yet, for one last night, unaware and weary, he slept the sleep of the young and the lighthearted.

## CHAPTER 17

# LOAD THE TORPEDOES

Cmdr. Mitsuo Fuchida had been chosen by Adm. Yamamoto to be the chief aviation commander, which meant he was in charge of all planes whose bullets and bombs would soon wreak death and destruction upon Pearl Harbor. He was surprised by his appointment. "At thirty-nine, my spirit was great but my stamina was fading," Fuchida recalled. He would have preferred to have been appointed the head of aviation and teach others to fly bomber and fighter planes until his retirement. Fuchida was not a bloodthirsty fanatic; yet he was a superior air commander who deified Emperor Hirohito. That meant he was not only duty-bound, he was eager to serve the Empire. After all, ever since he'd joined the naval academy twenty years earlier, the words "Your enemy is the United States" had been deeply embedded in his consciousness.

While Fuchida commanded the air, the sea operation was commanded by an old-school battleship commander who had little experience with naval aviation but had achieved seniority—Vice Adm. Chuichi Nagumo. And at that moment, Nagumo ordered the task force speeding toward Hawaii to be refueled by the nine oil tankers that followed the convoy on the open sea. They were also on hand to transfer fuel for the bombers and fighters. A rough sea made an efficient fueling effort extremely difficult.

The mission could not be successful without the oil tankers. The two main ingredients in modern warfare are blood and oil, and little

Cmdr. Mitsuo Fuchida aboard the *Akagi*. Fuchida, *From Pearl Harbor to Calvary*.

blood can be shed without fuel. It has been reported that the Imperial Japanese Navy was burning 2,900 barrels of fuel every hour; and that was just the navy. Japan also needed oil for its air and ground forces. With few oil resources of its own, a bloody chicken-and-egg situation had been created: war was necessary to obtain the oil necessary to levy war. Japan's march into French Indochina the year before had yielded little oil that could be refined into fuel. A successful Southern Operation would gain the oil fields of the Netherlands East Indies and Malaya, providing Japan with the fuel it badly needed. Operation Hawaii would protect Japan's navy from the US Pacific Fleet while it seized that oil. And so the oil tankers sailing with the great Japanese armada were much more than just supportive: they were an essential part of Japan's expansionist and militarist ambitions.

Around midday on December 5 (Hawaii time), the Japanese flotilla had reached a point six hundred miles from the northern tip of Oahu. Following its final refueling before the attack, the fleet broke away from the oil tankers and prepared to change course directly south. The flagship *Akagi* signaled to the other ships: "We pray for our good fortune in battle."

Throughout the day and into the next, while the fleet continued sailing south, a distance of about four hundred miles to the launch point two hundred miles from Oahu, mechanics aboard the aircraft carriers readied the torpedo bombers as teams checked the planes' spark plugs and oil. The deafening engines roared, forcing orange and blue flames mixed with smoke to shoot from the exhaust pipes. When the testing of the engines had been completed, sailors attached black cigar-shaped torpedoes underneath the planes. The maleficent torpedoes, seemingly as long as the planes' underbellies, had been specially designed by Cmdr. Fuchida for the shallow waters of Pearl Harbor. Soon, bombers with folded wings would be rolled onto elevators that would raise them from all decks to the top flight deck of each carrier. There, they'd be lined up with wings fully spread to await the signal for takeoff.

Cmdr. Genda's plan provided for up to four separate waves of planes to take off from the carriers, with the exact number to be flown depending on the extent of the damage inflicted at Pearl Harbor by the previous waves and the risk of counterattack from US fighters and submarines. The first wave called for bombers to be escorted by fighter planes. There would be a total of 183 planes in the air during the initial wave, and 167 on the second wave. Each torpedo bomber would be manned by three crew members and carry a single 1,760-pound torpedo.

That's why bomber crews busily attached the deadly torpedoes to the propeller-driven bombers: they would be needed very soon.

The first wave would take off for Pearl Harbor within hours. The attack on Pearl would be the signal for other surprise attacks to follow throughout the Pacific. Yamamoto's plan, an audacious strike in his mind and even more daring on paper, was nearing the point where it would be tested in the real world—a world that his gamble would change forever.

## CHAPTER 18

# GRIDIRON

---

Harry Olson hoped for a good seat as he walked along with the rolling mass of fans filing into Honolulu Stadium's gates that Saturday, December 6. He'd paid $1.10 ($22 today) for a reserved seat to watch the eleventh annual college football game to benefit the Shriners Hospital in Honolulu. Harry had heard on the radio that the game was a sellout—and, by the size of the crowd, he believed it would be. It was the biggest college football game of the year in Hawaii. An advertisement in the *Honolulu Advertiser* called it "The Biggest Game for the Biggest Cause." The University of Hawaii Rainbows would be hosting the Bearcats of Willamette University, a small college in Salem, Oregon, which boasted being the oldest college in the American West.

Harry didn't have to read or hear the advertisements in the newspapers or on the radio. The Willamette players and coaches, along with a few of their families and fans, about sixty of them in all, had filled the Moana Hotel where Harry was staying. Their presence changed the atmosphere of the luxury hotel from one of a quiet, relaxing island resort, as Harry had experienced during his stay there in July, to one filled with hoopla, loud voices, pushing and shoving, muscle exhibitions, and other silliness. A number of the young boys reminded Harry of his sons, Ted and Jimmy. He hadn't seen Jimmy in months, but he'd be seeing Ted in another week when he returned to Wake Island at the end of his vacation.

There were two additional college football games planned at Honolulu that December. On December 13, the Saturday following the Shriners game, the Hawaii Rainbows would host the Spartans of San Jose State College. The Spartan players and coaches were also staying at Harry's hotel, adding to the craziness. Then on Tuesday, December 16, a third game would be played between the Willamette and San Jose teams, with the proceeds going toward the two teams' travel expenses.

Assorted events had been planned for the visiting players' amusement. The Honolulu police even volunteered to chauffeur players to various tourist sites around the island. Once the games and fun were done, both football teams and their entourages planned to board the SS *Lurline* on December 17 and return to San Francisco. The entire trip to the island paradise had been carefully scheduled so that the visiting teams would be home in time for Christmas.

Harry located his seat and was satisfied. The stadium's wooden decking and supports had creaked loudly as he'd walked to his seat. The Shriners game that Saturday was played at Honolulu Stadium, on the corner of King and Isenberg Streets in the heart of Honolulu. Honolulu Stadium was the largest sports venue in Hawaii. Completed in 1926 of concrete block and wood, the stadium (later affectionately known as the Termite Palace) was home to the University of Hawaii Rainbows. The stadium's grandstands had recently been expanded to hold twenty-five thousand fans, just in time for the Shriners game and Harry's visit. It initially doubled as a football and baseball stadium but later drew various sporting, concert, and other entertainment events. By the end of 1945, the stadium would have seen its share of stars, like Joe DiMaggio and Irving Berlin.

The local newspapers urged fans to be seated at the stadium by 1:15 p.m. to watch a parade of fourteen local marching bands. Kickoff would be at 2:30 p.m. Harry was there and ready to watch. Everyone stood as members of the US Marine Corps Color Guard marched out on the field and presented the Colors. During the first half, the two teams, wearing their leather helmets and black high-top cleats, played each other to a close halftime score, with the Hawaii Rainbows leading 7 to 6. The bands performed again at halftime, led by the Shriners drill team in their green-and-red uniforms, while Harry and many other fans were busy purchasing hot dogs and pineapple ice cream. The most dramatic segment of the halftime entertainment was performed by the Nobles of the Aloha Shrine Temple, whose stunts were capped off by firing a human out of a cannon. The game resumed around four o'clock, and by game's end the smaller but faster Rainbows had trounced the Bearcats, winning 20 to 6. The Bearcats players blamed the loss on large-scale seasickness on the five-day voyage from San Francisco, a believable disadvantage for visiting teams.

After the game, players returned to their rooms in the Moana Hotel and prepared for a fun evening. Hawaiians looked forward each year to the Shriners benefit game and wholeheartedly extended their hospitality to the teams from the mainland with dinners, luaus, and galas, as they did that Saturday night following the game. Many players and chaperones had hikes and sightseeing tours planned for Sunday, December 7. Others planned to fish and surf. They couldn't wait. It would be a day they would always remember.

## CHAPTER 19

# SEA SERPENTS

The long, narrow submarines forged ahead under the ocean's surface like some terrible shadowy sea serpents of folklore as they sailed two hundred miles ahead of the Japanese attack group's main task force steaming toward Hawaii. Thirty-two large submarines surveyed the waters for American warships and submarines that conceivably could be closing in on the location of the task force—but were not.

Three submarines remained behind with the carriers and support vessels to provide underwater patrols as fighter planes patrolled the air. The mission of the aerial and underwater sentinels simply was to attack and destroy any plane or ship, military or civilian, before it could radio a message back to Pearl Harbor, alerting them of the task force's location. Even if an enemy vessel was destroyed, the task force would have likely turned around and returned to Japan rather than risk being attacked on its way toward Hawaii.

The advance expeditionary force of submarines also carried five Type A "midget" mini-submarines that would be deployed approximately ten miles from the mouth of Pearl Harbor before the main attack commenced. There were only two crew members aboard, operating each of the battery-powered midget subs, which were armed with two torpedoes each. Once released into the ocean, the tiny subs' objective would be to enter the harbor the night before the main aerial attack and wait until it began the next morning. Because Pearl Harbor positioned defensive submarine nets at the mouth of

World War II-class Japanese submarine. Unknown.

the harbor, the subs would have to time their entry to follow an American ship sailing into the harbor, which required the nets to be withdrawn. The large submarines would patrol the waters off Pearl Harbor, seeking any ships that either approached or tried to escape the harbor during the attack.

But for now, the dull black submarines, large and small, crept in the dark Pacific waters, snaking ever closer to the Hawaiian Islands, anxious to do their part in destroying the US Pacific Fleet.

## CHAPTER 20

# FRIENDLY FIREWORKS IN HONG KONG

Wrapping up his business in Hong Kong, Hank Marsman eagerly awaited the *Hong Kong Clipper*'s departure on Monday. He had flown from Manila to Hong Kong on December 2 and planned to return to the Philippines aboard the clipper on the eighth. At forty-nine years old, the Dutch-born US citizen owned multifarious business interests in the Far East. He'd fortuitously met a widow in the Philippines whose husband had succumbed to the 1918 Spanish Influenza, leaving her scores of gold mining claims that Marsman took over.

"I clippered to and from the Far East to attend to business interests," Marsman recalled. "I made a quick trip to Manila to inspect what our firms were doing in the Philippines and in other parts of the Far East where we were engaged in filling a number of diversified contracts. . . . The schedule was so arranged that I would be home in San Francisco to celebrate Christmas with my family."

Hong Kong had changed a great deal since Marsman's initial visit twenty years earlier. Hong Kong was second only to Shanghai as the busiest port in the Far East, but Shanghai was now under the control of the invading Japanese. Marsman had seen Hong Kong transform from a peaceful "Pearl of the Orient" to a chaotic "Island of Refuge" following the Japanese invasion of China in 1937. Four years since the Sino-Japanese War had begun, Hong Kong's population of one million had swollen to nearly twice that. However, the

Jan Henrik "Hank" Marsman. Marsman Drysdale Group.

number of Europeans, nearly twenty thousand, had been decreasing steadily during that time. Many Europeans withdrew to England, the United States, and elsewhere for fear of the war spreading to the fragile British colony. Hank Marsman had been one of those who'd joined the exodus. After years of living in the Philippines, Marsman moved his home to San Francisco in 1939, where he lived with his wife, Mary, and their eleven-year-old daughter, Anne. His retreat to the security of the US mainland forced him to make seventeen-thousand-mile round trips on Pan Am clippers to inspect his businesses in the Orient, at what would be a price tag today of more than $35,000 per round-trip flight.

This trip was his third to Hong Kong during 1941. Marsman spent his first few days in the Far East inspecting air raid shelters that his construction company had built over a seventeen-mile area in the Granite Hills. He'd also inspected a tungsten mining operation on Needle Hill on the Kowloon Peninsula and had spoken at a corporate shareholders' meeting. Marsman stayed at the Hong Kong Hotel, which was in the heart of the city and was a favorite among wealthy Brits and Hong Kongese who often stopped by for a meal or a drink simply to check the pulse of high society.

For someone of Marsman's business and political connections, his stay in Hong Kong wasn't all work. He'd set aside plenty of time for tea and crumpets and opulent white-tie dinners. On Thursday night, December 4, Marsman had attended the diamond wedding anniversary (sixtieth) of the multimillionaire Eurasian merchant Sir Robert Ho Tung. Marsman described Sir Robert as a "fabulously rich and white-bearded Chinese patriarch who was knighted by the British for his loyalty to their interests, and civil leadership, in Hong Kong." Everybody who was anybody in Hong Kong was there, as were dignitaries from around the world. Sir Robert received the guests in his mandarin robe while sitting in "an embroidery-covered throne in the ballroom inside the vast, glittering elegance of the ultramodern Hong Kong Hotel." It was one of the biggest social events ever held in Hong Kong. Gwen Dew, a foreign correspondent for the *Detroit News*, was also there that night, later remarking, "A thousand guests were invited, from the high-ranking . . . Governor-General to lowly me. . . . The candle was burning at both ends in Hong Kong . . . that first week in December."

Two nights later, Hank Marsman attended the China relief ball held at the Peninsula Hotel. United China Relief's fundraising parties, called "China relief balls" in support of the Republic of China in its war with Japan, were quite the rage for the affluent at that time, especially in the United States. The month before, *Life* magazine covered a China relief ball held not at Hong Kong, but at Shangri La, the Diamond Head coastal estate of tobacco heiress Doris Duke, known as the "world's richest girl." Several attending the Moonlight Festival had flown to the Hawaiian paradise on the *Anzac Clipper*. But the relief ball held at the Peninsula Hotel that

December was as fine as any. "Hong Kong of yesterday was never more brilliant than on Saturday night," Marsman wrote, "when the rich and grand and gay assembled for a China relief ball in one of the ballrooms upstairs in the Peninsula Hotel in Kowloon across Victoria Harbor." Marsman recalled mingling with other grandiloquent guests in the "flower-festooned ballroom, where the best orchestras in the Far East played sweet and hot, and the fair danced with the brave."

To support the relief effort that Saturday night, Madame Sun Yat-sen, the petite widow of the "George Washington of the Chinese Republic," attended along with her sister, Madame H. H. Kung, wife of the Chinese minister of finance, reported to be the richest man in China. Again, Gwen Dew was there and, in fact, served as one of the judges of costumes. The head of the American President Lines steamship company acted as the master of ceremonies and auctioneer for the evening. Hank Marsman was among the bidders, outbidding everyone for the racket of the young American tennis player Phillip Harman, who was in Hong Kong to play exhibition games before prosperous fans and royalty as part of the relief effort.

The Hong Kong festivities consumed all of that Saturday night and much of the early dawn. It was nearly daybreak on Sunday morning, December 7 (Saturday, December 6 in Hawaii and the US mainland), when Marsman finally settled into his hotel room. Sunday was a day for rest and recreation for many in Hong Kong, and Marsman decided he'd spend most of the day resting. He had yet another party to attend that Sunday night. He'd received an invitation from a Chinese banker to attend a dinner party in his honor. Though he'd have to catch the *Hong Kong Clipper* early the following morning, he figured he'd have plenty of time to rest on the five-hour trip to Manila, the first leg of his long clipper journey home to San Francisco.

"Sunday was always a busy day [in Hong Kong]," wrote Gwen Dew, "for there were countless parties, beginning with breakfast and riding, luncheon and sailing, and ending up with cocktails and dinner. . . . Whiskies and soda enjoyed their usual popularity. Military authorities enjoyed their usual round of social duties, as they did at Pearl Harbor."

And so, on that Monday morning, December 8, having completed his work and attended every party of consequence, a worse-for-wear Hank Marsman sipped coffee and smoked a cigarette on the upper terrace of the Hong Kong Hotel overlooking Victoria Harbor before boarding the *Hong Kong Clipper* for Manila. The old British ship HMS *Tamar*, first launched in 1863 with its masts and a steam engine, was a regular fixture floating in the harbor, its bottom thickly covered with barnacles. The Chinese junks sailed across the harbor's water in every direction as the misty mountains formed a picturesque backdrop along the Kowloon Peninsula. A sweet-smelling breeze drifted in from the harbor. There were few places more tranquil and exotic. It was a perfect Monday morning in Hong Kong.

## CHAPTER 21

# TAKING OFF TO GUAM

The smell of breakfast filled the dining room at Wake Island's Pan American Airways Hotel before sunlight had the chance to rise above the ocean's horizon. Mac and the others were awakened at 5:00 a.m. that Monday, December 8, to prepare for their journey to Guam. With fair weather and no mechanical hitches, Mac would be in Manila by Wednesday afternoon and the military passengers would land at Singapore on Thursday.

On Wilkes Island, along the western edge of Wake, a shrill whistle pierced the relentless sound of the surf to awaken Marines and sailors on Camp One, as well as construction workers and clerical personnel on Camp Two. Maj. Devereux was shaving in his tent and would soon join Cmdr. Cunningham and the other men sitting on what resembled rows of long picnic tables in the mess hall. Coffee, cigarettes, and the news were the order of the day. Bacon and eggs were also welcomed.

As the morning grew longer and the sun rose higher and with all hunger assuaged, the men drifted away from the mess hall. Some hopped in the beds of trucks, while others set out on foot for the construction sites. Harry Olson's son Ted was among them. The twenty-one-year-old had written his sister only days earlier, boasting of his tan and the fun he was having working on Wake. "Ah, life—it's wonderful," his letter concluded.

Camp Two's administrative office began to fill with engineers, supervisors, secretaries, and bookkeepers, all of them men, for what was expected to be another dull workday on the isolated island. Visiting US Bureau of Budget assistant auditor Herman Hevenor joined them. The Bureau's schedule called for Hevenor to spend a week on Wake Island reviewing construction records for his report. It was his first day on the job at the tiny island. Meanwhile, a member of the staff typed up the news and ran it through a mimeograph machine for distribution throughout the atoll, as he did each day. Many of the officers, including Cmdr. Cunningham and Maj. Devereux, continued to sip their coffee and linger, reading the latest bulletins.

At Pan Am's dock, which stretched three hundred feet into the lagoon, the ground crew had just finished refueling the *Philippine Clipper* using motorized pumps that sucked 100-octane gasoline from 55-gallon drumheads stored on the island at about 35 gallons per minute. The clipper carried 4,080 gallons of gasoline in its six fuel tanks dispersed inside the wings and sponsons. Refueling had taken more than two hours. Now Capt. Hamilton and his crew boarded to begin performing their preflight checks in advance of taking off for Guam.

While joking with all those within earshot, Charlie had just finished stowing cans and bottles in the galley cupboards. He had replenished his food stocks from Godfrey and the Pan Am supplies on Wake. He was anxious to see his friend Felix at Guam, where he'd purchase more provisions for the hop from Guam to Manila and catch up on the latest island gossip.

At the hotel, Mac and his four co-passengers finished their breakfast and drank their coffee while reading the morning's single-page newspaper, the *Wake Wig Wam*. They could hear the clipper's engines start and rev as part of the preflight checks. A sputtering engine required maintenance; thirty minutes later, it was ready to go. As the young waiters cleared away the dishes from the breakfast tables, Wake's airport manager, John Cooke, along with Mac and the four officers, stepped out of the hotel and walked down to the dock where the clipper waited. Pan Am's chief engineer and mechanic had already arrived to oversee the departure.

"As the Manager for Pan Am [at Wake]," Cooke recalled, "one of my duties was to accompany the aircraft to the seaplane area in our launch." Not long afterward, the Pan American Airways Hotel steward, Godfrey Free, escorted a handful of luggage carriers to the loading dock.

Despite the fact that the *Philippine Clipper* would carry just five passengers, it was heavily loaded with tires, mail, and other payload that had shifted during the flight from Midway and had to be repositioned and tied down. It was First Officer Bill Moss's job to make sure the plane was properly ballasted, which required Moss to calculate weight and center cargo at strategic points so the clipper could get up on the step during takeoff.

The morning was already hot and the skies overcast when Capt. Hamilton taxied the *Philippine Clipper* out into the lagoon. Cmdr. Cunningham recalled that he and Maj. Devereux heard the clipper lift off for Guam from inside the mess hall. It was early, 6:50 a.m. or so, when the clipper separated its belly from the lagoon's surface and climbed into the dawn, already behind schedule due to the morning's engine repair. Those onboard, including Mac, looked down at the island with its aqua-colored lagoon surrounded by sand and the dark blue ocean waters and got a bird's-eye view of the neatly landscaped Pan Am compound and new construction already underway that morning.

With the clipper flying out of sight, Godfrey and the young Pan Am luggage carriers returned to the hotel to finish scrubbing the kitchen and dining room before cleaning the departing passengers' rooms. The *Philippine Clipper* wasn't scheduled to return for nine days, whereas the *China Clipper*'s timetable called for her to take off from Treasure Island and land at Wake in four days. With the *Philippine Clipper* taking off for Guam and no other clippers due for days, the Pan Am personnel settled in for what they thought would be just another Monday on the scraggly little island, thousands of miles out in the Pacific.

## CHAPTER 22

# CLIMB MOUNT NIITAKA

Yamamoto signaled in code from aboard his ship, *Nagato*, at anchor at Hashirajima, commanding the task force to proceed with the attack on Pearl Harbor: *Niitaka yama nobore* (Climb Mount Niitaka). For those aboard the vessels steaming nearer to Pearl Harbor, the command was welcomed with glorious applause and cheers. "Hawaii seems to be just like a rat in a trap," a fellow admiral remarked to Yamamoto aboard the *Nagato*.

The Imperial Japanese Navy had planned and practiced for this moment; cadets had studied strategy and tactics at the Naval Academy always with the United States as the enemy; children had played war in parks and streets against Imperialist Americans—and now it was almost time to finally strike the long-awaited blow that would cripple the United States of America.

## CHAPTER 23

# A LATE WARNING

At 4:00 a.m. Eastern Time, on Sunday, December 7, a sleepless Ambassador Nomura and special envoy Saburō Kurusu finally received the last in a series of messages sent from Tokyo. The receipt and decoding of the entire series of parts had taken eighteen hours. The fourteenth and final part of the message read:

> The Japanese Government regrets to have to notify hereby the American Government that in view of the attitude of the American Government it cannot but consider that it is impossible to reach an agreement through further negotiations.

The message constituted Japan's answer to President Roosevelt's pronouncement two weeks earlier that the United States would only resume normal trade relations with the Japanese when the Empire of Japan pulled its troops out of China and Southeast Asia and ceased its military aggression.

Kurusu stood by the fireplace and stared into the jumping blaze. He was tired and disappointed. Japan's answer had broken off further negotiations with the United States. The militaristic Prime Minister Tōjō would have his way, Kurusu thought, or perhaps negotiations could resume following a brief cooling-off period, he hoped.

It wasn't long until a messenger brought in another cable that had been decoded. Kurusu was piqued by the telegram's mysterious direction. The Japanese Minister of Foreign Affairs instructed Kurusu and Nomura to deliver the fourteen-part message to Secretary of State Hull "at 1:00 p.m. on the 7th your time." The specificity of the time seemed sinister. One o'clock in the afternoon in Washington, DC, meant 7:30 in the morning in Hawaii, which was a half-hour time zone until 1947. Another telegram soon handed to him confirmed it. The embassy had been ordered to destroy its cipher machine. Kurusu and Nomura knew that meant war somewhere in the Pacific.

Just as the messages flashed through the airwaves from the Japanese Foreign Ministry in Tokyo to its embassy in Washington, DC, a US Navy communications station at Fort Ward on Bainbridge Island in the state of Washington intercepted the radio transmission. The PURPLE messages were decrypted by a MAGIC analogue machine at the Office of Chief of Naval Operations and passed to the US Army Signal Intelligence Service for translation. The message would soon be in the hands of Secretary Hull and President Roosevelt. Unfortunately, the PURPLE diplomatic code did not provide specific military information, so the White House still had no advance direct knowledge that a strike on Pearl Harbor was imminent.

Adm. Yamamoto may have conceived of the plan to attack Pearl Harbor, but it had been against his best judgment to enter a war with the United States. He'd held open the possibility of peace even as the task force drew nearer to launching its bombers to attack Pearl Harbor. "If the negotiations with the United States turn out to be successful, I will order the forces back before 0100 December 7. Upon this order each ship must withdraw immediately."

Tokyo's fourteenth and final part of the diplomatic message made it clear—Yamamoto would not be ordering the task force to return to Japan—the Imperial Japanese Navy would strike Pearl Harbor in just nine hours.

## CHAPTER 24

# THE CALM

Harry Olson didn't turn in early after the Shriners college football game. He returned to the Moana Hotel and rested before cleaning up and changing into his Sunday best. He went out to attend one of the sundry Saturday-night parties in Honolulu where Eudelle Russell, the wife of his friend and coworker, Pete Russell, would be. Russell had asked Harry to check in on his wife while vacationing in Hawaii. Days earlier, Pete Russell had ridden the crash launch out into Wake Island's lagoon to wave at Harry as he took off aboard the *China Clipper* headed for Hawaii. As the clipper flew past and gained attitude, Harry could see his friend waving from the lagoon.

Now in Honolulu, Harry and Eudelle, with her husband, Pete, still on Wake Island, hit it off that Saturday night enjoying each other's company, making the most of what any late-night island party had to give. Harry later wrote his wife, Katherine, at home in cold, wintry Oregon: "We had all been out on a lovely party, gay and formal. It lasted until 3:30." Harry, who wore a rugged look with balding head and a slight belly, failed to mention that a bit of kindling had sparked between Eudelle and him at the party. The spark would soon ignite an all-out fire of passion.

On that Saturday night, December 6, in Honolulu, sailors with their liberty passes and tourists like Harry weren't the only ones burning the midnight oil. Military brass from Pearl Harbor and other Oahu bases were out enjoying the evening. Much like corporate CEOs, the army and navy provided perks to their upper echelons.

Lt. Gen. Walter Short, the US Army commander responsible for the defense of US military installations in Hawaii, attended an annual charity dinner and dance called Ann Etzler's Cabaret at the Schofield Barracks Officer's Club. Officers sipped smooth wine and hard cocktails while enjoying a song-and-dance event put together by one of the captains' wives. After the party, many went out for nightcaps, but Lt. Gen. Short had an early golf game Sunday morning so he left the party to turn in for the evening. He drove past a well-lit and orderly Pearl Harbor on the way to his residence that night. He couldn't help but admire its majesty and power.

Short's golf partner for Sunday morning was US Navy Rear Adm. Husband Kimmel, who was the commander in chief of the US Pacific Fleet. He'd also been enjoying a festive Saturday evening, partaking of food and drink at the Halekulani Hotel where a dinner party was held that evening. He left around 9:30 p.m., looking forward to his morning of golf on the beautiful island where he'd showcase his skills amid beer and cigars.

US Army Air Forces officers weren't left out. They enjoyed a dinner party at the Hickam Field Officer's Club. Other officers enjoyed a dance at the Royal Hawaiian Hotel that ended at midnight.

———

It was a lovely evening in Honolulu as most bedded down for the night. Breezes rustled coconut palm fronds and delivered the aroma of warm ocean air. If there ever had been a calm before the storm, it was that Saturday night, December 6, 1941, in Hawaii.

## CHAPTER 25

# TORA! TORA! TORA!

The Japanese task force swung directly south toward Oahu and increased its speed to twenty-four knots—battle speed—lashing across the ocean's surface, casting spray high onto the ships' hulls. Fueled planes with their wings fully extended now lined the flight decks of the six carriers. The black surfaces of torpedoes and bombs strapped to the planes' underbellies reflected an eerie shimmer in the early morning light.

Fuchida stood high aboard the ship and looked out at the massive armada. "The overwhelming sight of the fleet—plowing the waves and churning up snow-white spray—was truly magnificent, and I was excited like a child despite my age. Turning my head to the east, I saw the sunrise. I prayed to no one in particular. I wished that for just one day, we will not be detected by anybody."

The sea was rough despite fair weather. Hurling waves splashed forty feet high upon the *Akagi's* top deck as the bow rose and fell hard into the ocean, splashing the already high waves even higher like giant geysers shooting up from the ocean's depths. The bow's pitch approached fifteen degrees, so much that if a plane attempted to take off while the bow was moving downward, the plane would fly straight into the churning ocean, where it would be plowed under the carrier's bow and ripped apart by the gigantic propeller at its stern.

Fuchida ordered: "We have to measure the timing of the pitching."

Empire of Japan task force heading for Pearl Harbor. US Navy, Naval History and Heritage Command.

The ensign in charge yelled in reply: "I think it will work if we release the wheel blocks one by one according to the pitching cycle."

Fuchida would be the first to take off and test the young ensign. He recalled the moment in his autobiography:

> In my flying togs I entered the operation room and reported to the Commander in Chief, "I am ready for the mission." Nagumo stood up, grasped my hand firmly and said, "I have confidence in you." . . . Waiting for me at the side of the plane was a senior petty officer from the air squadron's maintenance group . . . he handed over a *hachimaki* [a white headband marked *Hissho*, meaning "certain victory"] saying, "The maintenance crews . . . wish that they would like to accompany you to Pearl Harbor themselves. Please put it on and go with our wishes."

At 230 miles from Oahu, the *Akagi* turned into the wind roaring from the north. At that moment, the battle flag was hoisted to a position directly below the historic Z flag near the top of the mast. It was dawn—6:00 a.m., Sunday, December 7, Hawaiian time.

"Enjin o kidō shimasu! [Start your engines!]" the carrier's loudspeakers shouted out. The planes' propellers commenced spinning as the engines sputtered and then roared. The flight decks appeared full of swarms of miniature cyclones. Anxious pilots switched on their lights, which quivered from the vibration. The smell of pungent fuel exhaust filled the air.

"Ririku suru! [Take off!]" The order echoed from the loudspeakers, simultaneously with a green signal light swinging in a large circle from the command center for everyone to clearly see. The takeoffs were timed to coincide precisely with the pitch of the bow near its topmost position. One by one the planes roared off and upward into the dawn, as the sailors on board waved caps, handkerchiefs, and hands, shouting "Banzai! [Hurrah!]"

Cmdr. Fuchida lifted his Nakajima B5N2 "Kate" torpedo bomber off the flight deck of the *Akagi*. The timing of the bow's pitch had been perfect, and Fuchida's plane sped up and away, turning outbound as it climbed. As the commander of the entire air attack on Pearl Harbor, Fuchida circled his group of fifteen attack planes at 1,500 feet, directing the formation of the initial wave from above. Planes from the *Shokaku* and *Zuikaku* circled and formed in the rear, joined by planes from the *Kaga* and *Hiryū*, and lastly by planes taking off from the flight decks of the *Akagi* and *Sōryū*.

Once all the planes were airborne—183 in all—the fighters and bombers passed over the flagship *Akagi* to the cheers of those standing on the decks. "We flew through and over the thick clouds which were at 2,000 meters (6,500 feet)," Fuchida remembered, "up to where day was ready to dawn and . . . the brilliant sun burst into the eastern sky. I opened the cockpit canopy and looked back at the large formation of planes. The wings glittered in the bright morning sunlight."

Fuchida then ordered flight formation: the horizontal bombers directly behind the lead group at 9,000 feet; torpedo bombers to starboard at 8,500 feet; and dive bombers to port at 10,500 feet. He later recalled that moment:

> I was full of enthusiasm and courage in the lead position . . . shouldering the destiny of my country . . . I was surely born to be a warrior of the Japanese Empire. . . . My past days of youth were indeed just for this one day. I will leave nothing undone in today's command of the battle . . . I thought at that moment that I was glad that I was born a man.

Thirty minutes and seventy-five miles into their flight, the advancing Japanese bombers recalibrated their course five degrees as Fuchida zeroed in on radio signals of Hawaiian jazz music coming from Honolulu that Sunday morning. The US Army Air Forces had instructed the station to play music all night and into the early morning to guide a dozen Boeing B-17 Flying Fortress bombers arriving from the mainland. Concerned that Oahu might be covered by thick clouds, Fuchida turned the dial on his radio receiver once again. Incredibly, he found what he wanted—the morning's aviation weather report from an American radio broadcast in Oahu. "If things had been prearranged," Fuchida recalled, "the most needed information would not have come at a more perfect time."

Fuchida did not realize it, but the Empire's secret attack force had already eluded not one, but two discoveries by the United States that morning. The first came at 6:45 a.m., more than an hour before Fuchida's planes would reach Pearl Harbor: the USS *Ward* fired on a Japanese midget submarine near the entrance to Pearl Harbor. The US destroyer's commander sent an urgent message to Pearl that he had "dropped depth charges upon a submarine operating in defensive sea area," but his superiors wanted confirmation, which could take hours. The second opportunity for the United States came just seventeen minutes later at 7:02 a.m.—a US Army private manning a recently installed mobile radar station spotted large blips of what appeared to be more than fifty aircraft approaching Hawaii from the north. When he telephoned his lieutenant, he was told to disregard the observation, as a dozen Boeing B-17 bombers were expected from California to the east. The radar station then was shut off for the day.

Forty-five minutes later, the first wave of Japanese bombers and fighters reached Hawaii. Passing Waimea Bay on the north shore of Oahu at 7:49 on Sunday morning, December 7, Cmdr. Mitsuo Fuchida instructed his radio operator, Petty Officer 1st Class Norinobu Mizuki, to send the coded signal "To, To, To" (to charge), as he slid back the canopy and shot a single flare (a black dragon) into the sky. The bombers swept in. Four minutes later, Fuchida ordered Mizuki to send the code words to the flagship *Akagi* that complete surprise had been achieved—"Tora! Tora! Tora!"

## CHAPTER 26

# THE STORM

A lazy Sunday morning in Hawaii, there are few things better. Eager to enjoy his third full day of vacation, Harry Olson got an early start. "I awoke at six, got up, bathed and ate breakfast. Afterwards, I went for a walk through the grounds around the Royal Hawaiian." He strolled beneath a banyan tree shaped like a giant parasol on his way to the edge of the beach cooled by a stiff ocean breeze and tall palm trees. Harry had seen his share of sandy beaches, hot sun, and crystal blue waters at Wake Island, but that's where the similarities ended. Very few places on Earth could match the picturesque Waikiki Beach.

Harry's tranquil surroundings helped clear his mind, a mind clouded with concern. His son Ted was improving at his job on Wake Island, but he could be flippant about his work on occasion, and that could reflect badly on Harry. He didn't want to have to make excuses for his son. Then there was Eudelle Russell—his friend Pete's wife. Harry and Mrs. Russell had enjoyed each other's company way too much the night before. Pete had asked Harry to check in on his wife, not to woo her. But there was something there—a spark, a chemistry—whatever it was called wasn't important. It was something that Harry and his wife, Katherine, had not possessed for years, if ever. He and Katherine had not been happy for a very long time—that's one reason he accepted jobs far away and spent Christmas without her.

Harry decided to shake those troubling thoughts from his mind. After all, he was in Hawaii on a beautiful morning. Reclining in a lounge chair, he sighed relaxingly and looked out on the sparkling blue waters and cresting white breakers. He then lit up a smoke and closed his eyes.

Harry wasn't the only person soaking up paradise that Sunday morning. The sun and the waves were up, and the sand was raked. Beachcombers surfed or thrashed about in the ocean under the watchful eyes of the tanned, athletic men of the Waikiki Beach Patrol. Some planned beach picnics, steak fries, luaus, and barbecues. Others sought to lift their sails at the Yacht Club and cruise away into the blue.

Golfers already were teeing up on the surrounding courses. The commander of the US Pacific Fleet, Adm. Husband Kimmel, and Lt. Gen. Walter Short, responsible for the defense of military installations in and around Pearl Harbor, had a golf game scheduled that morning. Their creased slacks were draped from hangers and their golf clubs had already been buffed. Soon they'd be picked up by their drivers.

For those sleeping off Saturday night's fun, it was still quite early, even though bars and clubs had been required to close at midnight. Of the seventy-five thousand soldiers, sailors, and Marines stationed at Pearl Harbor, eleven thousand had been in Honolulu the night before, doing what young men do. Sunday morning found many of them aboard their ships, nursing hangovers.

For others, the cool indoors sounded like just the ticket—movies and local plays, restaurants, or simply sitting at home sipping beer or tea and listening to records or catching a football radiocast from the mainland. With Christmas fewer than three weeks away, shopping was on many minds. Newspapers and radio carried advertisements of Christmas specials such as GE washers with wringers, Sears, Roebuck and Company refrigerators, and "a 12-tube automatic phonoradio combination in a beautiful furniture console with 6 free records." And then there were sailors and civilians alike, primped and dressed on their way to church services.

Harry hadn't budged from his peaceful spot in the shade that showcased a view of the beach and Diamond Head. He opened and fixed his eyes on two young boys guffawing as they struggled to toss a net over a school of fish in a pool of still water. It was then, just before eight o'clock, when "I heard all this noise, a sort of wump, wump, continuously, but put it down to [US naval and air] practice. Finally one or two [bombs] fell close and I learned what it really was."

"Nobody knew what was going on," said a San Jose State college football player staying at the Moana Hotel. "Some of us thought it was maneuvers. Others saw spouts of water in the harbor and a waiter told us . . . it's a whale spouting." The players and coaches went out to the beach laughing and joking to watch the whales, not realizing that Pearl Harbor was under attack.

Ruth Bramham was awakened when her bed began shaking inside the Moana Hotel. She was expecting her husband, Jack, the host of Pan Am's hotel on Midway, in a few days on the return flight of the *Philippine Clipper* from Singapore. They were to be reassigned to another Pan Am base. After running outside to see what was happening, she "found people standing outside picking up fragments resembling bark from trees, which turned out to be shrapnel."

It was 7:55 a.m., and the first wave of Japanese fighters and bombers converged on Pearl Harbor from every point of the compass—level bombers, dive bombers, torpedo bombers, and fighters. Everyone on Waikiki Beach, including Harry, stood and faced toward Pearl Harbor as sounds of fantastic explosions could be heard, followed by thick clouds of black smoke rolling into the sky with terrific intensity. The onlookers quickly took cover as planes zoomed above Waikiki and Honolulu, banking and circling back to inflict further carnage on Pearl.

At 7:58 a.m., a message went out to all ships in the harbor: "AIR

RAID, PEARL HARBOR. THIS IS NOT A DRILL!" At 8:12 a.m., another message was sent to air and fleet commanders: "HOSTILITIES WITH JAPAN COMMENCED WITH AIR RAID ON PEARL HARBOR." The most infamous attack of World War II in the Pacific was underway.

Japanese Aichi D3A1 "Val" dive bombers, carrying a single 551-pound "land bomb," along with Mitsubishi A6M "Zero" fighters, first attacked Wheeler Army Air Base and Hickam Field and the seaplane base at Ford Island to prevent US fighters from engaging Japanese bombers in the air. Days before the attack, US Army Lt. Gen. Walter Short had ordered an alert against local sabotage from Japanese living on the island, concentrating most of the army's fighter planes wingtip-to-wingtip out in the open where guards could maintain watch. The US planes along the flight line were easy targets—bombed and strafed by the incoming Japanese planes, causing most to explode into flames on the field. The hangars and barracks also were attacked, killing several men. Only six US fighters had been able to take off to engage the Japanese in dogfights. In total, 188 US aircraft would be destroyed before ever leaving the ground.

Ships moored inside Pearl Harbor were prepared for Sunday worship with white canopies stretched above their bows to provide shade for those attending services. Just as the buglers sounded the eight o'clock Colors, Nakajima Kate bombers attacked the US warships. The largest bombers from the Japanese carriers, Kates were manned by a pilot, an observer/bombardier, and a rear gunner/radio operator. Their aim was deadly.

Cmdr. Fuchida was among the crew of the first wave of Kates to attack. The Japanese bombers flew in so low—forty feet above the water's surface—that many sailors aboard ships looked down at them from their vessels' decks as the bombers released their 1,847-pound Type 91 Model 2 torpedoes with 452-pound warheads. The deadly torpedoes splashed into the harbor and buzzed just below the water's surface, leaving an ominous trail behind them. The torpedoes had

Explosions at Pearl Harbor. Library of Congress.

been ingeniously modified with wooden aerodynamic stabilizer fins that broke away when they hit the water so the torpedoes would not sink into the mud of the shallow harbor upon release from the bombers. These self-propelled explosives would be the deadliest to the battleships at Pearl.

"Like a hurricane out of nowhere, my torpedo planes, dive bombers and fighters struck suddenly with indescribable fury," Japanese Cmdr. Fuchida recalled. "As smoke began to billow and the proud battleships, one by one, started tilting, my heart was almost ablaze with joy."

The torpedoes slammed into the ships' hulls just below the waterline. With a deafening explosion came gigantic geysers of water followed by a strong trembling and heaving of the entire vessel. The first torpedoes hit the target ship USS *Utah*, which capsized, and then the light cruisers USS *Helena* and *Raleigh*, before sinking the minesweeper USS *Oglala*. Then the Kates zeroed in on the majestic battleships moored in Pearl Harbor's Battleship Row. Seven battle-ships—USS *West Virginia, Maryland, California, Arizona, Tennes-see, Oklahoma*, and *Nevada*, lay anchored, mostly in pairs, side by side, without the deployment of torpedo nets around their perimeter. (Another battleship, USS *Pennsylvania*, commanded by John Cooke's uncle, was undergoing repair in Dry Dock #1.) Like the planes parked at the airfields, the moored battleships in Battleship Row were easy targets.

"As I observed the damage done by the first attack wave," Cmdr. Fuchida recalled, "the effectiveness of the torpedoes seemed remarkable, and I was struck with the shortsightedness of the United States in being so generally unprepared and in not using torpedo nets."

Within the first thirty minutes of the relentless attack, the battleship USS *West Virginia* had been sunk by torpedoes and bombs. The USS *California* also sank. The two battleships that received the most destruction and lost the most lives were the USS *Oklahoma* and *Arizona*. Within minutes of the first bombing wave's strike, the *Oklahoma* received nine hits and began to list to port before rolling over. Its superstructure (the tower bridge and tubular mast above the main deck) crushed into the mud of the harbor's floor thirty feet beneath the water's surface, halting the battleship's roll but leaving it capsized. A gigantic propeller eerily protruded from its stern above the water's surface.

The USS *Arizona* and its officers and crewmen suffered the worst from the attacks. Kates flying at both high and low altitudes dropped 1,763-pound bombs (converted naval shells) that hit the *Arizona* with tremendous force. One bomb penetrated the ship's decks and ignited the forward powder magazine. There was a brilliant flash of light, and then a cataclysmic explosion equivalent to the detonation of one million pounds of TNT ripped the ship essentially in two. A tremendous rush of wind shot out in all directions as if from an

Capsized USS *Oklahoma*. Library of Congress.

exploding volcano that could be felt miles away, shaking buildings in Honolulu. The concussion extinguished fires on an adjacent oil tanker and even knocked Japanese planes off their bombing runs. The immediate inferno melted the steel of the *Arizona* and instantly incinerated hundreds of sailors onboard.

"Suddenly a colossal explosion occurred in battleship row," Cmdr. Fuchida remembered. "A huge column of dark red smoke rose to 1,000 feet and a stiff shock wave reached our plane. . . . Studying battleship row through binoculars, I saw that the big explosion had been on *Arizona*. She was still flaming fiercely."

Most of the sailors aboard the *Arizona* were killed instantly by the massive explosion and its enormous ball of fire. Body parts rained down on nearby ships. Other sailors had been trapped inside and drowned. Still others had been blown off the deck into the oil-covered water of the harbor, whose ferocious blaze burned their

The sunken USS *Arizona*. Library of Congress.

bodies as they attempted to swim to safety. Sailors aboard adjacent ships recalled the piercing cries of fellow sailors on fire, a horrible sound that rose above the other horrific noises of battle.

The tumultuous bombing and barrage of bullets inflicted by the first wave lasted forty-five minutes, and then the shelling stopped. The sky was empty and eerily silent of the roaring engines of attacking planes. Only sirens, ship horns, shouts, and screams could be heard. The commander of the USS *Nevada* believed this was his chance to attempt a breakout through the channel to the open sea. Cheers from men on the other ships erupted as they spotted *Nevada* making its way along the channel. It was the high point in a morning of disaster; but it didn't last. No sooner had the *Nevada* commenced moving than it was caught and bombed by the second wave of Japanese bombers that soared in at 8:50 a.m., only minutes after the first wave had ended. The *Nevada* was hit several times and forced to ground on Waipio Peninsula opposite Hospital Point to avoid obstructing the harbor's channel if she sank there.

Though taken by surprise and under fire, and despite many antiaircraft guns being locked or disabled on Sunday morning, US sailors and Marines commenced returning fire the best they could. "As my group made its bomb run," Cmdr. Fuchida recalled, "enemy antiaircraft suddenly came to life. Dark gray bursts blossomed here and there until the sky was clouded with shattering near misses which made our plane tremble . . . I was startled by the rapidity of the counterattack which came less than five minutes after the first bomb had fallen."

Aerial photo of Pearl Harbor. US Navy, Naval History and Heritage Command.

Countless Americans exhibited outstanding bravery during the attack. One was US Navy Chief Aviation Ordnanceman John "Johnny" Finn. When Mitsubishi Zeroes converged on the Naval Air Station at Kaneohe Bay and commenced strafing the planes on the field, Finn raced from his home to the field and manned a .50-caliber machine gun on a tripod near the airfield out in the open. Continuously fed ammunition by other sailors, Finn fired for the duration of the attack, almost two hours, despite receiving twenty-one shrapnel wounds. He later remarked that he didn't have time to be scared because "I was mad as hell." Finn would be the first serviceman in the US Navy to earn the Medal of Honor during World War II and, seventy-five years later, a guided-missile destroyer would be launched into service bearing his name—USS *John Finn*.

George Youmans, who supervised Morrison-Knudsen Company's share of the CPNAB defense projects on Wake Island, lived in Honolulu with his wife. It was Youmans who'd recommended Harry Olson for the supervisory job at Wake. Youmans received a telephone call at 8:30 a.m. informing him that an attack was underway and that Morrison-Knudsen's operating base was in jeopardy. Youmans dropped everything and hopped in a car:

> Shortly after I left the house, I could see the dense black smoke rolling up from Pearl Harbor and drifting out to sea. . . . As we came closer to the yards, we could see the blaze of the hangars on Hickam Field and the blazing of the sunken ships in the harbor. . . . We were there only for about five minutes, when we saw about thirty planes approaching the harbor . . . they started to drop bombs all over the place. We ran for cover.
>
> The planes came over us in a group, flying slowly, and some of them were . . . so low that we could see the Japanese pilots and crew looking out. . . . All of them started up their machine guns and raked the main highway and housing area with a steady

stream of bullets. They then circled around . . . repeating their bombing and machine gunning. The planes then passed out to sea and out of sight.

The principal damage . . . was to the battleships that had been moored at Ford Island. Seven of them appeared to have been hit, and one had turned turtle up completely. . . . All of them seemed to be burning fiercely . . . from what I know personally, the loss [of life] on the sunk ships will be over 3,000.

Youmans's estimate was reasonably accurate—2,403 Americans killed, 1,143 wounded—military and civilians. Two-thirds of the servicemen killed had been aboard the USS *Arizona* and *Oklahoma*. Some families back on the US mainland bore more than their share of the loss. Thirty sets of brothers had been killed at Pearl, as well as a father and son. Three families lost each of their three sons during the attack.

Almost two hours into the bombing, a reporter for an NBC radio affiliate in Honolulu made an urgent telephone call to New York that was relayed live to radio listeners. It may have been reminiscent of when just three years earlier, many listeners believed that aliens from Mars were invading Earth as Orson Welles broadcast "War of the Worlds" over the radio. Though it may have seemed so, this was no fantasy.

Hello, NBC. Hello, NBC. This is KTU in Honolulu, Hawaii. I am speaking from the roof of the Advertiser Publishing Company building. We have witnessed this morning in the distant view a brief full battle of Pearl Harbor and the severe bombing of Pearl Harbor by enemy planes, undoubtedly Japanese. The city of Honolulu has also been attacked and considerable damage done. . . . It is no joke. It is a real war. The public of Honolulu has been advised to keep in their homes and away from the Army and Navy. There has been serious fighting going on in the air and in the sea.

Japanese forces lost only nine planes in the first wave and twenty in the second wave out of a total of 350 planes engaged in the attacks. All five midget submarines were lost. Sixty-four Japanese men had been killed and one crewman of a midget sub had been captured.

Notwithstanding the damage to US ships and the terrible loss of life, it can be argued that the Japanese attack on Pearl Harbor had been a strategic failure. Of the ninety-six American warships moored in the harbor, fewer than twenty had been damaged. Of the eight battleships bombed, six were later repaired and returned to service. Most importantly, no US aircraft carriers had been in the harbor during the attack. And although Cmdr. Fuchida had pleaded for a third wave of bombers and fighters to attack the submarine base, fuel storage tanks, and ship-repair yards, as well as to search for the carriers, a conservative-minded Vice Adm. Nagumo refused. Nagumo believed that the attack had been sufficiently successful and was fearful that planes from the undiscovered US carriers might locate the Japanese task force. Instead, Nagumo ordered the flags on the *Akagi* hoisted to signal that the task force was retiring from the theatre of battle and changing course for Japan.

Adm. Yamamoto's belief when he first planned the surprise attack on Pearl Harbor was that America's morale would "sink to the extent that it could not be recovered" if the attack was successful. But that did not happen—just the opposite. The bombing raid brought Americans together, all eager in their resolve to fiercely extract revenge for the "sneak attack" that killed 2,403 Americans. Although the famous quote attributed to Yamamoto in film likely was not actually spoken or written by him—*I fear all we have done is awaken a sleeping giant and fill him with terrible resolve*—it does accurately reflect the American people's response, which would be swift and severe.

## CHAPTER 27

# ROOSEVELT RECEIVES WORD

President Franklin Roosevelt had just finished lunch with top aide Harry Hopkins in the nautical-themed oval study on the second floor of the White House. Roosevelt was an avid stamp collector, a hobby he used to relieve stress. The servants cleared away the lunch plates, and Roosevelt laid out his stamp album to begin pasting. The study's telephone rang. It was 1:47 p.m. (EST). Secretary of the Navy Frank Knox instructed the White House operator that his call was of the utmost urgency. Roosevelt took the call. "Mr. President," said Knox in a distressed voice, "it looks like the Japanese have attacked Pearl Harbor." The attack on Pearl Harbor had been going on for twenty-two minutes. Roosevelt was heard to shout "No!"

Around 2:30 p.m. (EST) that Sunday, radios all over the world began broadcasting news of the surprise attack. The NBC Red network interrupted Sammy Kaye's music program, while CBS broke into a New York Philharmonic broadcast. The Mutual Broadcasting System, famous for its programing of *The Lone Ranger*, *The Shadow*, and professional sports, interrupted its play-by-play commentary of the New York Giants and Brooklyn Dodgers NFL football game to announce the attack.

We interrupt this broadcast to bring you this important bulletin from the United Press. Flash. Washington. The White House announces Japanese attack on Pearl Harbor. . . .

From that moment on, American citizens everywhere remained near a radio set. In the cities, many stood near outdoor public address (PA) speakers. Though most had heard of Hawaii, they'd never heard of Pearl Harbor and weren't aware that the United States maintained its Pacific Fleet there. But now they knew it; and they knew it meant war for the United States and their sons, brothers, fathers, and other loved ones.

## CHAPTER 28

# PLAN A

On that Sunday, December 7, Pan Am CEO Juan Trippe was at his Greenwich, Connecticut, estate, nursing the flu. He typically relaxed at his beautiful home on the eastern tip of Long Island between Georgica Pond and the Atlantic Ocean, but that was during summers, not December, when salt ice rims the shoreline. Just before 2 p.m., as Trippe sipped hot tea and read reports, the telephone rang—it was Frank Knox, the US secretary of the Navy.

Knox, who'd telephoned President Roosevelt merely thirteen minutes earlier at 1:47 p.m., commenced relaying details of the air strike to Trippe. The attack had been going on for thirty-five minutes. He informed Trippe that the reports coming in to his desk at Washington, DC, indicated that the Japanese bombers had inflicted terrible damage on the US Pacific Fleet, and the Japanese planes had taken off from carriers whose location was still unknown. When asked, Knox replied that he could not say with any confidence whether a land invasion was imminent, but that was the prudent theory. Knox also informed Trippe that based on radio monitoring and Japanese movements in the South China and Philippine Seas, additional attacks were expected at Hong Kong and the Philippines, where Pan Am maintained bases, planes, and personnel.

That was all Trippe needed to hear. Trippe's first order of business was to send a cable to Pan Am bases and planes in the air: "DE-CEMBER 7, 1941 EXECUTIVE MEMORANDUM 71 . . . ALL DIVISIONS

. . . Maintain all facilities subject emergency order US military authority your area. Plan A effective this order . . . proceed in accordance therewith."

Plan A, the shortened term for "Case 7, Condition A," was a coded signal for division headquarters and pilots to institute a prearranged action plan. It was a document enclosed in a large envelope labeled PLAN A that broadly addressed various scenarios in case of wartime or other impending danger. Pilots carried the document in their briefcases and stowed it in the cockpit if ever needed. Its objective was simply for planes to head to the nearest landing area where the crew and passengers would be safe and the plane secure. Radios were to be silenced, lights blacked out, and headings changed. Mail was to be safeguarded and Pan Am personnel evacuated from bases, if possible.

Trippe put down his tea and sped to the Chrysler Building on 42nd Street in New York where Pan Am maintained its headquarters. The lobby and offices in the second-tallest building in the world were typically empty on a Sunday afternoon, but Pan Am directors and employees had been called in and were congregating, such as Pan Am's representative to the Far East, Harold Bixby, who'd seen firsthand the slaughter that Japanese bombers and infantry had inflicted in China.

Trippe was the chief executive officer of Pan American Airways System; but as he sat behind his desk on the fifty-eighth floor of the Chrysler Building, he resembled Secretary of War Henry Stimson executing his war plans. Pan Am had 162 aircraft in operation and 192 ground bases, giving it the largest commercial fleet of aircraft anywhere, with thousands of employees in 62 countries and colonies around the world amidst war in Europe and Africa, and now in the Pacific. With the aid of Trippe's secretary serving hot soup and tea, his office remained lit throughout the night as telephone calls and telegrams bombarded the operators' stations. "President Roosevelt called Juan that night, asking Pan American to give every assistance," Juan Trippe's wife, Betty, later wrote. Trippe also spoke with several in Roosevelt's cabinet, members of Congress, and US military officers. He maintained constant contact with US officials and with officials in Hong Kong, Manila, Singapore, Brazil, Cuba, and New Zealand. "From that fateful Sunday on, all night, all day, those lights have burned [in Pan Am's offices] like a sleepless eye over Manhattan's skyline . . . a 7-day, 24-hour watch," a Pan Am periodical read at the time.

Reports from Pan Am's bases around the world—throughout the Pacific, the Atlantic, South America, Alaska, and elsewhere—arrived on Trippe's desk at all hours, as did the latest news from wire services and radio broadcasts. It was decided that all this information should be collected late each night, summarized in a confidential Pan Am bulletin, and disseminated by wire to Pan Am division headquarters throughout the world before nine o'clock the following morning. The result was "a last minute system-wide coverage that often gives Pan American's executives several hours' head start in meeting the day's contingencies." Public Relations Director William Van Dusen was placed in charge of the daily PAA BULLETIN, which was usually anywhere from two to four pages, single-spaced. One of the earliest bulletins, albeit a succinct one, was sent to President Roosevelt on the morning of December 8th. It read simply: "Guam lost. One S-42 lost. Gas at Guam . . . destroyed. Clipper now probably on its way."

Over the course of Trippe's numerous conversations that first day and the next, the US government made it clear that it needed Pan Am's flying boats, pilots, bases, and expertise, and needed them immediately. Trippe had known this was a possibility should the United States enter the war in Europe or should one break out in the Pacific; that's one reason why Plan A required that the planes be secured. Pan Am was eager to serve; but first it had to get its planes and their crews home safely.

## CHAPTER 29

# THE *PACIFIC* AND *ANZAC CLIPPERS*

## PACIFIC CLIPPER

The flight of the *Pacific Clipper* began as routine on the morning of December 8, west of the International Date Line. The flying boat cruised above the Coral Sea at 180 mph with six hours to go before it could touch down in Mechanics Bay at Auckland. That put the clipper's arrival around three o'clock, just in time for afternoon tea.

The clipper's first radio officer had handed over radio duties to a young trainee around nine o'clock that morning. "About an hour out from Nouméa, I was on watch," the trainee recalled. "It was common practice to assign ground radio operators to the crew as future flight radio operators." Wearing headphones, the trainee listened to a French-speaking station in New Caledonia, until the signal eventually faded into static. He switched frequencies and zeroed in on an English-speaking station from Auckland. The signal grew stronger as he turned various dials, and then:

> White House has announced that Japanese airplanes attacked the Hawaiian Island Oahu, also the Pearl Harbor naval base . . . Imperial Japanese headquarters announced that Japan was at war with the United States and Great Britain in the western Pacific.

Captain Robert Ford of the *Pacific Clipper*. National Library of New Zealand. Pan American Airways, *New Horizons*, Vol. 11, No. 1, October 1940, 11; U. Miami PAA.

The trainee yelled out. Fourth Officer John Steers, who was making only the second flight of his Pan Am career, succinctly described the moment in his flight log: "Radio operator listening in on press dispatches, intercepted news of Pearl Harbor attack." The crew patched in to the broadcast and heard the news for themselves. "At first, no one could believe it true," Steers recalled. "It seemed incredible that the news could be true," the engineering officer wrote. "[We thought] it might have been a mistake or maybe only a test."

The flying boat's captain, Robert "Bob" Ford, quickly but calmly began implementing the necessary precautions. "The captain silenced the radio, then posted watches in the blister, then altered course about 50 miles," Fourth Officer Steers said. The "blister" was the clear acrylic navigator's dome atop the fuselage between the wings. Watches were also posted at windows not occupied by passengers. "The Captain even got out his 38-caliber pistol," Steers added.

The captain realized that he was four thousand miles from Honolulu and four thousand miles from Manila. He hoped the immense distances would provide protection from Japanese task forces. Yet, the enemy could be anywhere; they'd already proven that. The skipper briefly deliberated with his navigator about altering their course, but there was no place to divert. Australia lay as far away as New Zealand, and there was no civilized speck of land between his plane and the two countries. It was at that time that the first radio officer received a Morse code message from Pan Am advising to implement Plan A.

From the pilot's seat, the captain reached for his black flight case filled with flight plans, weather reports, checklists, and other essential documents. He riffled through the case and withdrew a large envelope stenciled TOP SECRET: PLAN A.

"Our orders for future action came in part from . . . an envelope from [Pan Am Flight] Operations, carried by the captain," Capt. Ford later said. "For many months we had carried . . . a sealed envelope to be opened when war should break out in the Pacific. . . . We always turned our sealed envelope in again to the operations office on our return to San Francisco."

The captain wouldn't be turning those orders back in at Treasure Island following the flight. War had broken out in the Pacific, and Pan Am and the *Pacific Clipper* were now in the thick of it.

"'Plan A' meant a lot of things that are, of course, a secret," read a Baltimore newspaper two weeks afterwards. "But radios were silenced, the ship's lights were blacked out, headings were changed to predetermined courses. Flight crews, who knew their new rules by heart, changed over to war operations."

Once Plan A had been executed, Capt. Ford, like the captain of a great sinking ship, considered it his duty to tell the twenty-three remaining passengers onboard. The *Pacific Clipper* wasn't sinking, but it might if a machine gun from an enemy plane or a deck gun on a ship or submarine hit its mark. The captain called the passengers into the plane's lounge and informed them of the attack on Pearl Harbor. Before they could ask questions, he assured everyone that the likelihood of the *Pacific Clipper* being attacked was remote, but security measures still had to be implemented. He implored them to remain calm but vigilant. If they spotted any plane, ship, or submarine, they were told to report it immediately, even if it was simply a reflection or speck that seemed out of place. Aside from gasps and looks of disbelief, the passengers handled it all very well.

The remainder of the flight was practically silent, with all available eyes fretfully scanning the sea and the air. Everyone onboard had to have been contemplating within that eerie silence what the attack meant to them, their families, their businesses, and their countries. Would the Japanese attack the United States mainland? New Zealand? Australia? Would Hitler send forces to help the Japanese? More immediate for the crew was whether they could safely return to Hawaii and then to San Francisco. For the passengers traveling to Australia, could they continue their journey, or would they be trapped in New Zealand—if they made it there at all?

For the next six hours, everyone ruminated about their own distinct future and its uncertainty until, with a collective exhalation of relief, Auckland came into view. The *Pacific Clipper* passed over Warkworth, New Zealand, that Monday afternoon at "an unusually low altitude," an Auckland newspaper reported. Pan Am's Auckland airport manager, Bill Mullahey, was ready. He'd ordered a channel sweep and cleared the landing area of craft. He'd also alerted New Zealand's Ministry of Defence. No one wanted any of the Territorial Units or Home Guard mistaking the big Boeing for a Japanese aircraft with belligerent intent.

Around 3 p.m., as scheduled, the skipper brought the *Pacific Clipper* in for a landing in Mechanics Bay. Passengers disembarked and set foot in a world that had ominously changed since they'd boarded a mere eight hours earlier. They'd grown uncomfortably accustomed to the war in Europe eleven thousand miles away; but now there was war in their hemisphere that could possibly encroach upon their shores at any moment—and that was terrifying.

# ANZAC CLIPPER

Having taken off from Treasure Island on an overnight flight the evening before, it was now early morning, Sunday, December 7. The sun shone brilliantly across the *Anzac Clipper's* rudders and wingtips. One by one, the passengers awoke. With Honolulu three hundred miles away, everyone enjoyed a wonderful breakfast in the lounge or in their cabins, talking and laughing, anxious to land at the always-enchanting Hawaii.

Another hour passed. It was eight o'clock, and Pearl City now lay less than an hour away. Normally the clipper would have been preparing to land at Pearl City in the Middle Loch of Pearl Harbor, but because of the captain's attendance at his daughter's piano recital, the *Anzac Clipper* was nearly an hour behind schedule.

Capt. Lanier Turner left the bridge and joined the passengers on the lower level. "I had gone down below and was having breakfast," the captain recalled. Amid the morning hubbub, few noticed the first radio officer, his feet rapidly tapping the metal steps as he hurried down the spiral staircase to the passenger level. "His eyes were about the size of saucers," the captain remembered. The radio officer had tuned to Hawaiian radio station KGMB to listen to Hawaiian music, as was the crew's custom. This time, a news flash of an enemy attack cut in over the radio:

The island of Oahu is being attacked by enemy planes. The center of this attack is Pearl Harbor, but the planes are attacking airfields as well. We are under attack. . . . This is not a maneuver. This is the real McCoy! . . . I repeat, we are under attack by enemy planes. The mark of the rising sun has been seen on these planes. . . . This is not a maneuver.

"[The first radio officer] informed me of the [attack]," the captain recalled, which had been going on for more than half an hour. Without causing any alarm to the passengers, both men returned to the bridge. "I went back up . . . I put on a pair of [head]phones and at that time it was announced definitely the aircraft attacking were Japanese."

It was minutes afterward that the first radio officer received a coded message from Pan Am—PLAN A. He thrust the cryptic message in front of the plane's captain, who immediately withdrew the envelope marked PLAN A from his flight case just as the captain of the *Pacific Clipper* had done moments earlier some four thousand miles away. For a document requiring quick action, it was long—three pages and an appendix of authenticating flight maneuvers captioned "TOP SECRET."

Unlike the captain of the *Pacific Clipper*, the captain of the *Anzac Clipper* chose not to inform the passengers. No passenger noticed any change in the crew's demeanor or the captain's slow turn to starboard. Unbeknownst to the passengers, Hilo on the Big Island of Hawaii, two hundred miles from Honolulu, was now the *Anzac Clipper*'s destination. It was a perfect diversion point of little interest as a Japanese target. Hilo had no military installations and its airport wasn't large, mostly used by Inter-Island Airways (later Hawaiian Airlines), which served the Hawaiian Islands. The airport did have a marine terminal for seaplanes, though it was not a regular Pan Am stop. And as the second-largest city in the Hawaiian Islands, hotels were available to keep the clipper's passengers comfortable until the danger passed, if it passed.

The crew scanned the sky for Japanese planes and ships. At any moment they expected to see Japanese Zeroes zooming toward their slower, unarmed plane. After all, they were flying off the coast of the Hawaiian Islands with almost two hundred Japanese planes in the air and more on the way. If even a solitary errant Japanese plane spotted them, they would all be goners. Fortunately, the Japanese attack path was north of the islands, whereas the *Anzac Clipper*'s flight path was several miles south—but the crew had no way of knowing that, so they worried and watched.

Capt. Ford frequently asked his crew if they spotted anything, even though he knew they would shout out if it they did. The men also bantered about the attack and how it was all so fantastical. Talking among themselves seemed to relieve some of the tension that silence only amplified. After two nerve-racking hours, a snow-covered Mauna Kea on the Big Island slowly began to materialize through the clipper's enormous windshield. It wasn't long afterward that the captain and first officer spotted Waiakea Peninsula jutting out into Hilo Bay. As the *Anzac Clipper* approached, the captain commenced a series of "authentication flight patterns" per the instructions of Plan A to assure those on the ground that the plane was friendly.

"We landed cautiously . . . there had never been one of our aircraft . . . in that harbor to my knowledge," the captain recalled. He was concerned about not only obstructions in the water and Japanese attack but overzealous Hilo residents who might take potshots at a strange plane landing in their bay. "Anyway, we eased onto the water and taxied up and tied to a buoy available there."

Upon landing, stewards asked the passengers—who now knew they were at Hilo and not Pearl City—to meet in the plane's lounge and to leave their belongings behind for the moment. Most believed it was another malfunction. After all, they'd returned to San Francisco on Friday night because of mechanical problems. They couldn't have guessed the actual reason for this diversion.

Moments later, the captain and the first officer appeared in the lounge with their jackets buttoned and their caps straightened, looking very official. Capt. Turner then bluntly announced: "We have been informed that . . . planes are carrying out raids on the island of Oahu." Blank stares, dropped jaws, and anger filled the cabin. Everyone knew this meant war—likely another world war for the United States—the second in their lifetimes. For passengers who were residents of Honolulu, the attack meant the possibility of an invasion and their capture. Within days, paradise could become an internment camp. The others believed they too could be captured or killed. Even so, "there was no panic . . . of any kind among the passengers," the captain recalled.

A launch carried the passengers ashore, where vehicles arrived to transport the twenty-eight passengers and crew to the Naniloa Hotel, with their bags to follow. The foremost thing everyone wanted to do at the hotel was to contact someone—tell them they were safe, and learn more about the attack and whether an invasion was coming. But that wasn't going to happen. Telephone and telegraph lines were busy, or their operators were not responding. They were cut off from the rest of the world. The passengers would simply have to retire to their rooms or to the lounge and listen to a radio—and wait.

## CHAPTER 30

# NO THOUGHT OF SURRENDER

Imperial Japanese Forces had positioned themselves for an invasion of Hong Kong, codenamed Operation C, to begin shortly after the attack on Pearl Harbor. At least forty thousand soldiers, possibly thousands more, their bayonets fixed and blackened, supported by three battalions of mountain artillery, amassed just seventy-five miles northwest of Hong Kong.

Four years earlier, the Imperial Japanese Army had similarly gathered outside of Nanking (now Nanjing), the former capital of the Republic of China, preparing to strike. Weeks later, Japanese soldiers had beheaded, shot, stabbed, beaten to death, and buried alive an estimated three hundred thousand surrendering Chinese soldiers and civilians. Thousands of bloated bodies drifted along the Yangtze River, descending on the banks of villages downstream. Those atrocities, along with tens of thousands of rapes of Chinese women and children, as well as looting and destruction on a scale that left the city decimated, became known as the Massacre of Nanking. Now, a Japanese army crept along the countryside on the outskirts of Hong Kong, preparing to strike. Those inside the city well realized that much more was at stake than simply losing a battle.

On Monday morning, December 8, Lt. Gen. Sakai Takashi gave the order to attack. Three regiments of the 38th Infantry Division of the 23rd Army crossed the Sham Chun River into the New Territories north of the Kowloon Peninsula. The light cruiser *Isuzu*, commanded by Vice Adm. Niimi Masaichi, along with the destroyer *Tsuga* and the 15th Escort Squadron, also sped into position in the South China Sea.

Maj. Gen. Christopher Maltby commanded the British, Canadian, and Indian troops defending Hong Kong with the help of the Chinese militia. The mostly inexperienced defensive force totaled approximately fourteen thousand men. A lone destroyer, the twenty-year-old HMS *Thracian*, and a few gunboats and motor torpedo boats constituted Hong Kong's navy. Five obsolete Royal Air Force planes represented its air corps. The woefully ill-equipped Maltby had been assigned the mission to buy time for Great Britain to defend Malaya and Singapore. Though British Prime Minister Winston Churchill had informed Maltby that "there must be no thought of surrender," defeat in Hong Kong had already been preordained.

The Imperial Japanese Army Air Force would be the first to strike the Kowloon Peninsula and Hong Kong Island. At 7:20 a.m., three hours after the attack on Pearl Harbor had ended, twelve Kawasaki Ki-32 light bombers escorted by thirty-six Nakajima Ki-27 army fighters took off from Baiyun Aerodrome in Canton, China (not to be confused with Canton Island). Their attack plans called for the planes to strafe and bomb the Kai Tak Airport and other strategic targets in Victoria Harbor and on the Kowloon Peninsula. As the Japanese planes leveled off among scattered clouds, Hong Kong lay just forty minutes away.

———

The streets and harbor of Hong Kong came alive Monday morning, December 8. Shop owners laid out their ivories, linens, and colorful silks in neat piles. Markets displayed their fresh fish on planks and juicy produce inside shallow crates for passing customers to inspect. In Victoria Harbor, junks hoisted their sails and dropped their nets, hoping for a bountiful catch. Unmoored from the harbor docks,

Captain Fred Ralph of the *Hong Kong Clipper*. National Library of New Zealand.

freighters flying flags of almost every maritime nation carried their precious cargoes out of the harbor into the South China Sea, headed for faraway ports where merchants desired exotic goods from the Far East.

The Second Sino-Japanese War was entering its sixth year; and even though Japan had already taken the Chinese cities of Nanking, Shanghai, and Canton, the war had reached somewhat of a stalemate. The Hong Kongese and American and European merchants went about their lives, day after day, having grown accustomed to news of war and hardship. "We have had so many flaps and lived in a state of tension for so long that we have become blasé," British Brigade Maj. John Monro wrote in his diary on Sunday, December

7, the day before the attack on Hong Kong. "We live only for the day when the rather annoying precautions that interfere with our private amusements are once more considered unnecessary."

Among the morning's bustle, the *Hong Kong Clipper* floated, moored to Pan Am's dock beside Kai Tak Airport, restlessly waiting for its captain to take off for Manila. It was a perfect day for flying, as several are in Hong Kong during December—a cool, sunny, and pleasant sixty-one degrees.

Fred Ralph, the thirty-seven-year-old slender captain of the *Hong Kong Clipper* from Northeast Harbor, Maine, had arrived at Kai Tak Airport early that morning. He sat in the hotel and sipped coffee, read weather reports, and prepared for the morning's flight, scheduled for nine o'clock. Typically, it was an easy five-and-a-half-hour flight, and the clipper's captain expected that Monday's flight would be nothing more than routine. As the morning progressed, however, he began receiving mysterious and conflicting reports from Pan Am and CNAC representatives about whether or not he should take off. Figuring it had something to do with the Japanese, and believing Manila to be safer than Hong Kong, Capt. Ralph decided to advance the scheduled takeoff time from 9 a.m. to 7:20 a.m. just in case. He'd not yet heard of the attack on Pearl Harbor, nor had he received word of the diversion of the *Anzac Clipper* or the saga of the *Pacific Clipper*.

"I was in the Peninsula Hotel," First Officer John Strickland recalled. "They woke me up and said that our crew was to come to the airport immediately. They didn't tell us why or anything else and we got there and it was just gross confusion. Nobody knew anything."

Pan Am's office contacted and advised Hong Kong hotels to awaken and notify clipper passengers of the earlier takeoff time. Passengers forewent shaves and showers, tossing their clothes into suitcases and grabbing coffee on their way out. Pan Am's bus waited outside to carry them to Kai Tak Airport. Meanwhile, CNAC's ground crew rushed to get everything ready. "We were at the little shack out at the airport," the first officer recalled. "We'd taken all of the baggage and put it on the airplane and we were . . . completely fueled and ready to go."

The clipper's passengers, however, had run into a delay. It seems that the Hong Kong Hotel clerk had failed to call millionaire Hank Marsman to awaken him. Twenty-six passengers, mostly British, Americans, and Filipinos, sat inside the polished Bedford coach bus outside the Peninsula Hotel across the harbor, waiting for Marsman, a man of importance, to arrive so they could go to the airport. "I was the target for some disapproving glances and passing remarks from my fellow passengers when I hustled into the bus . . . because of my tardiness," Marsman wrote.

It was around that time that the *Hong Kong Clipper*'s captain received a warning from the British—Japan had declared war on Great Britain and the USA. It seemed that British intelligence had intercepted a Japanese Broadcasting Company transmission on Radio Tokyo:

> We now present you urgent news. . . . The Army and Navy Sections of Imperial Headquarters jointly announced at 6 o'clock this morning, December 8, [thirty minutes after the attack on Pearl Harbor ended] that the Imperial Army and Navy forces have entered into a state of hostilities with the American and British forces in the Western Pacific at dawn today.

The intelligence had been relayed at 6:45 a.m. to the British commander of the Hong Kong Garrison. It did not include news of the attack on Pearl Harbor, which had been over for more than two hours.

As the *Hong Kong Clipper* and its crew awaited the passengers, Capt. Ralph telephoned William "Bondy" Bond at his home on Repulse Bay on the south side of Hong Kong Island. Though Bond held many titles like vice president and director, he was

the operations manager of CNAC and had a solid working re-
lationship with Pan Am CEO Juan Trippe and Harold Bixby,
Pan Am's representative in Hong Kong. The clipper's captain
told Bond about the news of war that he'd just received from the
British. "I advised Captain Ralph to fly his clipper inland to a
lake near Kunming and that I'd have a CNAC pilot guide him,"
Bond later said, who'd realized that the safest spot to fly to was
inland China, north of the Japanese lines where the Chinese
government still remained in power.

Back at the Peninsula Hotel, Pan Am ground crew member
Chen Teh-tsan closed the bus door and began to pull away from
the hotel, headed to the airport with the clipper's passengers. "I was
already sitting in a Pan American Airways bus outside the Hong
Kong Peninsula Hotel," recalled Richard Wilson, a United Press
staff correspondent. "The bus moved off slowly. A Chinese clerk ran
out [and] scrambled aboard."

"Get out! Get out! The flight is delayed," the clerk shouted, relaying Bond's latest instructions.

"We piled out," Marsman wrote. "The boy's excitement seemed
greater than a commonplace delay justified and one of the passengers said he'd heard that war with Japan had finally burst over the
Far East. He was considered an alarmist and a rumor-monger, and
subsided under the weight of general disapproval."

Everyone went inside the Peninsula Hotel and waited in the
elegant lobby, frustrated that they'd been hastened out of bed
so early only to learn that the flight was now delayed. Marsman
located a friend who was the head of the American President
Steamship Lines, and they sat together for coffee inside the hotel. "I looked out the window and saw airplanes circling and diving over an airfield some distance away. . . . Columns of smoke
billowed from the area." Marsman and his friend differed on the
planes' origin. His friend insisted that they were British planes
on maneuvers.

As the passengers of the *Hong Kong Clipper* continued to wait in the Peninsula Hotel, speculating about the cause of the delay, Capt. Fred Ralph readied the flying boat for a flight, not to Manila, but in the exact opposite direction—without passengers. Flying over Japanese lines into inland China was dangerous during the day, but the captain believed that it was the safest course now that he'd finally received word of war with Japan.

"The crew and I [planned] to hide the plane by setting down on an inland lake," the *Hong Kong Clipper*'s captain recalled. "I was preparing to leave and standing beside the clipper when word of the [incoming] attack [on Hong Kong] came. The alarm sounded almost immediately, then planes appeared."

"I was in my hotel room," a CNAC pilot recalled a year afterward, "when something went whizzing by the window. Then explosions began occurring everywhere. I rushed down to the lobby and asked what all the excitement was. One of the bellboys informed me that Japan had begun war against the United States and Great Britain."

"Almost immediately planes . . . began diving on the field," the captain remembered. "Fortunately, nobody was aboard the clipper [though First Radio Officer Melvern "Mel" Orton had just escaped]. The crew and myself managed to scramble to safety [in the water] behind a dock pillar. The Japanese planes swooped within fifty feet of the field. There were so many they almost collided with each other at times. In fact, I saw one who was forced to halt his machine gun fire on the clipper to avoid shooting a comrade." The captain added that "I watched close enough to see, hear, and smell the bullets."

Phillip Harman, the young American tennis pro, was in the Gloucester Hotel when a shell exploded nearby. Harman recalled stepping out on his hotel balcony with a pair of binoculars to inspect the damage. "The horror of what I saw sickened me . . . dismembered limbs . . . writhing bodies . . . one small child crawling toward the gutter, leaving a long trail of blood in his wake."

A young English woman, who lived in a flat on Victoria Peak and drove an ambulance for the St. John's Ambulance Overseas Brigade, watched the bombing from her balcony. "Wham! Wham! Wham!" she later wrote. "The apartment shook and the windows rattled. . . . More explosions. . . . Black planes drifted across the blue sky, one by one they came diving down. I could see at the bottom of each dive a tiny shining object detach itself and come tumbling slowly earthward. . . . The Japanese were rapidly exploding the Kai Tak aerodrome into a mess of craters and rubble."

Another woman, Gwen Dew, an American journalist who had cheerily judged the costume contest only two nights earlier at the China relief ball, witnessed horrors that even a correspondent wished she hadn't. "A bomb made a direct hit on part of the Central Market . . . and I went to see the sad remnants. . . . On the corner lay a mass of something which had been a man."

"I saw planes diving in the distance and heard the sputter of machine guns," United Press correspondent Richard Wilson said, who'd stepped back inside the Peninsula Hotel. "Air sirens wailed but the 1.5 million residents, mostly Chinese, thought it was a drill."

Those who realized that it wasn't a drill ran for cover. "When the Japanese commenced their attack, we jumped down into this ditch that was alongside the building there," First Officer John Strickland recalled, echoing his captain's recollections. "The top of the walled ditch was right up even with our eyes. It was a drainage ditch . . . for a cloth manufacturing company and the dye was washing out into the bay. A stinking mess, it was." Despite the chemical stench, the walled ditch appeared to provide adequate cover for the clipper crew. The men stood in waist-deep water and watched as Japanese bombers zoomed past overhead. They felt relieved, but for only a moment, as they realized the enemy planes were turning to begin firing from the opposite direction. The ditch had a retaining wall only on one side, which meant the men's backs were exposed to the circling planes. Everyone climbed out and ran for their lives. "Back came the Japanese," read a Pan Am periodical's account of the event, "this time with machine guns roaring. Swerving like angry hornets, they swooped to within 50 feet of the ground." As the others scattered, the first officer discovered that not only was he the last one still in the ditch, no one had stayed to help lift him out from above.

"Bullets were hitting all around me, all over the place, kicking up water and everything like that," the first officer recalled. "It scared me to death. But I finally boosted myself out of that ditch . . . [I ran] inside a building they were using as a final passenger staging point . . . there wasn't a soul inside. So I lay down and slid under one of those benches alongside the wall . . . that they put the baggage out for inspection. And, God, there must have been some forty people . . . under those benches."

Wave upon wave of circling bombers and fighters wreaked havoc on Kowloon Peninsula and Hong Kong Island. Black, white, and gray smoke filled what had been a beautiful blue sky above the peninsula. The *Hong Kong Clipper*'s captain watched from behind a concrete pillar as the planes roared past, strafing and dropping their bombs, fervently killing those on the ground. He was a commercial pilot, not a fighter pilot. He had a young family at home in Devitt Hill, Pennsylvania—his wife, Sallie, his six-year-old son, Stevens, and his daughter, Sallie, just one and a half years old. Eventually, the Japanese zeroed in on the *Hong Kong Clipper*. "There were at least a dozen different strafing attacks on the clipper," Captain Ralph reported. But the clipper, its wing tanks full of fuel, stubbornly remained afloat.

Others watched the attacks on the clipper, praying that it survive. A CNAC pilot recalled: "From my bed, I could see the American clipper in the water. . . . All of a sudden I saw water spraying up. They were machine gunning that clipper."

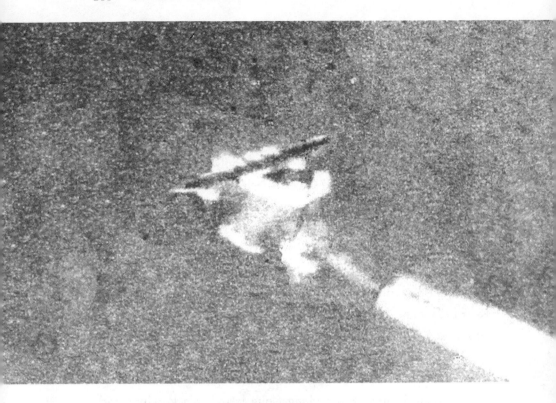

Aerial photo purporting to be a Japanese fighter attack on the *Hong Kong Clipper* while moored at the dock at Kai Tak Airport. Unknown.

The first officer's curiosity bested him, and he slid out from beneath the hangar's table. "I got a little courage . . . and looked out the crack of the door . . . just as I saw a Japanese plane attacking our plane. . . . The fuel was just running out all over the place. . . . One airplane caused a spark by shooting at it . . . or it might have been a tracer bullet that ignited the fuel. And then our S-42 . . . didn't make a big noise, just made a big 'poof' and went up in flames." The first officer quickly realized the jam he and the other crew members were in. "It was a heart-sickening thing to think, here I'm [nine] thousand miles from home . . . and there's no way . . . [back]." Many passengers and American and Filipino expatriates must have felt the same.

"The planes attacked the Kai Tak Airport," correspondent Richard Wilson recalled, "destroying the Pan American Airways clipper plane on which I was about to leave for Manila."

It seemed as if the machine-gun fire and bombing would never end. Resolute in completing their murderous surprise attack, the Japanese pilots banked and turned their planes and attacked again and again. People hiding behind or under objects cringed at the noises of the planes, bullets, and bombs, knowing that all it took was a single bullseye to end their lives and those around them. At last, the planes didn't turn but continued flying out over the South China Sea. It was nearing 9:00 a.m. The air strike had lasted forty-five minutes. As the bombing and strafing noises ended and the sound of the departing planes' engines faded, everyone cautiously ventured from their hiding places and watched the horrid planes fly out of sight.

Many people had taken cover inside the hotels. Civilians in their homes or hotels weren't targets—yet. Hank Marsman, who'd taken refuge inside the Peninsula Hotel during the course of the bombing, decided to return to the lobby to "chase a little information." His questions were quickly interrupted when the clipper's crew burst into the lobby, some drenched in dye, all agitated from the air strike. "Words tumbled over one another as they told how Japanese dive bombers had set their plane ablaze." Marsman added that the clipper's steward, whom he knew from frequent trips, had dived overboard and swum into a drain at the waterline. "He was still trembling violently, scarcely able to talk."

"When I returned to the field," Capt. Ralph reported, "I saw that they had succeeded in destroying a number of planes standing in the field." A journalist agreed. "I had gone outside to watch . . . bombers hammer the airport across the bay. They destroyed the *Hong Kong Clipper*, eight of eleven transports, and the entire RAF squadron— all on the ground."

The *Hong Kong Clipper* had not exploded, even though it was full of fuel, but instead had slowly burned to the waterline, leaving one wing underwater and the other draped over the dock's edge. When a final tally was taken, the Japanese had destroyed all planes on the ground except three CNAC commercial airplanes. Airport buildings were burning or had been obliterated, and runways and roads were obstructed by cracks, holes, and scattered debris. In addition, the area was littered with "subversive pamphlets," primarily aimed at persuading the Indian troops to give up fighting in support of the British.

"I found craters on the runway and also one bomb right through the center of the hangar roof," the *Hong Kong Clipper* captain recalled. But the bomb that hit the hangar was a dud. It had smashed through the roof, pierced the wing of a plane parked inside, and broken apart on the hangar floor, spewing pale yellow picric acid all over. The shimose powder shell caused those inside the hangar to gag and cough and turned everything it touched as yellow as a canary, even human skin. NBC reporter A. C. Taylor had his face badly seared with the acid.

All the while, CNAC operations manager William Bond had been trying to reach the airport from his apartment on Repulse Bay. His taxi crept along, stopping and weaving around the hellacious craters and debris in the road caused by the shelling. Once Bond reached the airport, he found CNAC and Pan Am pilots and mechanics hard at work. Men who'd never operated a tractor had hopped on and commenced pulling the three remaining CNAC planes—two Douglas DC-3s and one DC-2—off the field, one by one. The men ripped a hole through the perimeter fence and flattened objects that wouldn't allow a plane's wings to pass. When finished, they'd spaced the three planes three hundred yards apart, intermingled with peasants' huts and vegetable gardens along the base of Kowloon Peak. Several of the workmen spent the next two hours wiping and smudging the planes' wings and fuselages with mud and straw to camouflage them before the next Japanese air strike.

Bond ordered men to fill the craters in the runway and others to move fuel tanks away from the hangar and camouflage them. He directed other men to gather up as many spare airplane parts and supplies as they could find—communication equipment, instruments, tires, ailerons, tools, even two spare engines. With luck, the remaining CNAC planes would carry the spare parts and supplies to a safe location inside China in order to keep the airline operating.

As the men worked, Bond relayed to the crew of the burned *Hong Kong Clipper*—Ralph, Strickland, Shaw, De Wees, Orton, May, and Featherstone—that there would be an evacuation at nightfall aboard the three CNAC planes. "We're going to take you on a flight to Namyung," First Officer Strickland recalled being told. Namyung was two hundred miles inland, behind the Japanese lines.

An evacuation seemed futile to many, given that only three planes remained intact and there were thousands who warranted removal from danger. But Bond and the CNAC pilots were determined to transport all they could to safety, especially whoever and whatever the airline required to keep flying.

Bond eventually made his way to the Peninsula Hotel, where he set up "court" to assemble a list of priority passengers to be evacuated. His shoes and the hems of his dungarees were stained yellow and reeked of the shimose bomb that had spewed its foul contents inside the hangar. As the vice president and operations manager of CNAC, Bond felt obligated to remove CNAC personnel and their families to safety, and then consider additional priority passengers. Obviously, his mechanics and other technical and skilled employees would be onboard. And since Pan Am co-owned CNAC with the Chinese government, the *Hong Kong Clipper*'s crew should be aboard. Besides running CNAC, Bond had worked with Pan Am CEO Juan Trippe for several years. "I had a cable from Clarence Young, division manager of Pan Am's Pacific Division, reminding me of my promise to get the clipper crew out if and when trouble started," Bond recalled. "We had already told the clipper crew to be prepared to leave that night."

## CHAPTER 31

# SEEKING ANOTHER VICTORY

Aircraft from the Imperial Japanese Navy Chitose Air Group of the 24th Air Flotilla lined the runway on the island of Kwajalein in the Marshall Islands. It was just before noon on December 8 (December 7 in Hawaii). Their destination was Wake Island. The Chitose pilots had received word of their countrymen's successful attack at Pearl Harbor, and they were anxious to bring back a victory of their own.

A dozen ships—six Japanese destroyers, *Oite, Hayate, Kisaragi, Mutsuki, Yayoi,* and *Mochizuki,* along with three light cruisers and three transport ships, followed by an oil tanker and a submarine tender—hurried to join four submarines already circling Wake. The invasion force aboard the ships reviewed the attack plans and checked their ammunition. Some wrote letters home and stuffed them in their pockets in case they were killed while invading the small American-held island.

The attack plan called for fighters and bombers to strike first to "soften up" Wake Island, with their bombs blasting sites of strategic importance. Later, Japanese destroyers would launch a bombardment of the small island with their big guns, nowhere nearly as big as the guns on a cruiser or battleship but still big enough for this task, showering ruinous shellfire from miles out in the ocean. All would be in preparation for a landing by Japanese infantry.

Meanwhile, Wake Island was occupied by around 525 Marines and navy servicemen, most of whom had arrived ten days before, along with 1,145 unarmed civilian construction workers. None knew what was about to hit them.

## CHAPTER 32

# SCUTTLEBUTT

The tail fin of the *Philippine Clipper* reflected the early morning sun as it sliced through the ginger sky hanging over Wake Island. The morning haziness had lifted from the water's surface, though those onboard remained a bit heavy-eyed. More than 1,500 miles of ocean and eleven hours lay ahead as the clipper's crew settled in for the long flight to Guam. Since all had eaten breakfast on the island, Charlie simply filled coffee and chitchatted, being particularly careful since the plane was still climbing. Having made the flight numerous times, Mac reclined in his seat and read. Others conversed and gawked at the waves on the ocean's surface losing their distinctness. If they hadn't known better, the surface of the Pacific Ocean might've appeared like swells of snow blown across the plains, an illusion reinforced by the intensifying coolness as the plane's altitude increased. Soon they'd see nothing below them but a glimmering silver ocean and scattered white clouds.

Having just heard the clipper take off over the boom of the surf, Cmdr. Cunningham and Maj. Devereux stepped outside the dining hall to start their day. "As I walked to my pickup truck I saw a man running toward me from the radio shack," Cunningham wrote years afterward. "The radio man . . . waved his arms and shouted as he ran . . . He clutched a piece of paper . . . 'Commander, Commander!'" The young man pushed the radio message toward Cunningham, who snatched it from the radioman's hand. "PEARL HARBOR UNDER

ATTACK BY JAPANESE—STOP—CARRY OUT PREARRANGED PLANS."
The attack at Pearl Harbor was still raging. It would be another
thirty minutes before the second wave of Japanese bombers completed their sorties.

"It just came in from ComFourteen," the radioman told Cunningham, referring to Commandant Fourteenth Naval District at
Pearl Harbor. "The operator [at Pearl] said, 'This is no drill, this is
no drill.' Then he broke off communication." Cunningham remembered distinctly that "[The radioman] looked at me hopefully, as if
an island commander could surely put a stop to such an outrageous
thing."

Maj. Devereux called for "the Music" on the double, ordering
the bugler to sound the call to arms—an emergency call for the
Marine defense battalions to man their posts. Devereux watched
men lollygagging about, believing it to be just a Monday morning
exercise. He shouted to them: "This is no drill! Pass the word!"

Cmdr. Cunningham telephoned Maj. Paul A. Putnam, who
commanded USMC Squadron VMF-211, and instructed him to order
four of Wake's twelve Grumman Wildcat fighter planes to take off
immediately and patrol the skies surrounding the island. Neither
radar nor pre-radar listening horns had been installed on Wake like
at Midway, which meant the planes were the island's only eyes into
hundreds of miles of distant sky except for two 52-foot water towers
that were of limited use to spot oncoming aircraft and ships.

Someone reminded the commander that the *Philippine Clipper*
had taken off. Cunningham grabbed the telephone again and called
the dock, where Pan Am airport manager John Cooke had just returned aboard the launch. He told Cooke that he thought the clipper should return to base right away; otherwise, it would risk being
shot down by Japanese forces that were surely approaching. It was
7:01 a.m.

"I returned to the radio-equipped launch and called the clipper,"
Cooke later said. "*Philippine Clipper*, this is Wake. Return to base."

Captain John Hamilton of the *Philippine Clipper*. Jock Hamilton collection.

Questioned by Capt. Hamilton, Cooke told the Pan Am pilot that he'd explain once he returned. Notwithstanding that Cooke had called Hamilton at Cmdr. Cunningham's suggestion, it was Capt. Hamilton's decision to make. Hamilton began to swing the heavy plane around.

"We circled, dumped about 3,000 pounds of gasoline to get to our landing weight . . . returned to Wake and landed about twenty minutes after takeoff," Hamilton later told US Naval Intelligence. He believed the ground crew had forgotten to load something or someone on the plane since they'd been gone merely ten minutes when called to turn back.

Cooke waited on the pier as the big seaplane skimmed along the lagoon's surface to a stop and then taxied to the dock, where mooring lines were tightened. Capt. Hamilton stepped through the main hatch onto the pier, leaving the remainder of the crew inside. The captain noticed that Cooke appeared agitated; but before he could ask why, Cooke blurted, "Pearl Harbor's been attacked!" He handed Hamilton the radio message. A part of Hamilton logically believed Midway, Wake, and Guam would be next, but another part of him refused to believe Pearl had been attacked at all. It was too bold. The Philippines or Netherlands East Indies, that he could believe; but Pearl Harbor? Shaking his head, Hamilton turned toward the clipper and gestured for the rest of the crew to exit the plane.

As Hamilton and Cooke discussed what to do next, Cmdr. Cunningham drove up and joined them on the dock. "The commandant . . . asked that first we make a patrol flight [before continuing]," Capt. Hamilton later said. "Then I went with the commandant to his office to discuss the patrol." Cooke accompanied them to Cunningham's headquarters in the brush at Camp Two where Maj. Devereux and the CPNAP chief superintendent, Dan Teeters, were waiting. It was a nerve-racking meeting. The men expected that a Japanese invasion force would soon be hitting Wake's beaches. If that happened, they would surely be overwhelmed and captured, or maybe even wiped out. But Hamilton hardly wavered. He was a lieutenant in the US Naval Air Reserve and a Pan Am master pilot, described by fellow pilots as a "man's man," with broad shoulders and a seventeen-inch neck, who enjoyed skiing the Andes and hunting crocodiles. He could be depended on to fly reconnaissance and then fly the clipper home.

The remainder of the clipper's crew and its five passengers, including Charlie and Mac, sauntered back to the Pan American Airways Hotel, discussing news of the attack on Pearl among themselves. The island had grown quiet around them. Silenced were the usual shouting and chatter of workmen and the groaning of equipment. Seriousness had overtaken the morning after the dire news from Pearl Harbor. The Marines were receiving their orders, as were the naval pilots. Dan Teeters told the construction workers, including Harry's son Ted, to go back to work. Wake needed the defense installations built faster than ever. Teeters also told Cunningham and Devereux that he and many of his men would volunteer to help the Marines should the Japanese attack.

Meanwhile, Pan Am employees received word to unload the clipper's cargo and refuel the plane. Hamilton and his crew would be leaving at one o'clock to conduct "an apple pie search around the island," escorted by two fighters. Then the clipper would resume its flight alone, though now it looked like a return to Midway was likely rather than proceeding deeper over Japanese-controlled waters toward Guam. Guamanian workers had already begun pumping gasoline into the clipper's fuel tanks. They wouldn't be finished for another hour. Capt. Hamilton and the *Philippine Clipper* would have to wait and watch the skies.

## CHAPTER 33

# BEHIND THE SQUALL

Twenty-seven twin-engine Japanese attack bombers of the Chitose Air Group approached Wake Island. Flying at an altitude of two thousand feet inside scattered clouds, they had flown undetected by the four Wildcat fighters that Maj. Putnam had ordered into the sky. The Japanese planes flew in a tight V-formation of three groups of nine planes each. At five miles out, sheltered behind an approaching rain squall, they cut their engines and glided toward the island in silence, except for the wind whizzing past the planes.

A formation of nine bombers armed with one-hundred-pound fragmentation bombs would strike the airfield and the Marine fighter planes. The remaining two groups would follow to bomb the petroleum tanks and drumheads and destroy all buildings on the island. Now within range of Wake's antiaircraft guns, the Japanese planes restarted their engines and banked downward to launch their attack.

## CHAPTER 34

# EVERY MAN FOR HIMSELF

When the meeting at Cmdr. Cunningham's headquarters concluded, construction superintendent Dan Teeters told his driver, a Chinese man named Tommy, to drive Capt. Hamilton and John Cooke to the Pan Am compound in his station wagon. Hamilton had to prepare the *Philippine Clipper* for takeoff and perform a reconnaissance mission around the island before flying back to Midway.

"As I left his office to go back to the hotel," Hamilton recalled, "we had just arrived at a spot where workmen had been laying new drainage pipes." From there on, the road was closed. Hamilton, Cooke, and Tommy left the car and continued on foot. Nearing noon, the day had grown hot.

Everything Hamilton and the two others saw and heard on Wake looked and sounded the same as always—the surf pounding the coral reefs, the heat scourging the sand and brush, and the strong trade winds blowing in from the east. Despite the fact that nearly five hours had passed since word of the attack on Pearl Harbor had reached them, Wake's inhabitants were still in a state of disbelief. After all, Pearl Harbor and the US Pacific Fleet, guardians of the Pacific Ocean and all US islands and territories therein, had been caught by complete surprise and suffered an incredibly terrible blow. How bad a blow, no one on Wake Island yet knew.

To the west of the lagoon, however, Pan Am mechanic Jerome "Jerry" Eldridge shaded his eyes against the sun to get a clearer look at a line of specks in the sky. "Hey, you guys. Do you see what I see?" Eldridge asked two fellow mechanics. They quickly determined that the emerging specks were US bombers coming to protect Wake. "Boy, don't they look good!" Eldridge recalled shouting. Seconds later, they learned they'd made a terrible mistake. "Japanese!" Eldridge yelled. It was 11:58 a.m.

Engines roared as the planes flew in low before releasing their bombs. The oblong projectiles created a loud whistling sound as they dropped. Less than twenty yards from Eldridge, the first bomb made a direct hit on the stock room. It exploded in a cloud of smoke and dust with a booming, rumbling noise. Metal and wood splinters shot out in every direction. The concussion from the blast knocked Eldridge to the ground. He staggered to his feet with his ears ringing and struggled to run as bits of burning debris showered down on him, setting his shirt afire. "I plunged into a shallow trench and put the blaze out with sand . . . I could still see the clipper and I prayed nothing would happen to it. Just then a bomb sent a geyser of water up only fifty feet from it." The *Philippine Clipper*—the lone American transport plane west of Hawaii on which the men might have a chance of escape—had become a sitting duck full of 100-octane gasoline.

Not far away, Hamilton, Cooke, and Tommy stopped walking, frozen where they stood. "Shortly before reaching our compound we heard what sounded like more than the usual amount of construction-related blasting—and some of it uncomfortably close," Cooke recalled. "Tommy yelled, 'Here come the [Japanese]! We don't have a . . . chance!' . . . All three of us . . . looked for the nearest shelter. We were in the very center of a vast seaplane parking area which had recently been paved, with no sign of cover. The sky was crowded with aircraft, all wearing the red ball of Japan and spewing bombs and machine gun bullets indiscriminately."

It would be the first wave. With no radar and the wind and surf muting the sounds of the advancing planes' engines, everyone had been caught by surprise.

"At that moment," Hamilton remembered, "they came over . . . in closed pyramid formation. One squadron started by machine gunning the construction camp, the other launched the attack I saw. . . . The bombs fired the hotel, destroyed all other Pan American buildings and the dock."

Mac was at the hotel with seven crew members and four army officers waiting to board the clipper. "Suddenly, there was a terrific explosion," Mac recalled, "and the hotel began to crumple over our heads. Then came the rat-a-tat-tat of machine gun bullets. . . . The roar of engines, of bombs exploding and machine guns was deafening, shaking the earth. . . . We all yelled and ran out into the open." Outside, Mac witnessed the lurid bloody onslaught and horrific screams and cries amid the blasts of the dropping bombs and the zing of red-hot bullets. "The Chamorro workmen . . . were just standing there looking at the planes. We yelled to them. . . . A moment later three of them were cut in half by bomb splinters, and the others wounded." Mac remembered thinking: "This is the end—nothing can live through it." Thoughts of his young daughter, Doreen, must have raced through his mind, along with the fear that she'd soon be an orphan. Such thoughts made a horrifying situation a torturous one.

On tiny Wake Island, with its flat terrain and trees no higher than two dozen feet, there were few places to hide. One of Pan Am's employees on the island, William Ball, who believed "this is it," recalled that "some of the people began hiding under buildings, but were ordered out because the buildings were objectives of the bombers." A Pan Am meteorologist, Walter Nobs, crawled into a drainpipe and his right leg was grazed by a ricocheting bullet. Worried that his body would never be discovered if a bomb landed on the underground pipe, Nobs scampered out of the pipe to a nearby bush, only to encounter an army of unorthodox attackers. "I had rats up my sleeves, up my pants, scurrying across my face, all over me," Nobs remembered. "None of them bit me. They were as scared as I was."

Meanwhile, Hamilton, Cooke, and Tommy had scrambled into an unfinished Marine bunker. "Bombs were going off all around us," Cooke recalled. "Some fell within twenty feet. It was then that Hamilton yelled, 'It's getting too hot' and jumped up and sprinted to a nearby drainage ditch." Capt. Hamilton's older son Jock recalled his father saying that "sand jammed under his bloody fingernails as he dug into the sand for better cover."

"It was every man for himself," Mac remembered. Mac ran looking for a hole or a "crease in the sand." He fell behind a bush and buried his face.

Just as Charlie raced from the hotel, a bomb landed a few feet from him. The blast wave sent Charlie flying, tossing him into the sand and brush. Dazed from the concussive force and now unable to hear in one ear, Charlie slowly stood and staggered toward the lagoon, his pants ripped from the blast, covered in blood seeping down his legs. No sooner had Charlie gotten to his feet than Japanese fighter planes commenced their strafing runs. He could clearly make out the faces of the pilots looking left and right as they fired lines of bullets at those running for their lives, diving into the shallowest depressions for shelter. "Dad positioned himself on the sand parallel to the pattern of the bullets, which probably saved his life," Charlie's son, Gary, recalled. "He said that had he been lying perpendicular, the strafing would have undoubtedly cut him in two." The wounded Charlie hobbled to the lagoon, where he yanked off his shirt and shoes and dived in, painfully swimming to a small peninsula called Flipper Point to take cover in the thick brush and tend to his wounds.

First Officer Bill Moss, who'd run out of the burning hotel with Mac, Charlie, and the others, remembered yelling "Oh God" as he dived into the sand, trying to wiggle his way below the surface. He'd landed near Ajax Baumler, the young man on his way to join the Flying Tigers in China. Ajax had first heard the sounds of the Japanese attack while eating breakfast with the others. He'd run out immediately, as only Ajax apparently could. "The door opened inward, but Ajax opened it outward," recalled Col. Robert Scott, "taking most of the screen, the door, and most of the end of that . . . building with him." Bill Moss recalled that singular frightening moment taking cover beside Baumler: "I glanced over beside me and saw Ajax kneeling on one knee. Bullets were flying everywhere. One went through his cap and another grazed his lip. He was taking notes about the types and number of planes, the bombs they were using and so forth. . . . It was the bravest thing I'd ever seen."

Radio operator William Comer, who'd relieved Fred Streib before the attack so he could grab lunch at the hotel, had time enough to flash out a single word as the bombs began exploding around him: "Raid." Comer ran out for cover seconds before a bomb obliterated the radio shack. Six of the eight white-and-orange striped direction-finder poles had splintered and collapsed. Pan Am's radio and navigational equipment was now gone.

The attack on tiny Wake Island, consisting of two waves, lasted only ten to fifteen minutes but had wreaked deadly havoc. No landing was planned; it was solely an air strike—for now. The Japanese planes flew out to sea to refuel at Kwajalein in order to return for another strike. Until then, those on the island emerged from their hiding places, brushing off sand and dirt. The sky was filled with black and gray smoke, and the sea air smelled of gunpowder, sulfur, and fuel. They hurried to inspect the damage.

"The island was shrouded in great masses of smoke and flame," Mac said. "The hotel was blown to bits—the runway a mess—the fuel tanks blown to blazes. . . . The pier had a hole in the middle, where a bomb had been aimed at the Clipper. She was tied to the pier, but they missed her by a hundred feet, and although she had

[23] bullets in her, none had hit a vital part. . . . All over the island there were nuts, bolts, bits of stoves—anything and everything that could be used to fill a bomb. The [Japanese] were returning with interest the scrap iron we had been sending them for ten years."

John Cooke's residence, in which he and his wife, Isyl, and two young sons, Bleecker and Phillip, lived, had been hit by the bombing. "I couldn't even find my wallet or glasses among the wreckage," Cooke said. It was then that he realized how fortunate he was, regardless of what happened to him, that his wife and children had been evacuated to Honolulu three weeks earlier.

Ten of the forty-five young Guamanian men were dead, and several others wounded. First Radio Officer Don Mackay was nursing a calf wound, and Charlie, who'd waited out the attack in the brush of Flipper Point, was picked up by a small boat that carried him to the dock.

"The Pan American staff . . . carried wounded to the pier," Mac remembered. Some yanked mattresses off beds to use as stretchers. Those badly wounded were readied for transfer by any means available to the CPNAB hospital on Camp Two for emergency medical treatment. Those beyond help were collected and stacked in a cold storage room in a CPNAB storehouse.

Pan Am passenger Lt. Col. John Tamraz of the US Army Medical Corps tended to Charlie and Mackay on the pier. He cut Charlie's pants away and discovered that he had been hit by shrapnel in the left leg and groin when he'd raced out of the blazing hotel collapsing around him. "His trousers were so riddled with holes from the bomb that they had to be discarded," Charlie's son, Gary, recalled. Lt. Col. Tamraz used homemade poultices and a first aid kit from the plane to stop the bleeding of both crew members. They were given whiskey to ease the pain.

Men like Mac, who'd been present during the building of Pan Am's compound on Wake six years earlier and had returned to his "baby" many times since, were happy to be alive for now, but felt a bitter personal sorrow as they looked about. "Ironically . . . [Mac] was tragic witness to the . . . minutes that wiped out the super-human building efforts . . . in 1935," Pan Am reported later. All twenty-five buildings of Pan Am's Wake Island compound were either ablaze or destroyed. Men had grabbed the fire wagon in an attempt to douse the flames, but the water pump had been hit and was unable to force the flow of water through the hoses. It was disheartening to stand and helplessly watch what minutes earlier had been shining white buildings with red roofs and manicured shrubs that formed an integral part of Pan Am's system of luxury marine bases to the Far East. The burning and collapsing hotel was especially difficult to watch.

The combined US Navy and Marine Corps forces on the island, roughly 525 men, had fared little better. Of the twelve Wildcat fighter planes preceding the raid, only three could now fly. Of the fifty-nine officers and men of the USMC fighter squadron, only about two dozen remained on their feet. The pilots had tried to reach their planes, but were "machine-gunned . . . [and] cut to pieces by the bullets," Maj. Devereux recalled. Only one pilot made it to his plane. He climbed into the cockpit to start the engine, "but it never had a chance to move," Devereux wrote. "A bomb got it. A direct hit." Although the Marine defense battalion had suffered no injuries, the battalion's antiaircraft guns and scattered gunfire had inflicted little damage on the enemy planes and their pilots.

"It had been an utter surprise," Cunningham remarked later, "a surprise as effective as if we had not known the war had begun."

Capt. Hamilton and members of his crew ran to the dock to inspect the *Philippine Clipper*. Pan Am's chief mechanic, Jack Eagan, had already started and tested the four engines by the time the others arrived. As First Officer Bill Moss walked down the pier toward the plane with sore ribs from hitting the ground too hard for cover, he dropped to his knees and vomited. Except for a few battle-hardened Marines and men like Ajax, it had been the most harrowing experience of their lives. "Everybody seemed dazed, including myself, and

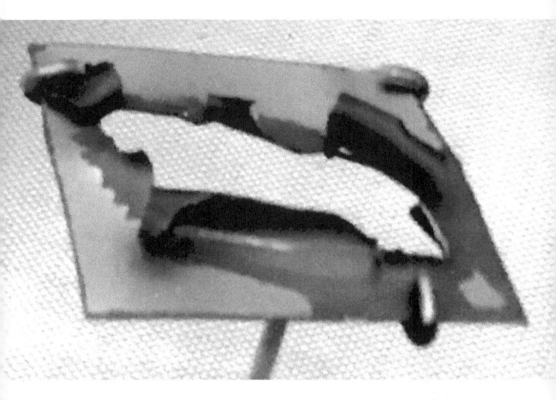

Bullet hole from *Philippine Clipper* cut out during repair. Photographed by author at the SFO Museum in San Francisco.

didn't seem to know quite what to do," recalled a CPNAB asphalt technician. Many others, however, were angry and had wanted to fight back during the raid, but were impotent without weapons.

A preliminary inspection of the clipper revealed nineteen bullet holes (four more were discovered later) piercing the top and starboard hull at a descending angle, each the size of a large adult thumb. Sunlight gleamed eerily through each hole, as if twenty-three flashlights were shining their beams of light diagonally into the interior of the plane. Luckily, none of the bullets had hit below the waterline or had inflicted damage to the four engines or fuel tanks. There was no smell of gasoline, and the controls reacted properly when tested.

It also was fortunate that the ground crew had refueled the clipper before the attack. "If we hadn't refueled that plane immediately after its return," Eldridge recalled, "we couldn't have refueled it afterward. The [depot's] fuel lines were broken [from the bombing] and there was no pressure." Gasoline had spilled on a portion of the dock and was ablaze during the attack. Once the danger had passed, men grabbed shovels and doused the fire with sand.

With the coordinated Japanese attacks in the Pacific, the *Philippine Clipper* flying on to Guam and then to Manila was now out of the question. Hamilton had overheard bursts of messages from Guam's operator, warning that Guam was also under attack. "There went the hotel," the Guam operator said with bombs dropping around him. "That one landed too close. I'm signing off." Hamilton realized that Hawaii via Midway was the clipper's sole avenue of escape now, provided Midway would still be in US hands should he be able to reach it.

The decision was made in accordance with Plan A to evacuate not only the plane's crew and passengers from the burning island, but all Pan Am personnel. Word circulated about the island that Pan Am employees were to board the clipper for departure right away. "The evacuees had been instructed to report to the airplane with no more baggage than they could carry in their pockets," Cooke recalled. The twenty-five to thirty dark-skinned Guamanian employees who weren't wounded or dead would not be allowed on board with the Caucasian Pan Am employees. They would have to wait for a way home to Guam; extremely unlikely under the exigent circumstances. "It seemed to me an unfortunate time to draw the color line," Cmdr. Cunningham later mused. Two Guamanian employees tried to stow away on the clipper, but were discovered and escorted off.

"Throw everything overboard that isn't essential to the flight, and do it fast," Cooke yelled. They jettisoned the plane's cargo, passenger seats, kitchen equipment—the whole kit and caboodle. Hamilton also burned the crew's papers and ordered that the oversized white duffel bags stenciled with US MAIL lying on the dock be burned. The two hundred tires intended for Gen. Chennault's Flying Tigers in China also were set ablaze, adding black billows to a sky already filled with dense smoke. Chennault, who'd been desperately needing those tires for his Flying Tigers, later commented: "When the [Japanese attacked] Wake, part of the booty was our shipment of parts." Nothing that might be of use to the Japanese could be left behind, since an enemy landing was expected at any time.

Pan Am employees drifted to the dock and waited as Cooke barked out a roll call. The wounded Pan Am personnel were carried aboard the clipper and stretched on the floor as comfortably as possible. In addition to the eight crew members and five passengers, another twenty-four Pan Am employees were ready to go aboard. "When we counted noses," Cooke recalled, "we were missing Waldo Raugust, one of our construction technicians. Capt. Hamilton told me to hold everyone . . . while he personally searched for Raugust, who was reportedly driving injured to the hospital."

As Hamilton set off to find Raugust in the lone vehicle available—a garbage truck—about fifty of the CPNAB construction workers marched down the three-hundred-foot redwood-spiked dock toward the clipper. Ajax Baumler volunteered to hold them off with his sidearm until Hamilton returned. When the leader of the group asked Cooke what they were doing, Cooke replied, "We are hoping to get in the air with quite an overload, head for Midway and hopefully Honolulu." Rather than attempt to rush the plane as had been feared, the man extended his hand and wished them the best of luck.

Hamilton soon returned, but without Pan Am employee Raugust. The young man had known the clipper was in a hurry to take off ahead of another air raid, but as Raugust had driven away with wounded men just after the attack, he'd bravely told a coworker that if he wasn't back in time, they should leave without him.

"After the bombing stopped I saw that a number of the Guamanian boys were wounded," Raugust recalled. "I put them on a flatbed and drove them over to the hospital. The doctor there said there weren't enough beds, so I drove down to the warehouse and brought back six cots. After the wounded were put to bed I went back to the base and picked up three that had been killed outright. . . . Somewhere along the way I remember looking across the lagoon and seeing the Clipper taking off."

The young Raugust had arrived at Wake aboard the *California Clipper* in February, traveling on the big, luxurious Boeing that to his delight had included Ernest Hemingway and his wife as passengers. Now he was stranded on an island surrounded by Japanese naval and air forces. Raugust would be captured when Wake fell on December 24 and would join forty-six other Pan Am employees captured from Guam and Manila who'd languish in a prison camp in Japan for forty-four months. Of those employees, one was shot and another beheaded. "I've never regretted it," Raugust declared years later. "I did a job that needed to be done."

The *Philippine Clipper* prepared to taxi into the lagoon without Raugust. "We could wait no longer," Cooke recalled. "All hands boarded the airplane and we kept our fingers crossed as each engine starter button was pressed. One by one the four Pratt & Whitneys started to sing their familiar song. It was beautiful music." Besides leaving behind Raugust, the *Philippine Clipper* would leave US Bureau of Budget examiner Herman Hevenor, who knew nothing of the clipper's departure, and Liberty Mutual Insurance Company safety engineer Edward Clancy. "It struck me as a rather drastic lesson in the wisdom of punctuality," Maj. Devereux wrote later.

Third Officer Elwood Leep released the bow's mooring lines and waved farewell to those still standing on the dock. Capt. Hamilton waved from his open cockpit window as he taxied the *Philippine Clipper* into the middle of the lagoon for takeoff. "It was a painful parting, to leave behind men of whom we were so fond," Cooke said of his escape into the air. Mac agreed. "It was hell to go away and leave [the servicemen] and the 1,100 employees of the Pacific air base contractors."

The *Philippine Clipper* was loaded to the brim with fuel and human cargo, carrying several thousand pounds beyond its maximum allowable takeoff weight. The crew continued to check the controls, and all indicated normal. Hamilton lowered his left hand and pushed the throttles forward, keeping his hand solidly on the grip. On the engineer's cue, the seaplane's propellers spun vigorously and pulled the plane forward faster and faster along the lagoon. The lagoon's launch area was two thousand yards long and contained red flags atop buoy poles near the end of the lagoon. Each flag warned the pilot of the diminishing water depth. If the plane passed the last red flag, the pilot risked colliding with coral reefs, potentially killing all on board in a somersaulting crash of hurling metal and flesh. Capt. Hamilton realized the clipper was approaching the flags at full takeoff speed without reaching the step. "My God, it's heavy," Hamilton grumbled as he pulled back on the throttles, slowing the vibrating plane to a drift. "Sound the hull tanks." Hamilton believed that water must have been gushing in through the bullet holes, but it wasn't. The captain then instructed everyone on board to jettison as much weight as they could. Men tossed out the navigator's table and stool plus the empty food and water containers stowed around the plane. They even ripped up floorboards and tossed them into the water, leaving nothing but a metal hull. "Keep on throwing everything out that you can," another crew member yelled.

Capt. Hamilton turned the plane around and zig-zagged as he returned to the starting point, trying to create waves as he went. Waves help a flying boat's belly separate from the ocean's surface during takeoff. The nose on a Martin M-130 was inherently heavy, and the plane's weight had to be distributed correctly to achieve a center of gravity specified for that model seaplane, which had been the job of First Officer Bill Moss. During the excitement, however, Moss had forgotten to calculate the plane's center of gravity. Moss's gaffe became evident on the initial run, so Cooke astutely moved five men from the front to the rear of the plane as Hamilton commenced his second run along the lagoon. This time the clipper rose up on the step when it reached the red flags, but wouldn't lift off the water. Hamilton pulled back on the throttles a second time. This run was better, but they weren't out of the water yet; and refueled Japanese fighter planes could be approaching any minute. The unenviable Capt. Hamilton turned the flying boat to attempt a third takeoff, and Cooke sent another five men to the stern. "The Flight Engineer advised [that] one more attempt at the same power setting might result in cylinder heads flying out through the engine cowlings," Cooke recalled. "In short, this time it had better work!"

On the third run, the clipper's engines were gaining thrust and lifted the plane up on the step, but it wasn't enough as the clipper approached the first and then the second red flag. The overloaded plane shuddered violently under the strain. "I shouted to Hamilton that he was now in one foot of water," Cooke recalled. "The airplane literally staggered out of the water, two feet, touched back on, almost stalled, dragged across the beach which was now three feet under our keel, . . . Straight ahead not more than a hundred yards was the still-burning hotel. We cleared it by a good six feet, and the heat rising from the building gave us a welcome boost, albeit a bit hot and smoky."

Everyone on board cheered as the plane continued to rise into the ocean air, just a half hour after the attack on Wake had ended. It was then that the passengers heard a loud whistling noise as a 130-mph wind squeezed through twenty-three bullet holes along the plane's fuselage. It sounded like they were inside a giant colander, but no one cared. They were thankful to be onboard and in the air, flying to somewhere they hoped would be safer.

The exuberance quickly faded, however, once those onboard remembered that Japanese fighters and warships might be just minutes away. To reduce the chance of being spotted in the day's sunlight, Hamilton decided to fly at an altitude between fifty and a hundred feet. The plane dropped so low at times that foam from the ocean's waves sprayed the windshield. It was 1,185 miles to Midway on a day when Japanese were "swarming like hornets." The communication equipment and direction finders at Wake Island had been destroyed during the attack, and who knew if the equipment at Midway would be operational when the *Philippine Clipper* neared the atoll; assuming, of course, that it would make it that far. Based on the clipper's flight speed and wind conditions, it would take approximately ten and a half hours to reach Midway—an eternity.

## CHAPTER 35

# THE *PACIFIC* AND *ANZAC CLIPPERS*

The *Hong Kong Clipper* lay burned and sunken in Kowloon Bay, with its crew stranded thousands of miles from home, while the *Philippine Clipper* attempted a brash but critical flight to Midway, trying to make it back to a devastated Pearl Harbor. Meanwhile, the crew of the *Pacific Clipper* was stuck in the Southern Hemisphere, cut off from the Pacific Ocean, and the *Anzac Clipper* was hiding in the Hawaiian Islands, which had just been boldly attacked by the Empire of Japan. No clipper crew was in an enviable position; they were all in danger, as were most of the passengers.

At the same time, Pan Am CEO Juan Trippe sat sandwiched between his two desks high above New York City, trying to help his clippers and their crews return home—worried that soon he might be attending several memorials.

## PACIFIC CLIPPER

Everyone who'd exited the *Pacific Clipper* at the Pan Am dock in Auckland was relieved to step foot on the soil of the British Empire. The attack on Pearl Harbor had ended seven hours earlier, but tensions were still extremely high. News of Japanese strikes throughout the Pacific kept trickling in, not only about Pearl, but the Philippines, Hong Kong, Thailand, Guam, Wake Island, and

Passengers deboarding a Boeing B-314. U. Miami PAA.

on and on. People were stunned by the coordination and magnitude of the Japanese strikes. They'd clearly underestimated the Empire of Japan.

Most clipper passengers checked into the Grand Hotel in Auckland; and after what should have been a good night's sleep, though most likely was not, those going to Australia gathered at the Tasman Empire Airways office the following morning, next door to the Pan Am offices. (Pan Am had not yet been granted landing rights in Australia.) They boarded Tasman's Short S.30 Empire Class medium-range flying boat on December 9 and were quite skittish of going up into the air unprotected once again. It was 1,340 miles to Sydney and would take nine hours to cross the Tasman Sea. Both Australian and New Zealand military intelligence had approved the flight, believing that the Japanese were not in the Tasman Sea or its airspace, at least not yet.

When the former *Pacific Clipper* passengers arrived in Sydney, Australia, on Tuesday, December 10, Alured Kelly spoke to newspaper reporters anxious to hear an account of having passed through Pearl Harbor just before its bombardment. "I am quite sure that when America recovers from her terrific shock, she will fight with great strength and as one people," alluding to those in the isolationist movement that had spoken out against the United States' joining the war in Europe.

Sir John Madsen, Alice Jackson, Muriel Heagney, and Alured Kelly caught a domestic plane from Sydney to Melbourne, where they reunited with their families that night. Alice Jackson wasted no time writing an article for the *Australian Women's Weekly*. The headline read "OUR EDITOR DODGED JAPAN'S BLITZ," with the subheading "Always just one hop ahead of danger in thrilling dash home." The editorial opened: "The memory of Pearl Harbor and its majestic warships was still in my mind when we heard the news on the Clipper of the Japanese raid. . . . The loveliest sight in the world was the sunlight on blue [Tasman] water as the Clipper taxied to its base on my return from abroad." It was a sentiment that had been felt by all aboard the flying boat.

But the Japanese were trolling the South Pacific islands like barbed stingrays. Soon their appetite would grow for bigger fish, like Australia and New Zealand. In four months, Japanese aircraft carriers would move into the Coral Sea, with their sights set on New Guinea and the Solomon Islands, only a hundred miles from the northern tip of Australia. And then would come the Battle of the Coral Sea and the Battle of Midway, which would determine the fate of the Antipodes. But for now, the *Pacific Clipper* passengers were simply happy to be home with loved ones.

# ANZAC CLIPPER

The passengers of the *Anzac Clipper* were safe for the moment at the Naniloa Hotel in Hilo on the Big Island of Hawaii. Unable to contact anyone, they felt cut off from their families and friends. Everyone was worried. Nobody knew if Oahu or the Big Island would be attacked from the sea or the air. Thousands of Japanese soldiers could be landing on the beaches at any moment.

Of further concern to the crew, enemy planes might fly over Hilo on their way to Pearl Harbor or back to their carriers and spot the *Anzac Clipper* floating in the bay. It had to be saved. "We pushed [the clipper] up into the bushes along the shoreline," Capt. Turner recalled. "In the old days of barnstorming, we used to mix buttermilk and lampblack together . . . and paint a sign on your airplane . . . to fly advertising messages." The captain and his crew rounded up gallons of buttermilk and plenty of soot and lampblack and, to give some degree of camouflaging to the plane, rubbed the concoction on the top surfaces of the wings and fuselage, which was no simple task. The crew decided to wait to refuel the clipper until morning. It seemed best to avoid having a plane full of fuel floating in the bay, albeit a camouflaged one.

One passenger objected to the plane being camouflaged and shoved into the bushes. "The premier of Burma [U Saw]," the clipper's captain recalled, "opened up his briefcase and offered me its entire contents, which he said was $1 million, to fly him back to San Francisco. I said to him, 'Brother, we're not taking anybody back to San Francisco [tonight].'" The captain could not have known that Prime Minister U Saw was at that moment hatching a plan to aid the Japanese. After his request for Dominion status had been deferred days earlier by Winston Churchill in London, U Saw had stopped at Lisbon, Portugal, where he met with the Japanese ambassador to strike a deal. He'd agreed to assist Japan should they invade Burma, in exchange for Japan's retaining him as prime minister. The Japanese strikes throughout the Pacific confirmed to him that he'd made a shrewd deal. His only mission now was to find a route back to Burma.

At seven o'clock the next morning, Monday, December 8 (12:30 p.m. in Washington, DC), everyone in the Naniloa Hotel gathered around radios and listened to President Franklin Roosevelt address a joint session of the US Congress. Transmitted live over the major radio networks, more than 81 percent of American homes tuned in, the largest audience in radio broadcast history. Roosevelt declared:

> Yesterday, December 7th, 1941—a date which will live in infamy—the United States of America was suddenly and deliberately attacked by naval and air forces of the Empire of Japan. The United States was at peace with that nation and, at the solicitation of Japan, was still in conversation with its government and its emperor looking toward the maintenance of peace in the Pacific.

A little more than an hour after the president's address, Congress declared war on the Empire of Japan and President Roosevelt signed the declaration.

Later that day in Hilo, moments before sunset, the time had come to attempt a flight home to Treasure Island. The clipper was too valuable to the US military to continue to risk being strafed or bombed in Hawaiian waters, or worse, captured. Capt. Turner and his crew of ten men boarded the *Anzac Clipper* from a launch—alone. None of the passengers wanted to join the crew, afraid that the Japanese would shoot the clipper down and everyone aboard would perish. The captain and his crew weren't keen on their chances either, but at that moment they believed the best option for the clipper was to deliver it to Treasure Island.

The camouflaged flying boat pushed away from the shoreline and the safety of tree cover and taxied into the bay. Then at five o'clock, as darkness approached, the *Anzac Clipper* took off for San Francisco, the top of its shiny silver fuselage and orange-topped wings drenched in the dull and dark gray and black mixture of buttermilk and soot that had been applied the day before. People watched from the dock and shoreline, including the clipper's former passengers,

Camouflaged Boeing B-314 (the *Pacific Clipper*). U. Miami PAA.

hotel employees, and the postmaster. As the clipper lifted off and passed out of their view, many wondered if they'd done the right thing by staying behind.

All aboard the *Anzac Clipper* were tense yet comfortable. If not for the uncertainty of the enemy's whereabouts, the flight would have been like any other, except without passengers. Unlike the strafed and stripped *Philippine Clipper*, the *Anzac Clipper* was fully functional and fully stocked. The stewards served beverages, snacks, and meals. There were plenty of restrooms. The plane's temperature was maintained at pleasant levels. Those onboard could remove their uniforms and dress casually. Despite the comforts, however, sleep was unattainable. Everyone who could watch for the Japanese did watch. Hours passed. It was exhausting.

"We were constantly on the alert during the flight," the clipper's captain told reporters afterward.

On Tuesday morning, December 9, after hours of flying into clouds and descending just above the water, the *Anzac Clipper* landed in San Francisco Bay at Treasure Island. The crew stepped out onto the dock looking as sharp as they could muster, given the circumstances. After a few minutes with their families, who'd been notified shortly before the men landed, anxious US Naval Intelligence officers of the Twelfth Naval District cut the family reunions short and "required some three or four more hours of my services," the captain recalled.

When the crew had been cleared to go home, reporters asked the men about their return flight as they stepped into the lobby to exit the terminal. "[The flight had not been] out of the ordinary," Capt. Turner told the journalists. "I saw no signs of war. I saw no ships. I saw no planes. I saw no warcraft of any kind. We definitely were not shot at. . . . We were pretty glad to get back safely."

Thirty years later, retired Pan Am captain Lanier Turner reflected on that particular flight of the *Anzac Clipper*: "The fact that I had delayed this departure by forty minutes [to listen to my daughter's piano recital] was exactly the time that I normally would have been into or over Pearl Harbor, and it goes without saying that we would have been the first [incoming plane] to be shot down. It was a big craft and they were shooting at anything they could see, and very effectively, too."

So, it seems that if not for his daughter's recital, twenty-eight people aboard Pan Am's big, luxurious *Anzac Clipper* may have been among the first casualties of World War II in the Pacific. What a marvelous tune Capt. Turner's little girl had played.

## CHAPTER 36

# ESCAPE FROM HONG KONG

With only three planes available to transport people out of Hong Kong to safety, the word circulated that CNAC's operations manager, William Bond, was the man in charge and that he could be found at the Peninsula Hotel. Chinese and British dignitaries cabled Bond, asking him to include their families and friends on the first plane out. Others showed up at the hotel and encircled him as he walked through the lobby. "I was pretty well tired out, with a bad cough and a game leg," Bond recalled. People talked over each other and waved documents purporting to prove how important they were and why they should leave Hong Kong immediately. Large sums in paper money or gold coin were offered. It was as if Bond were the officer of the last lifeboat of the RMS *Titanic* being lowered into the water—everybody wanted on. "It took the judgment of Solomon to decide," *Fortune* magazine noted.

Exhausted, Bond raised his hands and asked for quiet: "We have three planes remaining in flying condition. These three can carry a total of fifty-six passengers. . . . We have received telegrams from the Chinese government giving us the names of many important people who will be badly needed and whom we must get out. CNAC also has many of its staff and flight crews that we must get out. In other words, CNAC is now fully booked . . . and there is no way CNAC can take you during the next two nights."

Bond's evacuation plan provided for each of the three CNAC planes to fly out during the night to Namyung, China, return to the Kai Tak Airport to load more refugees, and then fly to Chungking, where the planes would remain parked through the following day. Once darkness fell again, the three planes would return to Hong Kong and repeat the process the following night, and so on until the Japanese captured the airport.

Most British and Chinese officials and businessmen, however, were not interested in escaping. Their decision to stay was not out of any deliberate demonstration of a stiff upper lip, but because they believed there was no need to leave, at least not yet. Hong Kong's governor had broadcast earlier that day that the Kowloon Peninsula could hold off the Japanese for a month and Hong Kong Island could hold out for three months. Many thought it would be much more dangerous to attempt an evacuation aboard an overloaded plane, passing over mountains and possible Japanese gunfire at night, than simply waiting and hoping that Chinese or British reinforcements would come.

But Hong Kong was already changing. The Japanese bombing strikes had quickly exacted a toll on the morale and decency of some in Hong Kong. Marsman wrote of "assassination, highway robbery, looting, wholesale killing of outlaws, and desperate chases of armed gangs of thieves." Those who'd traveled to Kai Tak Airport did so in the daytime to avoid holdups along the way—and the invading Japanese hadn't even set foot in Hong Kong yet. The real atrocities were still to come for those left behind.

Not satisfied with Bond's announcement at the Peninsula Hotel and lacking confidence in the governor's prognostications, the gold-mining millionaire Hank Marsman ventured on a Star ferry across the harbor to his hotel. The Hong Kong Hotel had the reputation of being the social center of the city—or, as Marsman called it that day, the "embattled information desk." Inside the hotel, scores of Europeans and Americans milled about. Marsman spotted his company's manager, George Dank-werth, United Press correspondent Richard Wilson, and several others. While at the hotel, Marsman wired Lt. Gen. MacArthur, Philippine president Manuel Quezon, and Philippine com-missioner Frances Sayre in Manila, requesting them to order Bond and CNAC to place him aboard a plane. Marsman had dined with all these important men before and believed they would come to his aid. They didn't; they had their hands full defending Manila against an ongoing Japanese onslaught.

Notwithstanding three more devastating air raids by the Jap-anese that afternoon and robbers that lurked along the roadways, Marsman and several other Americans traveled back across the har-bor to the Kai Tak Airport. They hoped to secure a seat even though they'd been told all seats had been spoken for. They weren't the only ones. Hundreds of people—mothers with babies lashed to their backs and others grasping bundles tied with string—encircled the Peninsula Hotel and the airport as the sun set at 6:10 p.m. on that first day of an embattled Hong Kong.

"Night fell and bedlam broke loose," a CNAC mechanic super-intendent recalled. "The hangar was a mass of pushing and shouting people who all wanted on the first plane. We had to . . . have the guards remove them, lock the gates and only allow authorized per-sonnel to enter. That gate turned into Hell."

Adding more tension to a chaotic situation, those waiting to board planes could hear the Japanese shelling in the distance, along the New Territories, on the mainland side, the same side as the airport. Many screamed or cried, asking one another, much like attempting to judge the distance of thunder, if the bombing was drawing nearer.

What had begun as another beautiful day had become one of fear, desperation, injury, and death. It was that way on many islands and provinces throughout Southeast Asia and the Pacific. "The [Jap-anese] pulled a gigantic surprise on us," British Maj. John Monro wrote in his diary. "We had no idea that he was as good as we found him to be. Before the war we looked down upon him, considering ourselves more than his match both in physique, training and equipment. To our consternation we found him better than ourselves in all respects."

Unlike the others, those waiting at Kai Tak Airport with earmarked seats clutched to a reasonable chance of escape. "Under double cloak of darkness and overcast," the first CNAC pilot climbed into a DC-3 as the passengers shuffled into the plane between armed Chinese guards posted by the hatch door. People and materials were stuffed into the plane, though the overall weight was carefully measured. It was almost as chaotic inside as it was out, but everyone soon settled down during the two-hundred-mile flight to Namyung. "I had no idea, they just said, 'Namyung.' I didn't know where Namyung was at all," the *Hong Kong Clipper*'s first officer John Strickland recalled. "We were the last ones on. They put us in the back."

At seven o'clock, the plane, overloaded with people and airplane parts, struggled to lift off from the bomb-ravaged and muddy runway. Inside the plane, the disheveled but well-dressed, wealthy, and powerful refugees—men in suits, ties, and fedoras, women in dresses with pearls, and others in uniform—clutched bags that typically would be carried by their servants or aides. More than a third of those onboard were children who sat in their parents' laps or clung to their shoulders. The plane was noisy and uncomfortable, babies cried, and those standing or squatting in the aisle constantly leaned or fell against those seated beside them as the plane dipped and rolled through the cold mountain gusts. To make matters worse, the plane's exterior lights and beacons and all interior lights were shut off throughout the flight, plunging those inside into complete darkness. Everything was blacked out "as dark as the inside of a whale," Bond recalled. Eventually, after hours of fear and darkness, there appeared light.

"We're circling some place and then we saw little spots of light show up on the ground," First Officer Strickland recalled. "They were lighting fuel in drums that were outlining the airstrip. We got off and the airplane left and someone took us into town." They'd made it to Namyung, two hundred miles north of Hong Kong, in territory still held by the Chinese.

Within thirty minutes, two other CNAC planes lifted off from Kai Tak Airport, fully loaded with refugees and heading for—and reaching—safety in Namyung. The three planes returned later and took off again in total darkness. The next evening, December 9, the planes returned to Kai Tak Airport around ten o'clock to begin the process all over again.

The boardings and takeoffs went smoothly and according to plan except for one passenger—Madame Kung, the wife of Dr. Hsiang-his Kung, said to be the richest man in China. Madame Kung told Bond that she wanted a private plane for her small party and her numerous large trunks and bundles that weighed over half a ton. A quick-thinking Bond placed Madame Kung and her party and some of their bags on a plane without any additional passengers, except for four CNAC pilots and crates of essential spare parts and tools, to give her the impression that she was on a private plane. She was told her excess baggage would follow. It didn't.

None of those who'd flown into Hong Kong on December 7 aboard the *Hong Kong Clipper* or who had planned to fly out on the clipper to Manila on December 8 were among those who escaped aboard the three CNAC planes, including Hank Marsman. "My husband is a resourceful man," Mary Marsman told reporters from San Francisco, "and if there is a way to get out of Hong Kong, he will find it." She believed what she said, but she was obviously deeply worried.

Bond, who'd taken the last plane out of Hong Kong, cabled Pan Am's Harold Bixby, who was with Pan Am CEO Juan Trippe at the Chrysler Building in New York: "Entire clipper crew [out of Hong

Kong] . . . advise [Pan Am district manager Clarence] Young . . . doing well so far." Bond also cabled his wife: "I am safely in Chungking and feeling fine. All our Americans are here. Have plenty of everything I shall need . . . and the goose is hanging high. Love, Bondy."

Much was owed to Bond and the CNAC pilots. The pilots had already earned a reputation of being some of the best anywhere, primarily because they flew during bad weather or at night over treacherous mountains to avoid Japanese fighters. It was said that CNAC was the only airline in the world that canceled flights on account of good weather. Capt. Fred Ralph would remark that it was "the sweetest job of flying I've ever seen."

The *Hong Kong Clipper*'s crew had successfully escaped a frenzied and dangerous Hong Kong, though they were without their flying boat, whose half-burned fuselage still remained moored with one scorched wing jutting out on the dock. Their ordeal was far from over: they were near enemy territory and more than sixteen thousand miles from Pan Am's headquarters in New York City—on the other side of the world.

## CHAPTER 37

# A WILL-O'-THE-WISP

Japanese destroyers *Ushio* and *Sazanami* with the fuel tanker *Shirya*, all part of Destroyer Division 7 of the Imperial Japanese Navy 1st Air Fleet, had deployed from Tateyama Naval Air Station on December 7. The two destroyers steamed swiftly toward Midway Atoll at thirty-five knots, proudly flying the flag of the Rising Sun. Their objective was to neutralize Midway's air base by destroying its planes and damaging its airfield. Midway's planes consisted primarily of US Navy PBY Catalina flying boats (patrol bombers). The base was expecting a Marine squadron of Vought SB2U Vindicator dive bombers to be delivered by the USS *Lexington*. The US aircraft carrier had sailed out of Pearl Harbor with its naval escort two days earlier but had not yet arrived.

At 9:31 p.m., thirteen hours after the attack on Pearl Harbor had ended, Japanese destroyers began their bombardment of Midway's Sand Island, which was defended by a small garrison of US Marines. The destroyers' five-inch guns wreaked havoc as the Marines scrambled, ultimately returning fire and repulsing their attackers. When the Japanese destroyers withdrew to the southwest at 10:25 p.m., their bombardment had killed four men and wounded several others but had not achieved its primary objective—Midway's Navy PBYs had escaped, largely undamaged. With broken water mains and damaged fire-fighting equipment, the PBY hangar, command and communication centers, power plant, and other buildings blazed wildly. The inferno painted the night sky a brilliant orange.

⸻

Darkness was a welcome relief for those onboard the *Philippine Clipper* who'd fled a blazing Wake Island and were now trying to reach Midway. No longer did Capt. Hamilton have to fly below a hundred feet. He climbed to an altitude of six thousand feet, far away from the ocean's waves and to a cooler temperature. For those in short pants and short-sleeved shirts, the higher altitude brought an unwelcome chill. However, the cooler air eased the suffering of the wounded and others drenched with sweat. "That night and the following day were bad," Mac recollected. "There was almost no ventilation . . . just the stink of half-naked, sweaty bodies and the groans of the wounded. There was no sleep for any of us as we had to sit or stand upright."

Gone was the steward in the starched white jacket and bow tie serving delicious four-course gourmet meals in fine china on linen tablecloths and setting up berths for those who wished to sleep. The cooking equipment, supplies, tables, chairs, china, silverware, and fine bedding were piled up on the dock back at Wake Island. Charlie Relyea, the purser, could be found with First Radio Officer Don Mackay on the plane's floor, groaning and sipping Pan Am's whiskey to help ease the pain of their wounds. Gone were the bathroom mirrors, davenports, soundproof upholstery, walnut tables and doors, carpet, and wardrobe closet. They, too, created a pyre on Wake Island's dock. There were no Phoebus Apollo certificates for crossing back over the International Date Line or a silly costumed crew member distributing them. All the pomp and grandeur were gone. All that remained were two wings and several prayers.

Though it was night, as rotten luck would have it, the moon shone brightly. There had been a full moon just four days before. Now the moon was in the phase called a waning gibbous, which meant it was about 80 percent illuminated. Capt. Hamilton ordered a man at each window to act as lookouts throughout the night. "Twenty-two pairs of eyes stared anxiously [through the windows] for an enemy plane or an aircraft carrier," Mac recalled. Despite the perfectly clear night, nearly full moon, and lack of sleep for those keeping watch, the farther they traveled, the safer they began to feel. "By this time a certain optimism had replaced our earlier apprehension," John Cooke recalled.

Even the wounded were feeling better. Having been medicated with whiskey and treated by one of the highest-ranking medical officers in the Pacific arena, Lt. Col. Tamraz, Charlie kidded with those around him. Wrapped in a blanket because his shredded trousers had been tossed away, Charlie joked that dinner would be served a little late that evening. He also laughed with the all-male passengers about the location of one of his wounds—his groin. Rather than spewing complaints, Charlie's courageous humor may have made some forget the ever-present danger for a while. Grimacing as he repositioned his body, Charlie also struggled to tell how when he was ten, he'd been administered the Last Rites by a priest at the Brooklyn Home for Boys when he was deathly ill from the Spanish flu; if the flu didn't get him, neither would the Japanese. Eventually, acute pain from his two wounds returned, and it was time for rest and quiet—and more whiskey.

Because of radio silence and the damaged directional equipment at Wake, the course of the flight was totally dependent on Second Officer John Hrutky's celestial navigation skills. Reminiscent of clipper ships in the mid-nineteenth century, both Hrutky and Capt. Hamilton took readings using an octant and compared them to each other. With radio silence, John Hrutky's brother, Second Radio Officer Ted Hrutky, who'd taken over for the wounded Don Mackay, had little to do for now except don his headphones and listen.

Forty miles southwest of Midway, at around 10:45 p.m., Capt. Hamilton and First Officer Moss spotted two ships traveling on a course away from Midway. Both were cruising south-southwest toward Wake. "Our spirits soared . . . when the cockpit announced the sighting of two surface vessels traveling at high speed on a reciprocal course," Cooke wrote later. "We cheered what we believed to be the US Navy en route to Wake."

Some on the plane tried to follow the ships' churning wakes that shone white in the moonlight, hoping to find any sign of Midway close behind. Hamilton knew he was in the vicinity of Midway, but the direction finder on the atoll apparently wasn't working. He decided to briefly break radio silence in an attempt to reach the base, using a special code that identified either Midway's radio operator by name or the clipper's estimated time of arrival. Neither worked; there was no response. Shortly afterward, passengers noticed something in the night's sky. It was dim at first but grew more intense with each passing mile. "Approaching Midway, we saw a brilliant light," First Officer Moss recalled. "We couldn't tell what it was." As the plane drew nearer, the crew was disheartened to discover that it was a burning airplane hangar lighting up the night sky. "The burning buildings on Midway served as a beacon for our approach," Cooke remembered.

Before attempting to land, Capt. Hamilton wanted to help those on Midway Atoll identify the clipper as a friendly aircraft, so he ordered all of the plane's beacons and landing lights, even its interior lights, switched on. He then brought the clipper in low and made a visual pass over the island prior to starting a left-hand circle, a maneuver that he performed twice to show friendly intent. Despite Hamilton's efforts, at least two skittish antiaircraft gunners fired .50 caliber shells at the clipper. Those onboard could see tracer rounds and flashes from the guns as they fired in the darkness; fortunately, their aim was poor.

A night landing on Midway's lagoon under the best of circumstances would have been challenging. Not only did the pilot have to determine the plane's distance above the water seconds before touchdown, but, more importantly, obstructions floating on or barely beneath the water's surface were invisible in the darkness. The firing of aerial flares from mortars by Pan Am's ground crew would have helped greatly, but they had not expected the clipper. Midway Atoll's lagoon was especially dangerous that night. The buoy lights weren't working, small craft were adrift, and all types of debris littered the lagoon, hurled into the water by the Japanese shells exploding on land. In fact, not long before the clipper approached, a group of US Navy PBYs landed in Midway's lagoon. Tragically, one struck a buoy that had been cut loose by machine gun fire. The collision killed the pilot and copilot.

As the clipper descended toward the lagoon, Capt. Hamilton ordered everyone to hold on to anything they could. He aimed the nose for the far edge of the lagoon in an attempt to avoid floating debris. As the plane descended, the orange glow from the burning buildings illuminated much of the lagoon's surface. Hamilton masterfully completed a frightful yet safe landing. Applause mixed with cheers rang out from those onboard and on Midway's dock. With a sigh of relief, Hamilton taxied the clipper toward a man waving a bright light from the landing barge. It was a welcome sight. Ground crew on the dock wasted little time mooring the plane. Everyone onboard, except the wounded, stepped through the hatch onto the dock to stretch their legs and breathe fresh air—happy to be alive.

Hamilton's first order of business was to meet with Marine base commander Lt. Col. Harold Shannon. He asked for any information that Shannon could share about Pearl Harbor and the enemy's location between Midway and Hawaii. Shannon knew little. They discussed the Japanese attack and the Marines' valiant response. Shannon shared with Hamilton that his twenty-six-year-old second in command, 1st Lt. George Cannon, who'd only been on the island three months, had died of wounds when refusing to leave his command during the attack (he was posthumously awarded the Congressional Medal of Honor, the first to a US Marine in World War

II). Hamilton had met the handsome young platoon officer only a couple of days before, and the news of his death saddened the clipper captain.

"When we landed," Mac recalled, "we heard what had happened. Up to thirty-five minutes before we got there, two warships shelled the island from opposite sides. They did it methodically, laying their shells in turn on one important building after another." But unlike Wake, Midway had a radar station and was somewhat more prepared when the two ships began firing on the island. The ships had been the destroyers *Sazanami* and *Ushio*, the same ships that those onboard the *Philippine Clipper* had mistakenly believed to be US naval destroyers on their way to aid Wake Island.

Pan Am's ground crew commenced refueling the clipper, while the chief mechanic and his crew gave the plane a quick once-over. Refueling would take an hour and a half. As he waited, Capt. Hamilton met with Pan Am airport manager Don Walker, while those onboard were given food and drinks. A member of Midway's medical staff who had access to medical supplies attended to Charlie's and Mackay's wounds. Walker asked Hamilton to evacuate Midway's twenty-one Pan Am employees, but Hamilton explained that the plane was already dreadfully overloaded. He did, however, agree to take Midway's port steward, Jack Bramham, whose wife had been evacuated three weeks earlier and was anxiously waiting for him in Honolulu. (All Midway employees would be evacuated to Honolulu in early 1942.)

With more than an hour's wait, Ed Barnett used the time to seek out information about the Philippines. He'd heard the buzz on the atoll about a widespread attack throughout the Pacific that included the Philippines eight hours earlier; but beyond that, no one knew more. He suddenly regretted that he hadn't insisted that his wife, Cecile, evacuate with other American civilians when she had the chance; yet, he still believed that Lt. Gen. MacArthur and the American and Filipino forces could repel the Japanese. Ed wouldn't

US soldier standing in bomb crater near Pan Am terminal at Cavite Harbor, Philippines. Pan American Airways, *New Horizons*, Vol. 12, No. 7, April 1942, 9; U. Miami PAA.

learn until later that despite hours of advance knowledge of the attack on Pearl Harbor, the Americans had been caught by surprise in the Philippines and lost half their planes on the ground within forty-five minutes. When all was said and done, many considered the fall of the Philippines months later under MacArthur's command as the worst military defeat in US history.

Like Ed, Mac was worried, too, but at least he knew that his daughter, Doreen, was safe in California. Mac simply didn't want his daughter to become an orphan; that would be too cruel and unfair for her, to lose both parents within six months. Despite his fears, the reserved and calculated engineer kept his thoughts to himself.

With refueling completed, the time had come once again when those onboard the *Philippine Clipper* had to say goodbye, this time to the Pan Am employees stationed on Midway who were being left behind. At two o'clock on Monday morning, December 8 (east of the International Date Line), the clipper lifted off from Midway's lagoon for Hawaii. "This time we had to take off in total darkness, with God knew how much floating wreckage in the way," Mac recollected. "Tough, swell master pilot that he was, Capt. Hamilton made it, but it was touch and go. . . . We made three attempts there too—finally got three feet off, by the end of five minutes were up to fifty feet. Another ten and we had climbed to eighty feet. The skipper recollected that he had shoved her nose into the air half an inch at a time—if he had given her any more she would have broken in two from the overload."

Capt. Hamilton gradually leveled the clipper at six thousand feet and again ordered each window manned by a pair of eyes. Midway was much more northeast than Wake Island, farther away from the Japanese mandate islands near Guam and Wake on which Japan had built military bases. Yet the danger of a Japanese attack was very real, as evidenced by the earlier shelling of Midway. That meant crew members had to stay sharp, despite having gone nearly twenty-four hours without sleep. Japanese fighter planes could fly twice as fast as, and were much more maneuverable than, the big unarmed *Philippine Clipper*. This was especially true given the string of bullet holes that created drag along the starboard side of the fuselage, combined with the enormous weight from the overload of the plane. If that wasn't enough, a battleship or destroyer could accurately shoot down the clipper up to an altitude of three thousand feet at a range of just over a mile. With all that to consider, Hamilton had no choice but to decrease his altitude once again as the sun began to rise.

The sun soon radiated off the plane's exterior, causing the temperature inside the fuselage to climb. It became excruciatingly hot. "Dawn came with the stench getting worse, less ventilation, increased agony of the wounded," Mac reported. "With daylight, there was added danger of detection by bomber squadrons or aircraft carriers. We flew at 1,500 feet; the cloud banks gave us some protection. When they parted by the sun's rays and burned away, we ducked from cloud to cloud, and at times, when the cloud bank settled, just above the waves."

Hamilton wondered whether the *Philippine Clipper* would hold up mechanically on the long flight to Hawaii. The plane had not received the extensive maintenance at Midway that customarily would have been provided. Midway's mechanics had inspected the bullet holes for further damage and checked the control lines. That's all they could do in such a short time, especially with their hangar still ablaze.

The clipper's crew also wasn't sure where they could land. According to the Plan A document, Hamilton's "operational scenario [would] be determined by the status of [the] flight at the time it becomes necessary to implement these instructions." With Pan Am bases and US and British ports under attack by Japanese southwest of Hawaii, Hamilton figured the safest and most sensible destination was Hilo on the Big Island of Hawaii, which was 1,525 miles and eleven and a half hours from Midway Atoll. He wasn't aware that the *Anzac Clipper* had landed at Hilo on the morning of the attack. Pearl City was 210 miles closer, but Hamilton didn't know whether it was possible to land in the Middle Loch so soon after the attack. His radioman Ted Hrutky had been trying to reach Pearl to receive orders that would sort out the mystery for the skipper; but so far, there'd been no response. "The officers kept calling Honolulu—no answer. Guam, Midway, Wake—no answer," Mac recalled.

Despite the clipper's difficulty communicating, Pan Am CEO Juan Trippe had informed Washington, DC, what was happening with his bases and planes to the extent he had information. Because the *Philippine Clipper* had yet to communicate with Hawaii, all Trippe knew was that the clipper had departed Wake and was still in danger.

Even if those aboard the clipper made it to Hawaii, no one knew what to expect once they arrived there. Rumors circulated that Pearl Harbor was in ruins. The dark subject consumed those onboard, some even believing it possible that Hawaii was now under a Japanese flag. The clipper's copilot, First Officer Bill Moss, a baby-faced graduate of Brown University, was among those who doubted the accuracy of the rumors. "There was speculation of a terrible disaster at Pearl Harbor. We didn't really believe it because we knew the navy had expected trouble." When landing instructions without elaboration finally did come over the radio hours later, however, they caused the clipper's crew much concern: "Go Hilo." "Hilo" meant Hilo Bay alongside Hilo Airport on the eastern side of the Big Island. Everyone wondered if the command to fly to Hilo meant that Pearl Harbor was still under attack, or that it had indeed been devastated.

As the clipper neared the northern tip of Oahu on its way to Hilo, Pearl Harbor sent out a cable to military posts on Oahu: "8 DEC 41 . . . PAN AMERICAN CLIPPER . . . WILL FLY OVER OAHU SHORTLY AFTER 11:00 FROM MIDWAY TO HILO . . . DO NO FIRE UPON."

The *Philippine Clipper* passed the location where it would normally prepare for an approach to Pearl City and continued its course for Hilo, "ducking and dodging" in and out of clouds and up and down near the ocean's waves, speeding through tempestuous weather. Because those onboard hadn't eaten or slept for hours, many became airsick. The bile and its smell in the sweltering plane made conditions even more intolerable.

First Officer Moss recalled, "After eleven and a half hours, we'd made it to the northern tip of the Big Island when we received another message, this time to land at Pearl." When the crew received the message, the *Philippine Clipper* had already flown 175 miles past Pearl Harbor in a bullet-ridden plane with wounded aboard. "We made a 180 back to Pearl," Moss said. The mix-up had added over two hours to their already long flight.

"PANAM CLIPPER DUE OVER OAHU SHORTLY AFTER NOON

MAY LAND AT PEARL," was Pearl Harbor's latest cable message to its posts. "DO NOT FIRE UPON."

Anticipation grew among those onboard as they flew nearer to Honolulu. They'd wondered since leaving Wake if the rumors they'd heard were true; they'd soon see for themselves. Around noon, those aboard the *Philippine Clipper* spotted black smoke hovering over Oahu from miles away. At long last, they'd reached Pearl Harbor. It had been just over two days since the clipper had taken off from Pearl for Midway. On that joyful Friday, December 5, as the *Philippine Clipper* had begun its ascent for Midway, the revered US Pacific Fleet and Pearl Harbor and its enthusiastic young sailors had combined to show their strength and majesty to those onboard the clipper. On that day, the spectacular view had been worth the price of their plane tickets. But on Monday, merely twenty-six hours after the attack, as the *Philippine Clipper* descended to make an unceremonious landing, those onboard filled every window, not to search for the Japanese as they had continuously done since leaving Wake and Midway aflame, but to gaze upon the ghastly devastation in the harbor.

"As we circled over it, we could see the turrets of the *Arizona* sticking out of the water," Mac recalled. "The *Oklahoma* was nearly bottom side up, it was a smoldering naval pyre and great masses of smoke hung in the air."

Silence filled the clipper's fuselage, interrupted by gasps and murmurs of horror. Gravity tugged the passengers' hearts a little harder. Then came bursts of expletives . . .

"We could see smoke rising from the harbor," First Officer Moss recalled. "We flew past Ford Island and could see Schofield. Oh, it was terrible. You couldn't see a whole plane. And the harbor was full of ships with their masts pointing in different directions and one was upside down. The *Arizona* was still burning as we passed over. It was a terrible shock."

"It was unnerving . . . the worst thing I have ever seen," Captain Hamilton recalled.

## CHAPTER 38

# MARTIAL LAW

The City of Honolulu had been damaged and civilians killed during the attack on Pearl Harbor. Some of the bombing and strafing had come from Japanese planes; however, many shells from US antiaircraft fire had fallen into populated areas. The resultant fires and chaos created civil unrest. Most citizens believed that the surprise attack was a prelude to the full-scale invasion of Oahu.

Knowing he was in a precarious situation over his head, Hawaii's territorial governor held a meeting with Lt. Gen. Walter Short and Lt. Col. Thomas Green. The governor then announced to the public over the radio that afternoon: "I have called upon the army to place the Territory under martial law." (Hawaii would not become a state for eighteen more years.)

Lt. Gen. Short commanded US Army and National Guard forces to take control of Honolulu and all of Hawaii. Having instituted martial law, he ordered the military with the help of citizenry to begin fortifying the island for an oncoming onslaught of Japanese soldiers landing on the beaches and parachuting inland. Short announced "that every male citizen in the Territory will be required to construct a bomb shelter for the protection of himself and his family, using his own tools and materials." Stretched coils of barbed wire, wooden barricades wrapped in wire, and barbed wire fences ten feet tall soon spanned the length of a once-inviting Waikiki Beach. Schools were closed to prevent mass casualties in the event of another bombing attack. Everyone over seven years of age was issued a gas mask and expected to take part in drills to learn its use.

Martial law attempted to safeguard against the potential threat of not only invasion but espionage and sabotage from any of the 160,000 Japanese and Japanese Americans living in the Territory of Hawaii, representing 37 percent of the population. Everyone older than age six was fingerprinted, registered, and required to carry military-issued identification certificates that resembled drivers' licenses. A strict curfew barred anyone from being on the streets between 9:00 p.m. and 6:00 a.m. unless carrying a curfew pass issued by an employer or other authority. People of Japanese descent had to be in their homes by 8:00 p.m. The military maintained intelligence reports on a vast number of Hawaiian residents, especially those of Japanese extraction. Honolulu police and detectives took Japanese consul Nagao Kita into custody and closed the consulate. Provost courts replaced civilian courts, and the writ of habeas corpus was suspended. Hundreds of Japanese community leaders were taken into custody, and 1,700 were sent to internment camps on the US mainland without due process of law.

Lt. Gen. Short announced that "a total blackout will be in effect all night and every night till lifted." All lighting in whatever form—bulbs or flames—had to be extinguished at nightfall. People covered their windows at night, and they were instructed to paint their car headlights dull red and their taillights blue to dim them. All businesses had to close by 4:30 p.m. so workers and shoppers could make it home before dark. "Motion picture houses, theaters, and other places of amusement" were closed at night. Cinemas advertised Hollywood movies for noon and 2:00 p.m. showings only. Residences and businesses couldn't display Christmas or other holiday lights at night. Those in violation of the blackout were arrested. Military, National Guard, police, and volunteers enforced the blackout. Even the Willamette and San Jose college football players, who now found themselves trapped in Honolulu, volunteered to patrol communities. "We're happy to help," Willamette coach Keene remarked. "If they equip us with rifles or guns, I hope our boys will shoot straighter than we did with our passes against Hawaii Saturday night."

With food and fuel in short supply and dependent upon shipments from the US mainland, gasoline was rationed, and hoarding and price gouging were forbidden. The governor explained to reporters that "this means that you may buy from your regular supplier in your customary amounts but no more." The sale of medical supplies, especially poisons and drugs, was also regulated. All bars, pubs, and taverns were closed, and the sales of liquor, wine, and beer were forbidden. According to Lt. Col. Green, the principal reason for the ban on liquor was to prevent intoxicated men from hunting Japanese residents, since feelings toward Japanese were at a boiling point. "Vigilante committees" had already sprung up, shooting out lights and threatening citizens. Some even boasted of being "Japanese exterminators." Many Chinese wore signs around their necks that read "Me Chinese" to avoid being mistaken for Japanese.

Censorship also was instituted. Army and navy censors reviewed everything going out of Hawaii. Newspapers required licenses to operate, and no publication was allowed to be printed in any language except English. The telephone company and cable and radio offices were commandeered by the military, and all outgoing mail and telegrams were censored. Long-distance telephone calls were monitored and could only be made in English. People of Japanese descent weren't allowed to own shortwave radios. Photographs of beaches and other sensitive areas were forbidden. All sales of radios and equipment, cameras, and photographic supplies were regulated.

It seemed that Lt. Gen. Walter Short and the US Army and Navy had everything under control. Most wished they had been as prepared defending Pearl Harbor against the attacking enemy as they had been instituting and enforcing martial law over the local citizenry.

Harry Olson had witnessed the initial chaos in Honolulu after the attack on Pearl Harbor and then the eventual order under martial law. He and other Morrison-Knudsen Company workers had remained after the attack and were quickly assigned to help repair or rebuild the destruction around Pearl Harbor and elsewhere. With his Waikiki vacation cut short, Harry began supervising divers and welders working on damaged ships in the harbor.

Some of the contractors were given the grim task of excavating trenches for burial of the dead that could not be identified, referred to simply as the unidentified or unknown. "And it is a sad and terrible sight to have to do this," George Youmans wrote. "Most of the bodies are burned to a crisp from the terrific heat from the burning ships. The odor is terrible and the flies are there by the millions." The majority of those aboard the sunken USS *Arizona* had been incinerated from the immense heat of the blast and fires that melted the ship's steel. Their remains were left aboard their ship, which later became a wartime memorial.

News of Japanese attacks on Guam, Wake, Malaya, Thailand, and Hong Kong had filtered into Hawaii. Later, word of the attacks on the Philippines and Midway also reached those in Hawaii. Harry's son Ted was still on Wake. Harry had helped his son get the job despite his wife Katherine's reservations. Ted had accepted the position with the idea of avoiding the draft and the war in Europe. Now he found himself on a tiny Pacific island under Japanese attack without his father there with him.

Harry wrote Katherine, "You know it is only a miracle that I am not down there [on Wake] with them." He had moved in with Dr. Tom Barrett, who'd left Wake with Harry on December 3 for a vacation. The two men shared an apartment with Mrs. Eudelle Russell and another friend's wife whose husbands were now under attack at Wake. When Dr. Barrett returned to the US mainland once the all-clear was given, Harry stayed behind with his two friends' wives. In a letter to Katherine in Oregon later that December, Harry frostily mentioned his "small harem" and that "the girls are so very good to me and I have never lived so well. So I can't really say the war has done me any harm."

Harry's son Ted would soon be interned at a Japanese prison camp in Shanghai and later moved to Japan. Harry's friend Pete Russell would be held captive on Wake and tortured by the Japanese.

Katherine busied herself trying to find Ted's whereabouts and his condition following his capture. She also readied the house for Harry's return. His job in Honolulu was nearing an end and there were few jobs in the Pacific, except for men willing to wear an American uniform. When Harry's work was finished in Hawaii, he accepted a job back on the mainland in Idaho. Despite the fact that he'd been away for a year, he didn't visit Katherine or his son and daughter in Portland, Oregon, making an excuse that it was a rush job without provision for a family residence in Idaho. Harry had the time, however, to hire Pete's wife, Eudelle Russell, as his secretary and move into a hotel room together.

---

Harry would file for divorce in 1942. With little money, Katherine, who'd never held a job outside the home, took a job with United Air Lines working at the Portland airport.

Of the 1,145 civilian construction workers captured on Wake Island, 34 were killed during the attacks on the island, 114 died in prison camps, 97 were bound and murdered by machine gun on Wake, and 5 others died or were killed elsewhere. Ted Olson was one of the survivors. When the war was over and Ted was released from prison camp in August 1945, Katherine met him in San Francisco and brought him home to Oregon. She had not seen her elder son since he'd left to work with his father on Wake Island four years earlier.

Pete Russell also returned from captivity in 1945. He'd been treated badly by his Japanese captors and burned from American bombs dropped on a Japanese shipyard where he had been forced to work. He was met by his wife, Eudelle, who'd been living with Harry since the attack on Pearl Harbor. She, too, asked for a divorce. Harry and Eudelle would marry and live in Spokane, Washington, while Pete went back to his first wife. Katherine eventually married a man she'd met while working at United Air Lines. Though the Olsons and Russells had survived the war with Japan, their lives had been changed forever because of it.

## CHAPTER 39

# HOMEWARD BOUND

Families of those onboard the *Philippine Clipper* agonized for any shred of news about their loved ones' location and welfare. The opening day of war in the Pacific had been nerve-racking for the families who knew that their husbands, sons, brothers, and uncles were likely in the thick of it. Since Sunday, they'd heard about the Japanese attack at Pearl Harbor on their radios, in the newspapers, and on telephone calls with family and neighbors. News bulletins continued throughout that first day and night and into the next, bringing word of bombardment, death, and capture all over the Pacific, including islands where Pan Am maintained bases and personnel.

The crew members' families repeatedly telephoned Pan Am's Pacific Division at Treasure Island to learn more about the *Philippine Clipper*, but there was little to be learned. The emotional calls to Treasure Island had drained forty-three-year-old Californian Valeda Lee, whose principal job was arranging Pan Am flight schedules and doing secretarial work. Because of her compassionate voice, she'd been enlisted to field telephone calls from families. The old saying "don't shoot the messenger" certainly applied in her case. For two days she'd been telling families that she had nothing to report, and then she'd have to explain why she did not. Much of the information was classified, because its dissemination might endanger not only Pan Am crews and passengers but also US Army and Navy servicemen. Families were told to stay near their radios for further bulletins and they'd be contacted as information came in.

But on the evening of Monday, December 8, things changed. Pearl City's airport manager Bill Eldridge watched the *Philippine Clipper* as it circled the loch and landed, taxiing to the dock. Having communicated with Capt. Hamilton on its approach, Eldridge wasted no time contacting Pan Am's office at Treasure Island. He cabled division manager Clarence Young that the *Philippine Clipper* had just landed safely in Honolulu. At last, Valeda could begin returning calls with good news. "We've heard from the boys," she told First Officer Moss's wife. "I can't tell you where they are, but they're okay." She repeated the same message to the families of the others.

Still over 2,400 miles away from the crew's families, the *Philippine Clipper* came to rest and was safely moored to the Pan Am dock at Pearl City. The forlorn men, whose whereabouts and well-being had been in doubt for two days, stepped from the plane onto the dock as if they'd just returned from the moon. Bill Eldridge stood on the pier to greet everyone. Unlike the typical disembarkment when passengers dressed like they were "Puttin' on the Ritz," those now standing on the dock were a ragtag bunch, many in filthy short pants and short-sleeved shirts, disheveled hair, and all in desperate need of a shave and a shower.

The first thing the men noticed as they emerged from the clipper's hatch was not the vivid firmament and tropical scent of Hawaii, but the smell of burning fuel from ships still ablaze in the harbor, billowing black smoke into the air. As the group of Pan Am refugees stood and gazed across the East Loch at what typically was a majestic view of American military might, their faces withered with sorrow. To help ease their suffering, if only for a little while, Eldridge offered shots of scotch as he escorted the men into the comfortable terminal. He also arranged for a driver to take Charlie Relyea and Don Mackay to the US Naval Hospital.

John Cooke Jr. Phil Cooke Collection.

"Pan American Airways base was practically deserted," Mac said later, "except for four bottles of Scotch and some soda," which the airport manager circulated.

Bill Eldridge was especially delighted to see one of the passengers—his brother Jerry—who'd been Pan Am's assistant chief mechanic at the besieged Wake Island. Unlike Jerry, Bill had been relatively safe at the Pearl City marine base. It had not been attacked by the Japanese planes, even though it was very near Battleship Row. Eldridge recalled later that during the attack, he "never got a scratch but was plenty scared." Yet Eldridge had maintained sufficient nerve to send Pan Am's Pacific Division at Treasure Island a coded message during the attack: "Condition Seven," which meant "we are under enemy aerial attack."

Also among those waiting to greet the thirty-seven men exiting the clipper was John Cooke's father, John Bleecker "JB" Cooke, who was the commanding officer of a naval section base at Pearl Harbor. The young Pan Am airport manager had also been in the US Navy. He had learned to speak Japanese while serving as a member of the "On the Roof Gang," a select group of men who'd learned to intercept and analyze Japanese radio communications from the roof of the US Department of the Navy building in Washington, DC. In fact, Cooke had descended from a long line of naval officers. Besides his father serving as a commanding naval officer, Cooke's uncle, Charles Cooke Jr., was a commander of the Pacific Fleet's flagship, USS *Pennsylvania*, which happened to be in drydock undergoing renovations when the Japanese attacked Pearl. His uncle had ordered antiaircraft fire from every gun on the deck of the *Pennsylvania*, which had been bombed but stayed afloat in its drydock. His uncle eventually rose to be a four-star admiral in command of the Seventh Fleet. Another of Cooke's uncles had been a naval commander who'd been killed in a plane crash scarcely nine months earlier. And there were others, like Cooke's great-great-uncle who'd been a rear admiral and founded the US Naval War College in 1884.

It was because of the Cooke family's long and honorable naval heritage that Rear Adm. Husband E. Kimmel, the commanding officer of the US Pacific Fleet, asked Cooke's father to relay a message that day on Pan Am's dock: "Admiral Kimmel requests Captain Hamilton and [John Cooke] to report to him at 0900 hours [on Tuesday morning] to brief him on what you've seen."

For the rest of that Monday, December 8, the crew and passengers simply wanted a shower, some good food, and lots of sleep. They hadn't slept for thirty hours. "We were tired and in shock," First Officer Moss remembered. "An hour and a half more and we made Honolulu by car to find the city completely blacked out. . . . In spite of it all, Honolulu looked pretty good to us." Hamilton and most of the others checked into the crew's cottages reserved by Pan Am at the Moana Hotel on Waikiki Beach, a beach that now was lined with wooden and concrete barricades and barbed wire.

Rather than checking into the hotel with the others, John Cooke joined his wife, Isyl, and two young sons, Bleecker, age four, and Phillip, age twenty months, who were now living in Honolulu with relatives. It was one of those times in life where families truly hug, kiss, and squeeze one another, when escape from death reminds loved ones to appreciate their time alive together. Cooke's wife and children had been evacuated from Wake Island just three weeks earlier. If not for the evacuation, they easily could have been killed, since their house on Wake had been struck by bombs and obliterated.

Flight engineer Ed Barnett wasted little time prying information from Eldridge and others who might have news about the Philippines. Those with access to the navy's formal channels of communication wouldn't speak, and Eldridge knew little more than was in the newspapers—news of bombings, submarine sinkings, and men killed. Ed wouldn't learn until later that his wife, Cecile, at the age of twenty-five, had been captured by the Japanese and would be imprisoned at Santo Tomas Internment Camp in Manila. Three and a half years later, in May 1945, she arrived at San Pedro, California, aboard the SS *Eberle*. During the two-month cruise, an emaciated Cecile and her friend had gained their weight back and looked quite lovely upon docking in California. She told a reporter with a chuckle as she and her friend disembarked, "We've gained twenty pounds each, and we have to do something about that."

Despite the exhaustion of those on the *Philippine Clipper* who'd just disembarked, many couldn't sleep soundly that night. With martial law and a blackout in force in Hawaii, the National Guard, state and local police, and volunteer air raid wardens often caused a ruckus raising false alarms while trying to keep Honolulu dark and quiet. "Honolulu Spends Anxious Night—Many Alarms," a *Honolulu Star-Bulletin* headline read. Many residents simply didn't obey the blackout rules; and their neighbors had no qualms about turning them in. Honolulu police received "thousands of complaints about lights" being on in residences or people breaking curfew and driving with their automobile headlights on. By 10:00 p.m., the authorities' patience had run out. "Attention, all cars. Arrest anyone whose home has a light on," a police transcript reported. "Do not give them a break. Arrest them. . . . If you can't turn the light out, shoot it out."

Then there were those who believed they'd spotted a Japanese soldier or saboteur behind every palm tree or primrose willow. Hundreds of reports came in. With islanders afraid of the possibility of an imminent invasion—a very reasonable fear—they spotted the Bogeyman around every corner. Several saw "parachutists," others reported "a man on a roof" or "a man with a rifle," and some saw "a man flashing a light" or "a man using short-wave radio," and so on. And then there were the shouts and the gunshots and the chases, not by the police but by citizens or volunteers who believed they'd hunted the enemy down only to discover that it was merely their neighbors or innocent passersby.

"There were plenty of amateur air raid wardens who were making the night miserable," recalled Mac, who stayed at the Moana Hotel. "They were shooting out any lights seen—and if someone got in the way of a bullet, it was just too bad. A lot of people were killed as a result before the regular police got the situation under control."

And it wasn't simply trigger-happy civilians who made the night menacing. "At Fort Russy [not far from the Moana Hotel], the night was punctuated with machine-gun bursts and antiaircraft discharges," Mac remembered, noting that identifying an "enemy" was apparently in the eye of the beholder. But morning came and the sun rose over the island, and so far, the Japanese weren't invading.

The *Philippine Clipper* was scheduled to take off that afternoon from Pearl City around five o'clock. The clipper had been checked out by Pan Am mechanics, but the bullet holes would have to await repair in one of the huge hangars at Treasure Island. The mechanics discovered that one of the big .50-caliber shells had lodged in the A-frame of the main structure. It was a vital part of the plane that helped hold the wings to the fuselage. With continuous vibration for a long period of time, the chance of a wing breaking away in flight was within the bounds of possibility; nonetheless, a thorough repair would have to wait.

Mac would be the only passenger returning to Treasure Island with the clipper's crew. He wanted to be home with his daughter, Doreen, until further orders came from Pan Am. One of the first things Mac had done upon landing at Pearl City was to send a telegram to relatives in Alameda to inform Doreen that her daddy was fine in Honolulu. The censors redacted the line that he would be coming home the following day on the *Philippine Clipper*. All of the other Pan Am employees had decided they'd had enough ducking and dodging in a bullet-ridden plane, at least until the US Navy determined where the Japanese were.

Charlie Relyea and Don Mackay would remain in Honolulu for about two weeks to receive medical care and stave off infection. Pan Am notified their families that they were all right. "[Relyea] is making very satisfactory progress in the US Naval Hospital and was hospitalized solely to guard against the possibility that complications might arise. This was on instructions of an Army surgeon [Lt. Col. Tamraz] who was a passenger . . . and attended Relyea on the return trip to Honolulu."

———

After a delicious breakfast at the Moana Hotel, the first since Capt. Hamilton and his crew had taken off for Guam three days earlier, John Cooke's father picked up his son and Capt. Hamilton to drive them to Pacific Fleet headquarters in the Administration Building near the submarine base at Pearl. As they stepped out of the car, the men could see the submarines moored at their base projecting out into the harbor, untouched by the Japanese bombers, a mistake that would prove to be to the Empire's detriment.

Situated on the top floor, Adm. Kimmel's office faced the harbor. The men walked in. Cmdr. Cooke and Capt. Hamilton, a naval reservist, stopped three paces from Kimmel's desk and saluted, whereas the civilian John Cooke stood at ease. Adm. Kimmel's office was as they'd expected. Besides the American and US Pacific Fleet flags on floor stands, an enormous map of the Pacific Ocean and the various islands and continents that touched it covered one wall. Two other walls were adorned with paintings of ships that Kimmel had served on, framed black-and-white photographs of the admiral with military and political men of importance, and framed commendations of significance. A large window looking out on Pearl Harbor filled nearly the entire remaining wall. The window would soon be painted black so that the men in Kimmel's office could work at night without violating the blackout.

The visiting men were invited to sit and, following sparse pleasantries, began responding to the admiral's questions in the presence of another officer, who took notes. Capt. Hamilton commenced a narrative account of everything that he had witnessed at Wake Island—the number of enemy planes, their direction of flight, the size of the bombs dropped, and the damage exacted. He also recounted the two destroyers spotted off Midway and the damage inflicted on that island's installations. Cooke piped up as necessary, both making as complete a report as they could. Following the briefing, Adm. Kimmel spoke words of acknowledgement and then unexpectedly commenced taking barbs at John Cooke in his father's presence.

"Cooke, Cooke, let me see. Didn't you and [Dan] Teeters raise a fuss about our pulling your families off Wake?" Kimmel was referring to an order to evacuate women and children from the island bases after Japanese movements in French Indochina increased.

"Yes sir," Cooke responded.

"That's the trouble with you civilians," a smug Kimmel reportedly lectured. "You ought to know that we navy people have far better information than you do, and that we know exactly what we're doing."

Cooke later recalled that the remark made him very angry, particularly after what had happened at Pearl Harbor two days earlier. "I couldn't think of anything appropriate to say, so I merely turned my head and gazed out his window which overlooked Pearl Harbor and the still-burning remains of the once proud Pacific Fleet." The Japanese attack was the worst single day's attack upon the United States by an enemy up to that time, outside of the US Civil War.

Cooke's father relayed to his son later that afternoon that Adm. Kimmel didn't appreciate Cooke's behavior in his office when he implied, by turning to look upon the terrible carnage, that Kimmel had been negligent in his defense of Pearl. It didn't matter. Along with Army Lt. Gen. Walter Short, Kimmel was relieved of duty a week later and would be replaced by Adm. Chester Nimitz. In six weeks, a presidentially appointed commission to investigate the attack on Pearl Harbor would conclude that Kimmel and Short had been guilty of dereliction of duty during the events leading up to the attack. In 1944, a naval court of inquiry virtually cleared Kimmel, placing more of the blame on Adm. Stark in Washington, DC, for his failure to effectively provide information of Japan's movements to Adm. Kimmel; but Kimmel's reputation had been forever tarnished.

———

Capt. Hamilton returned to the Moana Hotel after meeting with Adm. Kimmel and then was driven to Pearl City. It was nearing time for takeoff. The *Philippine Clipper* and its crew had one more flight to make to reach home. Without credible reports of the whereabouts of the Japanese aircraft carriers, Hamilton knew the flight could be extremely risky at best—and suicidal at worst.

In spite of the risk, Capt. Hamilton and his crew boarded the flying boat to run through the preflight checks. The *Philippine*

*Clipper* lifted off the surface of the Middle Loch of Pearl Harbor on Tuesday, December 9, at 5:15 p.m. as the Hawaiian sun began to set, though few noticed its beauty. Those onboard witnessed once again through the encroaching darkness the devastation that lay below them—ships leaning in every direction and clouds of black smoke still surging into the sky. There was the capsized USS *Oklahoma*, rolled over, trapping more than four hundred of its sailors underwater; and the USS *Arizona* resting on the harbor's shallow bottom, its mainmast rising like a crucifix high into the air, marking the watery graves of 1,102 sailors inside its hull. "It was the grimmest thing I'd ever seen in my life," First Officer Bill Moss remembered.

The captain pointed the flying boat's nose toward home and climbed to a comfortable altitude. He ordered the shades drawn and all unnecessary lighting extinguished as sunset commenced shrouding the clipper in darkness. And once again, like twenty-three boiling teapots, the familiar noise of wind whistling through the bullet holes filled the fuselage.

The captain instructed Second Radio Officer Ted Hrutky to listen to Hawaiian radio, not for its lovely island music typically enjoyed by arriving and departing clippers but for bulletins of attacks, bloodshed, and war. Hrutky also listened for signals from ships and other planes as well as surfaced submarines, whether friend or foe. Under no circumstances could Hrutky transmit without first clearing it with the captain.

Ordinarily, the *Philippine Clipper* would make the return flight full of passengers scattered throughout the luxurious staterooms with a mountain of mailbags in its cargo hold. But only a single passenger, Mac, was aboard on this trip, and he worked for Pan Am. A handful of letters that had been given to members of the crew to deliver to the San Francisco post office were also aboard. One of those letters had been written by Harry Olson to his wife, Katherine. "The Captain said they may take off for the coast today and he will take this personally for me." The two men had met inside the Moana Hotel.

As the clipper and its crew drew nearer to the California coast, Ted Hrutky began picking up troubling reports of sightings of Japanese planes, ships, and submarines. Capt. Hamilton and the crew wondered if the Japanese task force had continued beyond Hawaii and was now attacking America's West Coast. While maintaining radio silence, they discussed what to do and decided to continue their course, with reservation. "[We] were prepared to land anywhere from Seattle to Mexico," the captain said later. Those aboard the clipper had not yet figured out that communities along the North American West Coast had contracted "invasion fever," calling in alerts for every boat, plane, or mirage sighted.

For example, on Monday, December 8, rumors spread of a Japanese aircraft carrier, like the *Akagi* or *Kaga*, loaded with bombers, being sighted off the coast of the San Francisco Bay Area. As a result, radio communications were shut down in San Francisco and a blackout was instituted throughout the city for three hours. The next day, the sighting was brushed aside as a test or a mistake. However, Lt. Gen. John L. DeWitt of the US Army's Western Defense Command adamantly disagreed, telling a Los Angeles newspaper that his station had tracked enemy aircraft up to one hundred miles off the coast. "Last night there were planes over this community. They were . . . Japanese planes!" It was amid this chaos that the *Philippine Clipper* continued on its course to Treasure Island.

Disturbing rumors of enemy threats persisted on Tuesday, December 9, as the *Philippine Clipper* roared closer and closer to the mainland. The Eleventh Naval District had relayed to the US Army Air Forces that thirty-four enemy ships were floating off the coast near Los Angeles, waiting for the fog to lift before staging their incipient attack. When the fog cleared, Army reconnaissance planes discovered that the well-equipped and indomitable Japanese task force was merely a group of American fishing boats casting their nets in the identical location. That same day, whales and floating logs were mistaken for enemy submarines.

"Nearing the Pacific coast, we learned of the [sightings and] blackouts," the captain said. "That worried us." As one California newspaper reported, "The radio which brought [the crew of the *Philippine Clipper*] word of the Oahu attack also told them of the air raid alarms in San Francisco last night as they approached the west coast."

The clipper and all those inside had been shielded by darkness for a dozen hours, but with the dawn came bright sunlight straight ahead from the east. Capt. Hamilton had no choice but to descend to within a hundred feet of the ocean's surface, just as he had many times since leaving Wake Island. Even with tinted windows and sunglasses, the ocean's glare and the constant scanning of the sky and water for enemy planes and ocean vessels felt as if holes were being slowly burned through the men's retinas. They rubbed their eyes and strained to maintain focus on the sea and the sky for the smallest of objects, ever the more difficult when red-eyed and weary.

As the clipper neared San Francisco, the clipper's captain broke radio silence for the first time and notified Treasure Island of his estimated time of arrival. He was given the all-clear. The captain requested Pan Am's motorboats to sweep the channel for obstructions and clear the area of surface craft. He also engaged in a set of course alterations that would be identified by military coastal radar and plane spotters as a US commercial plane.

After almost nineteen hours had passed since taking off from Pearl City—hours filled with anxiety watching for Japanese ships and planes—the California coast came into view. Capt. Hamilton and his crew recognized the coast and the reddish-orange glow of the Golden Gate Bridge—it had never looked grander. When they flew over the Bridge, they knew they'd soon see their families at Treasure Island. Valeda Lee had called the crewmen's wives and some parents, just as she had for those aboard the *Anzac Clipper* the day before. She told them that Pan Am expected the clipper to touch down around three o'clock that afternoon and to come beforehand and wait in the terminal lounge.

Just as Valeda had reported, shortly before three o'clock the sound of the clipper's Wasp engines could be heard in the distance. Family and Pan Am employees looked toward the sky, some with sunglasses and others shielding their eyes as they scanned the horizon for the source of the distinctive humming. A black dot emerged against the backdrop of a gray sky. It wasn't long until the silhouette of a Martin M-130 flying boat formed below scattered clouds. Sounds of excitement grew as the clipper cruised above the suspension cables between the San Francisco-Oakland Bay Bridge towers. Minutes later, they anxiously watched as Capt. Hamilton and his crew circled and then brought the clipper in for a smooth landing in Clipper Cove at Treasure Island.

The families ran out to greet them, some carrying babies and holding the little hands of toddlers bundled up against the cold wind as they made their way down the walk. All were so happy to see the men alive, unlike so many families who'd lost someone over the past three days. The men stepping off the clipper were allowed to embrace their loved ones before undergoing hours of questioning in the Pan Am offices. The crew of the *Philippine Clipper* had been the first to arrive on the mainland who had witnessed firsthand the attack on Wake Island and the devastation of Midway and Pearl Harbor, as they'd flown almost five thousand miles over the Pacific *after* the attacks. The *Anzac Clipper*, which had returned the day before, had not seen Pearl Harbor or anything beyond safe and intact Hilo. US military intelligence was extremely interested to hear what Hamilton and his crew, as well as Mac, had seen and heard, even though they'd already been questioned in Honolulu. Pan Am's Col. Clarence Young and Capt. J.W. Gates of the Twelfth Naval District Headquarters in San Francisco, along with several other army and navy officers, asked question after question, requested drawings, and wanted plane, ship, and bomb descriptions. One special moment

Previously wounded Charles Relyea and Don Mackay standing over newly placed chevron on nose of the "wounded" *Philippine Clipper*. Pan American Airways, *New Horizons*, January 1943, 27; U. Miami PAA.

took place when Capt. Hamilton handed over the American flag that had been lowered from the pole beside the charred remains of Pan Am's hotel and its soot-filled fountain on embattled Wake Island.

At last they were finished. As they stood, the crewmen were sworn to silence. "We were not to tell anybody what we had seen, even our wives," First Officer Moss recollected. Later that day, the US Navy and Capt. Hamilton released a joint statement for the newspapers that described the attack on Wake Island without revealing any classified information. Hamilton described the treacherous flight from Wake Island as "routine."

Reporters had photographed the crew members walking with their loved ones along the dock when they first arrived. "Mrs. Hamilton joyfully embraced the pilot as he stepped ashore," reported the *Arizona Republic*, complete with photograph. John and Geraldine Hamilton appeared so handsome in his Pan Am uniform and her fashionable dress that many might think they'd just attended a dinner party rather than weathering three and a half days of stress and worry. Newsmen photographed them again as they stepped out of the terminal on their way home.

While still back in Honolulu in a naval hospital, Charlie Relyea learned that his friend and Guam shop owner, Felix Torres, had lost his wife to the Japanese, leaving him a widower with an eighteen-month-old child. Felix, still in Guam, was subsequently imprisoned, beaten, and forced into labor, but survived the war. Charlie eventually would make a full recovery from his wounds and go on to marry and father a family of his own with seven children. Capt. Hamilton later wrote Charlie to thank him for his "fortitude" without "complaints." Pan Am also added a chevron to the nose of the *Philippine Clipper* to signify that it had been "wounded" during the war.

With the questioning by military brass over, Mac left the Treasure Island airport eager to see his daughter, who was staying with family during his absence. It was late by the time he reached her; he was told she was sleeping. He walked into her bedroom and woke his young daughter. Despite Doreen's grogginess, she wrapped her arms around her daddy's neck and hugged him tightly. She'd heard he was coming home; but, despite trying really hard, she couldn't stay awake. Mac gathered her things, and then father and daughter drove across the Bay Bridge into Alameda, where they parked in front of their quaint Tudor home on Calhoun Street, a few blocks from San Francisco

Bay. Mac opened the car door, and Doreen slid across the car's bench seat. She was too big for him to carry now, or at least she thought so, so they walked into their home holding each other's hand. They'd get her things out of the car in the morning. As she crawled into her bed and they said their goodnights, little Doreen couldn't imagine how far her daddy had come and the many dangers he'd faced to be back home with her. He would have endured so much more to keep his promise—that he'd be home for Christmas.

## CHAPTER 40

# CHRISTMAS IN WASHINGTON

Washingtonians outside the Japanese embassy watched gray smoke rise lazily into Sunday's Indian summer sky as smoke continued to surge over a frenzied Pearl Harbor, 4,800 miles away. Within minutes of the news of the Japanese attack on Pearl Harbor reaching the nation's capital on that December 7, Tokyo ordered Ambassador Nomura at Japan's embassy to burn all sensitive documents and destroy its cipher machine, code manuals, and anything else that might be helpful to the United States. It's a common procedure at embassies around the world when trouble arises, but this instance seemed particularly wicked. Reporters shouted questions through the bolted ornamental gate to tie-wearing men burning papers in open bonfires on the embassy's lawn. "Burning love letters," one Japanese was reported to have uttered as he shooed newsmen away from the iron gate.

If ever salt were rubbed in a wound, it was watching an enemy that had just killed hundreds of Americans by a surprise attack during peacetime now destroy secret information on American soil under the protection of diplomatic immunity. Angry citizens had to be held back at the gate by a line of policemen. This was the same embassy that housed special envoy Saburō Kurusu, who had visited Secretary of State Hull earlier that same day to deliver Japan's answer to President Roosevelt's counterproposal. Kurusu's answer broke off peace negotiations, but, due to a slow typist, had not been delivered before the Empire of Japan's task force had already commenced bombing Pearl Harbor.

On what should have been a restful Sunday in the federal capital, people stood outside the Japanese embassy shouting "murderers," "cowards," and similar words frequently laced with expletives, obscenities, and racial slurs. Newspapers echoed the angry mob's name-calling, describing those inside the embassy in crude and degrading language. Kurusu was also sarcastically referred to as the "peace envoy," and was accused of masterminding a "treacherous trick" or a "smokescreen" while his country's military killed young sailors and Marines at Pearl Harbor without warning as part of a "sneak attack."

Inside the White House, however, President Roosevelt realized that although Japan constituted an enormous threat in the Pacific, Germany remained a threat to the entire world, and therefore the war in Europe would have to be given priority. On December 11, Roosevelt's belief was confirmed when an emboldened Adolf Hitler declared war against the United States. Hitler believed that the Japanese attack strengthened his chances of ultimate victory in the East and the West. "I am thankful that [Providence] has entrusted me," Hitler declared as he addressed the German Reichstag, "with the leadership in a historic conflict that will be decisive in determining the next five hundred or one thousand years . . . of the history of Europe and even of the entire world."

When learning of the attack on Pearl Harbor, Prime Minister Winston Churchill was thankful because Britain was no longer alone in the fight in Western Europe. He later wrote: "Being saturated and satiated with emotion and sensation, I went to bed and slept the sleep of the saved and thankful." To ensure that Roosevelt did not deploy all US resources to avenge Pearl Harbor, Churchill visited the White House that December. "We could review the whole war plan in light of reality and new facts," he wrote Roosevelt before arriving. Risking German U-boats, Churchill and his entourage traveled ten days across the Atlantic aboard the British battleship HMS *Duke of York*. He would stay three weeks with the Roosevelts at the White House, celebrating Christmas and New Year's with Americans. Newspapers pointed out the irony of Churchill residing in the presidential mansion that British troops had burned during the War of 1812. The two legendary figures spent their days together, mostly in conferences mapping out the fight across multiple continents, cementing a close friendship.

Soviet Ambassador Maxim Litvinov, who'd visited the White House that December to meet with Roosevelt and Churchill on behalf of the Soviet Union, was also thankful. Two months earlier, the German Wehrmacht launched Operation Typhoon to capture Moscow and end the war on the Eastern Front in Adolf Hitler's favor by Christmas, but subzero weather and a Soviet counteroffensive now had Hitler's German army on the defensive for the first time. Though Litvinov wouldn't be celebrating Christmas in the Russian embassy due to religious restrictions within the Soviet Union, he would celebrate a very similar holiday on New Year's. There'd be no references to Jesus Christ, but a secular celebration that included the decoration of a tree, festive decorations and meals, gift exchanging, and a visit by Grandfather Frost, who'd leave presents under the tree—the Soviet solution to eliminating Christmas.

At the White House, on the other hand, Christmas would be celebrated more sincerely than ever. Roosevelt stood on the South Portico accompanied by Churchill and presided over the lighting of the National Christmas Tree. "Our strongest weapon in this war is that conviction of the dignity and brotherhood of man which Christmas day signifies—more than any other day or any other symbol," Roosevelt said to those gathered. "Against enemies who preach the principles of hate and practice them, we set our faith in human love and in God's care for us and all men everywhere." Roosevelt also asked Churchill to say a few words. The following day, Churchill would become the first foreign leader to address a joint session of

Congress, to raucous applause, especially when he closed with his trademark V-for-victory hand gesture. He would return to England aboard a British Boeing B-314A flying boat, the *Berwick*, that Pan Am had sold the British government to assist with the war effort.

Even inside the Japanese embassy on Massachusetts Avenue, a Christmas celebration of sorts was underway, surprising since the holiday was viewed as such a significant part of American culture. Newspapers reported that "two turkeys and a Christmas tree" were delivered to the embassy on Christmas Eve. "The turkeys will be eaten by Ambassador Nomura and 'Peace Envoy' Kurusu," the *Detroit Free Press* read, "who tricked the United States into the lethargy which permitted the disaster of Pearl Harbor."

The Christmas dinner was as much a farewell dinner to Washington, DC, and their embassy as it was a traditional celebration—because three days later, Nomura, Kurusu, and about eighty other Japanese diplomats and their aides, staff, and families would be rounded up and placed aboard a special US State Department train traveling under guard to a remote location, where they'd be safe and comfortable, though confined. It was a little too comfortable to suit most Americans—the Homestead, a historical luxury resort boasting natural hot springs, beautiful scenic mountains, and opulent hotel accommodations in Hot Springs, Virginia, a beautiful spot resting near the West Virginia state line in the Allegheny Mountains. Closed to the public during the Japanese confinement, more than seven hundred other Japanese diplomats within the United States would soon join them there.

## CHAPTER 41

# ANZAC AND *PACIFIC CLIPPERS* REACH HOME

## ANZAC CLIPPER

With the day's shadows drawing longer, the *Anzac Clipper* floated calmly at its marine base in Treasure Island, safe from attack. It was early Tuesday afternoon, December 9. Capt. Lanier Turner and his crew had already arrived at their homes in Alameda and Oakland, where they caught some much-needed shuteye.

More than 2,300 miles across the Pacific at Hilo, the clipper's former passengers listened intently to every newsflash with increasing concern. They'd heard that the *Anzac Clipper* had landed safely on the mainland. It was bittersweet news. They wondered if their refusal to climb back aboard had left them ensnared in a historic trap. None knew how or when they would be going home, and an invasion could come at any moment.

Those staying at the Naniloa Hotel who lived in Honolulu wasted little time seeking means by which to return to their homes. Most caught passage on one of the small inter-island ships like the SS *Hawaii* that cruised fourteen long, worrisome hours from Hilo to Honolulu. Others chartered yachts that would speedily take them there.

For former *Anzac Clipper* passengers who did not reside in Hawaii, returning home would be exceedingly difficult. The gloriously festive Boat Days in Honolulu were no more, at least for the foreseeable future. The SS *Lurline* that Harry Olson had watched cast off during the last Boat Day on December 5 had sailed 800 miles into open ocean before it received word of the attack at Pearl. Too far out and too dangerous to return, the ship had no choice but to continue on to San Francisco, still 1,600 miles away. Compelled to blacken windows, silence radios, confine passengers to their staterooms, and zigzag off course at forced draught (i.e., maximum power), the ship's captain completed the "thrilling dash through a war zone," arriving safely in San Francisco on the morning of December 10.

The tribulations of the *Lurline* splashed over the front pages of Honolulu newspapers and radio broadcasts. After that, no one was anxious to board another ocean liner any time soon. They couldn't, even if they'd wanted. For days after the attack, the US Army and Navy fretted that the Japanese might be maintaining a strong naval force between Hawaii and the West Coast. They didn't want to underestimate the Japanese a second time, so they restricted ship movements until they could conduct reconnaissance and collect intelligence. Eventually they determined that no Japanese naval force remained east of Hawaii; however, submarines were still being sighted.

Japan had assigned a group of nine submarines to troll about Hawaiian waters and inflict damage on merchant ships. They also hoped to sink the biggest prize of all—a US aircraft carrier returning to Pearl. Although the enemy subs didn't sink a carrier at this time, they did wreak havoc and stir fear throughout the Hawaiian Islands. For instance, the Matson Line freighter SS *Lahaina*, which left Hawaii on its way to San Francisco, was torpedoed by a Japanese submarine on December 11. On the fourteenth, the Norwegian motorship *Heough* was sunk as it approached Hawaii. Two days later, the SS *Manini* cargo ship departed Honolulu for New Zealand and was sunk by a torpedo the next evening. There were several others. The attacks revealed that the Empire of Japan had chosen to engage in unrestricted submarine warfare, meaning the submarine commanders drew no distinction between military and civilian vessels. To combat the submarine menace, the US Navy sent several ships and planes out to patrol the waters off the coast of Hawaii, with scattered success. During December, US ships engaged in fifty-two depth-charge attacks on Japanese submarines around Hawaii. By mid-January, Japan had withdrawn its submarines from Hawaiian waters; not necessarily because of the depth charges, but because they simply were needed elsewhere.

Submarines or not, there were no ocean liners available to carry ticketed passengers to the US mainland. The United States government had requisitioned the white ocean liners of the Matson Line—the SS *Lurline, Matsonia*, and *Monterey*—to deliver men and materiel to Honolulu. The ships formed convoys guarded by a light cruiser and two US destroyers armed not only with deck guns, but with sonar, torpedoes, and depth charges. The first convoy arrived in Honolulu on the twenty-first. The Matson liners, as well as ocean liners from the American President Lines, carried soldiers, weapons, and ammunition; fresh and dry provisions, lumber, steel, clothing, bedding, and salvage gear; and machinists, electricians, pipefitters, welders, and other skilled workers needed to repair the ships and docks at Pearl Harbor.

On their return voyages back to the mainland, the ocean liners carried wounded, military wives and children, and marooned tourists. One grounded *Anzac Clipper* passenger boarded the SS *President Coolidge* and sailed with its convoy from Honolulu just before noon on December 19 for San Francisco. Other *Anzac Clipper* passengers departed Honolulu on the 26th aboard the convoy of Matson liners returning to San Francisco with their US naval escort.

With submarines still occasionally sighted in the shipping lanes between Hawaii and the West Coast, the sea wasn't necessarily the safer route back to the US mainland. That left only one other route—the sky. Once it was determined with reasonable confidence that no Japanese planes or ships remained in that area, Pan Am resumed flying back and forth to Honolulu, with priority given to military officers and stranded Pan Am employees and their families. Large American flags donned the clippers on the tail, the front of the fuselage, and on the top and bottom of each wing and sponson. There was no way that anyone on the ground, on the sea, or in the air could confuse the planes' country of origin. The six large flags painted on the exterior of a Boeing B-314A, for example, covered more than 450 total square feet.

One of Pan Am's big Boeings, the *California Clipper*, was the first to trek across the ocean to Hawaii, landing at Pearl City just one week after the attack. Six former *Anzac Clipper* passengers boarded the *California Clipper* to return to Treasure Island. Among the passengers was John Cooke, the Pan Am airport manager from Wake Island, along with his wife and two young sons, and Jack and Ruth Bramham, the former host and matron at Midway. Other stranded Pan Am passengers boarded the *China Clipper* on December 19 for San Francisco.

Burma Prime Minister U Saw also reversed course but did not fare as well as other passengers. After arriving in San Francisco aboard the *California Clipper*, U Saw traveled to Bermuda, Cairo, and then to Haifa in British-controlled Palestine (now in Israel) on his way to Burma. During his travels, British intelligence discovered incriminating papers relating to U Saw's nefarious communications with the Japanese. He was arrested in Haifa in January and interned in Uganda until the Japanese surrender in 1945. After the war, U Saw returned to Burma and masterminded the bloody assassination of a political rival, Gen. Aung Sun, and six cabinet ministers. U Saw was arrested, found guilty, and hanged.

Though many Americans had fled Honolulu for the West Coast amid constant rumors of an eventual invasion, the Hawaiian people's morale remained strong. When the much-anticipated invasion did not materialize, those in Honolulu settled into life under martial law in a naval port city buzzing with sailors and soldiers deploying all over the Pacific. Even a kind of normality returned; for example, one former *Anzac Clipper* passenger, Dr. V. G. Clark, made the local news for officiating a pineapple-cutting contest at the beautiful Bellows Field luau, complete with "pig, poi, coconut pudding, and all the trimmings."

# PACIFIC CLIPPER

With his passengers disembarked and headed to their homes, Capt. Ford of the *Pacific Clipper* found himself still on the ground in Auckland unable to take off, a predicament that he was not accustomed to tolerating. Twenty-two passengers possessed tickets to fly aboard the clipper on December 9, but the plane was grounded until the captain received his orders. He'd spent each day for a week at the US consulate attempting to obtain those orders. The United States military, by way of Pan Am, had access to only nine of the big Boeings that could traverse oceans at the start of the war. The *Pacific Clipper*'s importance caused a good deal of deliberation between Washington and New York on how best to return the clipper home safely. The possibility of the militarily valuable flying boat being shot down by the Japanese over the Pacific had to be avoided at all costs.

At last, the clipper's captain received his instructions: "Strip all company markings, registration numbers, and identifiable insignias from exterior surfaces. Proceed westbound soonest your discretion to avoid hostilities and deliver NC18609 to Marine Terminal LaGuardia Field New York. Good luck."

Because the orders omitted any particulars, the captain wondered how in the heck he was going to fly from New Zealand to New York City while avoiding the Pacific Ocean. Jules Verne, author of *Around the World in Eighty Days*, could hardly have written a more mystifying tale than what lay ahead of the *Pacific Clipper* and its crew. Bill Mullahey recalled their solution. "With the captain, we

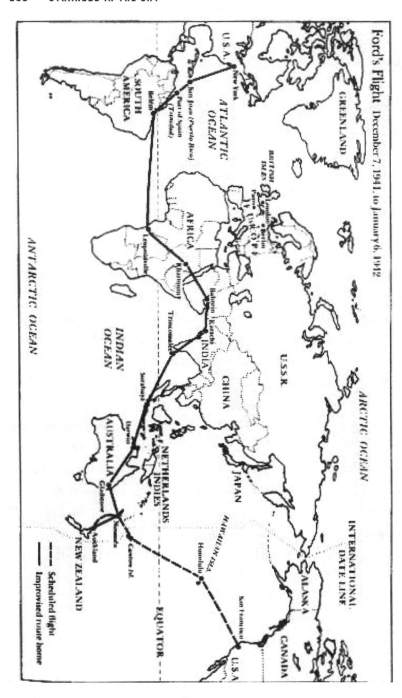

Map of the 31,500-mile escape route of the *Pacific Clipper*. U. Miami PAA.

went down to a high school and got a geography book." The clipper's crew returned to Auckland's Grand Hotel with the textbook. They sat around the library materials at a large table "and laid out a course back to New York."

The course agreed upon would take them across the South Pacific Ocean, Australia, Timor Sea, Netherlands East Indies, the Indian Ocean, Bay of Bengal, Arabian Sea, Persian Gulf, Red Sea, the Nile, Congo, and Amazon Rivers, the Atlantic Ocean, South America, and the West Indies before touching down at LaGuardia's marine terminal in New York City. It would be the longest continuous air route ever attempted by a commercial transport plane, especially during wartime and without routine maintenance. They'd be flying above Japanese-infested waters and German- and Italian-embattled lands without any support from the US military and very little from Pan Am.

"I had no information about his whereabouts at the time," recalled Fourth Officer John Steers's wife, Mary. "Gracious sakes, this was wartime, and during wartime no one called around and gave information about where anyone was. All Pan Am told me was that if they had any information, they would let me know."

On December 14, six days after the attack on Pearl Harbor, the ground crew camouflaged the *Pacific Clipper* and loaded various spare parts and supplies, including a crated engine and a barrel of engine oil. The first leg of the journey, albeit backtracking, landed at Nouméa, New Caledonia, to pick up Pan Am employees and their families, twenty-two in all, who had to leave their belongings behind. "It was pretty traumatic for those people, but they had to admit that it was better than falling into the hands of the Japanese," the captain said.

The big clipper unloaded the Nouméa employees and their families in Gladstone, Australia, before flying on to Port Darwin in northern Australia, "crossing some of the most desolate country one could find anywhere," Fourth Officer Steers recalled. He described

Port Darwin as "one of the toughest spots we ever saw." According to Steers, a shipment of beer had arrived that day and the town had metamorphosed into a free-for-all, like the Wild West of American folklore. So concerned was the crew about the clipper's safety that it remained tied up to buoys away from the dock with two guards posted.

While Port Darwin slept off the night's fun, the clipper set out early the next morning for Surabaya, Java. Though the captain had instructed the US consulate in Port Darwin to notify Dutch authorities of the clipper's upcoming arrival, the message had gotten "tied up in red tape." As the clipper neared, American-made Brewster F2A Buffalo fighter planes, flown by the Royal Netherlands East Indies Army Air Force, intercepted and flanked the clipper on its approach, unable to identify the large seaplane. Worse, the clipper's radio could receive but not transmit on the frequency used by the fighter planes. Fortunately, just seconds before firing, one of the fighters flew above the clipper and spotted a partially effaced US flag on one wing that the crew hadn't completely scraped away. A superior ordered the pilots to hold their fire but remained suspicious as the fighters escorted the clipper in for a landing. But the clipper's danger wasn't over. "It turned out that we had landed right in the middle of a minefield and [the men on the launch that came out to lend a hand] weren't going to come near us until they saw we were through it."

Once safely moored at Surabaya, Capt. Ford ran into an old friend, Willard "Jess" Reed, whose wife and infant child had just evacuated. Jess threw Ford and his crew a cocktail party that evening, sharing stories about flying and their mutual hometown of Cambridge, Massachusetts.

From Surabaya, the *Pacific Clipper* flew across the Java Sea, through the Sunda Strait into the Bay of Bengal, then along the southwest coast of Sumatra headed for the harbor at Trincomalee on the northeastern side of Ceylon (now Sri Lanka). As the *Pacific Clipper* neared Trincomalee, the captain ducked below the clouds looking for landmarks to get his bearings. No sooner had the clipper cleared the clouds over the Bay of Bengal than the captain spotted a Japanese submarine that had surfaced directly below them. The submarine's deckhands raced for their deck gun and spun around to take aim, but at 150 mph and with a pull of the yoke, the *Pacific Clipper* disappeared into dense clouds.

It was around this time that Capt. Ford learned that the Japanese had captured Surabaya, killing the Dutch officers he'd just met, including, sadly, his old friend Jess who'd thrown the crew a party. If Ford and his crew hadn't taken off when they did, they could have been among the dead. "All night I kept thinking sadly of [those lost]," Capt. Ford recalled.

After spending Christmas in Trincomalee repairing an engine damaged from using low-octane automobile gasoline, the clipper took off and flew 1,500 miles across India to the Gulf of Oman and over the water to Karachi (now in Pakistan). The men checked into the Carleton Hotel that afternoon for decent meals and deep tub baths—both welcome amenities.

The *Pacific Clipper* took off once again, this time for Khartoum, crossing the Arabian Desert despite being warned to fly around it. "The Saudis had already caught some British fliers. . . . The natives had dug a hole, buried them in it up to their necks, and just left them," the captain remembered. Despite the warnings, the captain flew the clipper above the clouds over a long stretch of the desert, which wasn't a suitable place for a flying boat regardless of the hostile Saudis. "We flew for several hours before there was a break in the clouds below us," the clipper's captain continued, "and damned if we weren't smack over the [Great] Mosque of Mecca! I could see the people pouring out of it. They were firing at us, but at least they didn't have any antiaircraft guns."

The crew was delighted to finally spot water—the Red Sea. Once across the Red Sea, they maintained a course westward above the sand dunes of Anglo-Egyptian Sudan that seemed to undulate like waves across the ocean. The clipper then followed the Nile until it split into the Blue Nile and White Nile, landing on the ancient tributary outside of Khartoum and spending New Year's Eve anchored on the river. The next day, they lifted off from the Nile, their first takeoff of 1942, and traveled to Leopoldville (now Kinshasa) in the Belgian Congo where Pan Am was building a base. Fourth Officer Steers wrote in his log that "Leopoldville is just 4 degrees off the equator and hot as blazes." Fortunately for the hot and thirsty crewmen, Pan Am had stationed a handful of employees there who passed out ice-cold beer. "That was one of the high points of the whole trip," the captain recalled.

From Leopoldville, the *Pacific Clipper* made its longest hop—twenty-four hours and 3,583 miles over the Atlantic Ocean to Natal, Brazil, in South America. They flew north to Trinidad, where they refueled, and then the weary men flew up the East Coast of the United States to LaGuardia Field in New York. Capt. Ford approached the marine terminal in darkness on January 6 at 5:54 a.m. He radioed the control tower:

"LaGuardia Tower, Pan American Clipper NC18602, inbound from Auckland, New Zealand, Capt. Ford reporting. Due arrive Pan American terminal, LaGuardia, seven minutes."

The tower control operator had not received advance notice from Pan Am or the military and didn't believe that it was possible for a Pan Am clipper from New Zealand to be landing in New York. He informed Capt. Ford that the seaplane base in Bowery Bay was closed until 7:00 a.m.—another hour. After a month and 31,500 miles grappling around the globe against all odds, the *Pacific Clipper* and all aboard were forced to circle above New York for another hour until given clearance to land.

Unlike the hot and humid air of the Amazon, when landing at LaGuardia Field "the water splashed up on the sea wings and froze solid," Fourth Officer Steers recollected in his notes. "The hawser [rope] on the buoy was like a chunk of ice. Coldest weather in the world." The fourth officer was almost right, because the *New York Times* reported the weather on January 6 to be: "The coldest temperature of the Winter—10 degrees at 8:30 A.M.," and that wasn't accounting for the chilling wind gusts across the bay. As the captain and his crew disembarked from the plane that had been their home for a month, they didn't bother dropping to the ground to kiss it. It was frozen solid. Instead, the men wrapped themselves in blankets to be met by Pan Am's Atlantic Division Manager John Leslie and Public Relations Director William Van Dusen, as well as a number of military intelligence officers who rushed them inside the terminal.

"He was gone for nearly six weeks," recalled Fourth Officer John Steers's wife, Mary. "When the good news finally came, that they arrived in New York and they were safe, you can imagine, it was a glorious day."

The *Pacific Clipper*'s flight set several world aviation records: (1) the first round-the-world flight by a commercial plane; (2) the longest continuous trip ever made by a commercial plane; (3) the first round-the-world flight by a plane following a route near the equator; and (4) the first aerial crossing between New Caledonia and Australia.

The *Pacific Clipper* also compiled additional statistics during its single trip that were simply astonishing during that era of aviation—an era that just four years earlier had witnessed Amelia Earhart notoriously fail at her attempt to fly around the world in a specialized airplane. The flight (beginning from Treasure Island) had required one month and four days (Dec. 2 to Jan. 6); had touched all but two (Europe and Antarctica) of the world's seven continents; had crossed three oceans; had made eighteen stops under the flags of twelve different nations; had spent 209½ hours in the air, including the longest nonstop flight in Pan Am's history at that time (3,853 miles from a port in West Africa to the northeast coast of South America); had crossed the equator six times; had flown 6,026 miles over desert and jungle country; and had flown 8,500 miles over territory new to

Pan Am's planes. All accomplished without the benefit of advanced weather reports or sea bases where the clipper could be properly fueled and serviced according to Pan Am's standards. In fact, mechanics on the grueling flight had scavenged for parts and even fashioned their own tools to keep the big plane flying.

If not for the recently declared wars, the *Pacific Clipper* crew would have likely been given a tickertape parade along lower Broadway in New York City, just as aviation pioneers Lindbergh and Earhart had received. But now there were thousands of American heroes, like those fighting in the Pacific and soon to be fighting in Europe. Men like 1st Lt. George Gannon, who posthumously received the Medal of Honor for giving his life on Midway Atoll; Chief Aviation Ordnanceman Johnny Finn, who received the Medal of Honor for courageously firing at Japanese fighters and bombers on Oahu while being wounded twenty-one times; and even Pan Am employee Waldo Raugust, who chose to drive the wounded on Wake Island to the hospital rather than escape aboard the *Philippine Clipper*, and who was captured and imprisoned for his efforts. Still, Capt. Ford and the crew of the *Pacific Clipper* had accomplished something truly heroic and remarkable, akin to orbiting the Earth two decades later.

Fourth Officer John Steers's son Steve Steers recalled later: "This was only my father's second trip with Pan Am, and it was a trip he talked about all his life. The older he got, the more strongly he came to look back on it as one of the defining moments in his life, . . . It's only later, looking back, that we can see how historic and heroic what they accomplished really was."

# CHAPTER 42

# THE EXCHANGE

Safely evacuated from Hong Kong, the exhausted *Hong Kong Clipper* crew found themselves in Namyung in the middle of the night, except for Capt. Ralph who had taken a separate CNAC flight directly to Chungking. They were escorted to a small, overcrowded "hotel" where the men shared a single room. Four men slept in a bed while two slept in chairs, rotating from bed to chairs throughout the night. "Instead of something soft to sleep on," First Radio Officer Mel Orton remembered, "they had ceramic pillows," a tradition begun in the Sui Dynasty to keep the slumberer's head cool. Another crew member recalled being offered nothing but cabbage soup to eat.

Although the CNAC pilots had grown accustomed to such primitive accommodations, Pan Am crews had not. They regularly stayed in the finest hotels and ate three- and four-course meals when traveling. Worse, the crew's bags had burned inside the strafed *Hong Kong Clipper* and their current lodging boasted few amenities. Without soap, razors, combs, and brushes, the men quickly grew whiskers and a strong odor not becoming of Pan Am crew members like those flaunted in the airline's brochures.

There wasn't much to do in Namyung besides hide during the frequent blasts from air raid sirens. The *Hong Kong Clipper* crew members just sat around, played cards, and talked with crews of CNAC planes that flew in and out. Unlike in Hong Kong, hardly anyone spoke English. One night, after finishing off more cabbage soup, the clipper's crew retired to their bed and chairs for sleep. "Someone came by and woke us up," First Officer Strickland remembered. "I thought, 'Well, they're going to take us out and shoot us' . . . because we were loaded into an old hearse." The hearse turned out to be nothing nefarious, simply Namyung's version of an airport shuttle. "They took us out to the airport and we got on a plane and I asked, 'Where are we going?' Nobody knew . . . we were just going."

They were going to Chungking, China, inside a CNAC Douglas DC-3. The CNAC planes had evacuated all that they could from Hong Kong—275 persons, including about 100 children. It was no longer safe to return for more. In just three days of fighting, the Japanese had fought their way across the New Territories to the Kai Tak Airport gate; so much for the Hong Kong governor's prediction of the defense of the Kowloon Peninsula lasting a month. All of Hong Kong fell within just eighteen days. The CNAC had no choice but to move its base from Hong Kong to Chungking.

After flying for three hours, the DC-3 with the Pan Am crew aboard descended into the Yangtze Gorges, comprised of three very scenic but remote gorges that span almost two hundred miles. All that anyone could see from the plane's windows were jagged mountains that soon gave way to steep riverbanks, hundreds of feet high. The CNAC pilot cut the engines near the confluence of the Jialing and Yangtze rivers, and the DC-3 glided in for a landing. The plane touched down and bounced roughly along a two-thousand-foot cobblestone runway scratched out on a sandbar in the middle of the Yangtze River—the Sanhupa Airport. It was an incredible oddity. Yellow water carrying silt from inland China rushed through the gorge on both sides of the sandbar where the plane now rested among a handful of shacks.

A wooden footbridge led across an eddy of the river from the runway to the base of a gray rocky cliff. Above the rocky cliffs lay the old walled city of Chungking. The city had become Generalissimo Chiang Kai-shek's provisional capital of the Republic of China,

CNAC plane parked at the Sanhupa Airport on a sandbar in the middle of the Yangtze River. Gregory Crouch, *China's Wings*.

which caused the city to be a prime target for Japanese bombing raids. The Japanese advance had caused the primitive city to swell beyond its bounds to over two million people; people who had to suffer frequent incendiary bombing without any retaliatory or air defense forces.

As those onboard the CNAC DC-3 stepped out onto the sand-and-cobblestone runway, sedan-chair bearers raced up and placed their chairs at the feet of each of the passengers, motioning for them to sit. With a carrier in front and another in back with a pole over each shoulder, a line of chair bearers carried the *Hong Kong Clipper* crew up some 250 steps carved into the cliff wall.

Chungking, China, around the time of the *Hong Kong Clipper* crew's escape. Gregory Crouch, *China's Wings*.

The clipper crew met up with their captain in Chungking. Some stayed at a three-story hotel called Shu Teh Gunza, which was larger, but similar in discomfort, to the hotel in Namyung. CNAC pilot Hugh Woods not-so-affectionately described it as "a dirty, filthy, rat-infested dump." Others stayed in the cellar of the Chaling House. The two hotels would be the crew's home for three weeks. They'd sleep at the hotels and, to avoid more cabbage soup, they'd eat most of their meals at a CNAC hut on the Yangtze River sandbar that served decent food. At night, the men played poker and shot craps. Women were available for anyone who dared. In time, they found themselves celebrating Christmas, feasting "on three ducks that the pilot of another outfit" had purchased on the street. New Year's Day passed in similar fashion.

At last, on January 2, the moment had come for the crew to leave Chungking. They'd received word that Pan Am's *Capetown Clipper*, a Boeing B-314A assigned to the Atlantic, would be in Calcutta, India, during the first week of January, trekking back to New York. It had delivered tires and parts for Chennault's Flying Tigers, which the *Philippine Clipper* had tried to do when it was attacked at Wake Island.

The CNAC DC-3 took off from the cobblestone runway and slowly climbed above the steep cliffs of the gorge. The Pan Am crewmen looked out the plane's windows and rejoiced as the Chinese city that had been their custodian for almost a month faded into the mountains. This would be the first leg of a route all the way to New York that was similar to the one the crew of the *Pacific Clipper* used once it had reached China—Kunming; Lashio; Calcutta, Karachi; over Ethiopia and the Horn of Africa to the Gulf of Aden at the tip of the Arabian Peninsula; Khartoum; Leopoldville; Lagos; over the Atlantic to Natal, Brazil; Belém on the mouth of the Amazon River; Port-of-Spain in Trinidad; and finally unceremoniously landing at LaGuardia Airport in New York City at 6:30 p.m. on January 9, 1942. Thirty-three days had passed since the Japanese had destroyed their *Hong Kong Clipper*.

The crew of the long-gone *Hong Kong Clipper* was painstakingly interviewed in New York by US military intelligence. After questioning, the men shied away from reporters. They wanted to telephone loved ones and get some much-needed rest. Pan Am would give the men two weeks off before requiring them to climb aboard another clipper. Until then, they would have a "do-over" for Christmas and New Year's and savor their time with family during a period when the world's future was uncertain, as theirs had been for thirty-three days. But now they could stretch out to relax on a couch or bed with soft feather pillows, and feast on ham, turkey, dressing, and all the trimmings with their families—minus the cabbage soup.

---

Just three days after the *Pacific Clipper* had arrived in New York City, the crew of the destroyed *Hong Kong Clipper* had landed there, too, aboard the *Capetown Clipper*. Both were incredible feats of travel under the harshest of conditions. But the passengers who had intended to board the *Hong Kong Clipper* on the morning of the attack were still stranded in Hong Kong, shielding themselves from relentless bombing while awaiting the inevitable. They wouldn't have to wait long. The Japanese took the Kowloon Peninsula and tightened their grip on Hong Kong Island. The British would surrender on Christmas Day, 1941—thereafter called Black Christmas.

With more than two million citizens and refugees in Hong Kong, Japanese soldiers couldn't toss everyone into internment camps. Most Hong Kongese carried on as usual, subject to random robbery, harassment, and assault. The British, Canadian, Indian, and Chinese soldiers who'd surrendered their weapons became prisoners of war. The Japanese conquerors then rounded up political prisoners. Thousands were executed, and thousands more were interned in prison camps and tortured. For British, American, and Dutch expatriates, they were imprisoned on the Stanley Peninsula in the southwest corner of Hong Kong Island, about ten miles from the city itself.

Most were taken to Camp Stanley straightaway, though there were some, such as diplomats, journalists, and foreign businessmen like Hank Marsman, who were held in hotels under guard until being imprisoned later. Rather than celebrating Christmas with their families, Marsman and others staying at the Repulse Bay Hotel were forced, on Black Christmas, to march ten miles to barges that ferried them across Victoria Harbor to the Kowloon Peninsula. From there, they were herded into the Kowloon Hotel, where they would be held on the fourth floor under guard until being transferred to Camp Stanley. The Kowloon Hotel, a second-rate lodging that had been looted of most of its furnishings and amenities, stood within sight of the luxurious Peninsula Hotel now used by the invaders as the Japanese High Command headquarters. Marsman shared his room with four others, including *Detroit News* journalist Gwen Dew and United Press correspondent Richard Wilson. The windows had been thickly papered over. Only a chair, mattress, and remnants of pleasantries remained in the room. Each of those inside were provided five tablespoons of rice each day and drank from a common pail of water until Marsman's Chinese friends on the outside began smuggling food in for him and his roommates.

Life under such conditions continued for a month until the time had come to move the Kowloon Hotel prisoners to Camp Stanley. Doing as their shouting captors ordered, everyone nervously shuffled with bowed heads into lines outside the hotel, including Marsman. Prodded by the bayonets of grinning soldiers, they commenced loading onto barges that would carry them across the harbor back to the Hong Kong Island side. It was while preparing to climb aboard a barge that Marsman sneaked away and returned to the hotel, where he remained hidden for hours. Dew, Wilson, and the others continued on the barge to Camp Stanley. When Marsman resurfaced, the former Manila resident convinced a Japanese officer that he was Filipino due to his knowledge of the Philippines. As such, he obtained a pass to reconnoiter about the city, where he met with prosperous Chinese friends and plotted his escape. When a Japanese military hearing to review Marsman's nationality neared, he decided the time had come to run. "Marsman," he said to himself, "this is the toughest spot in fifty years of tough spots, but you're going to make it . . . never doubt that."

Incredibly, Marsman was able to obtain 125,000 Hong Kong dollars from wealthy Chinese friends (about $31,500 USD, equal to $625,000 today). "There were friends and more friends," Marsman recalled. "It seemed that nobody could do enough for me." One of those friends volunteered his nephew to guide Marsman 650 miles to Chungking. The nephew utilized an intricate Chinese underground that involved miles of walking, hiding, and paying or bribing guerilla guides, sampan and barge boatmen, bandits, and truck drivers until Marsman finally crossed into a Chinese-controlled area. From there, he boarded a train to Kweilin (now Guilin) about 300 miles inland. Then, much like the *Hong Kong Clipper* crew had done in Namyung, Marsman caught a CNAC plane that carried him to Chungking. After procuring additional assistance from friends and higher-ups in Chungking, CNAC and British planes carried him to Lashio, Karachi, Calcutta, and Cairo. In Nigeria in March 1942, Marsman boarded the camouflaged *Pacific Clipper*, which had been conscripted into the Atlantic service with a new crew. The clipper carried him across the Atlantic to Brazil and then north along the American coast to New York City. Marsman's wife, Mary, and daughter, Anne, who'd been contacted while he was en route, traveled from San Francisco and met him at LaGuardia Airport on March 28—110 days after he'd sipped coffee on the terrace of the Repulse Bay Hotel when the bombing of Hong Kong first began.

"I was a little late for Christmas," Marsman wrote, "but in time for a plenty happy Easter."

Most weren't as fortunate as the well-connected Dutch businessman flush with gold. Folks like Joe Alsop Jr., Richard Wilson, George Dankwerth, Phillip Harman, and Gwen Dew were still imprisoned at Camp Stanley. During that time, Japanese atrocities mounted, from indiscriminate murders, theft, beatings, starvation, and widespread rape to organized torture and executions. Those in the camp would have to suffer until the Japanese surrendered on August 15, 1945 (August 14 in the US).

But during the summer of 1942 (and again in 1943), a hand-picked group of diplomats, foreign journalists, businessmen, missionaries, and their families would be released as part of a prisoner exchange. According to the agreed-upon rules of exchange, prisoners from Hong Kong would board the Japanese ship *Asama Maru* and cast off on June 26 for Lourenço Marques on the Portuguese East African coast (now Maputo, capital of Mozambique). Once docked, the prisoners would then disembark and board the MS *Gripsholm*, which had carried Japanese diplomats and other repatriates to the same Portuguese city.

Phillip Harman, the tennis player who'd been among the beaten and tortured at Camp Stanley, recalled disembarking from the *Asama Maru* pursuant to the exchange: "When my feet touched the ground of neutral Lourenço Marques, I knelt and pressed my lips to the earth and muttered some incoherent little prayer of thankfulness."

Harman also recalled the joy of strolling about Lourenço Marques and visiting cafes and shops and buying a few items, like decent clothing to wear, before he was due on the MS *Gripsholm* that evening. He described walking into the Hotel Palano, the most luxurious hotel in the city, to write and mail a letter to his sweetheart. It was there that he noticed an elegantly dressed and coiffed Japanese man standing in the lobby. "I realized that he was Mr. Saburō Kurusu!" Harman wrote. "It seemed hardly possible that I was gazing at one of the arch traitors of all times . . . a man who would go down in history as the betrayer of all that was decent and right."

Despite the fact that Harman's disdain for Kurusu was shared by most in the free world at that time, Kurusu would ardently maintain for the remainder of his life that he had not known of the oncoming attack. "It must seem absurd to you," he later told a reporter for the International News Service, "but it's true. The militarists kept their secret extremely well." In his memoirs, former Secretary of State Cordell Hull said he believed that Ambassador Nomura, with whom

Kurusu worked, did not know of the oncoming attack. And Maj. Devereux later wrote, "I felt in talking to [Kurusu] that he hoped sincerely to avoid trouble between the United States and Japan."

But on that July 1942 day in the Palano Hotel lobby, there was no question in Harman's mind that Kurusu was evil. Harman walked up to the former special envoy who'd disembarked from the MS *Gripsholm* and drew his attention. "Mr. Kurusu . . . I was beaten nearly to death by the Japanese soldiers in Hong Kong and practically starved to death in your concentration camp at Stanley. . . . Tell me, were you tortured and beaten in America while you were waiting to be returned to your country . . . were you slapped and kicked like an animal?" Without answering, Kurusu slipped off and lost himself in a crowd in the hotel's lobby. He would board the *Asama Maru* on its return voyage to Japan, but he would be returning to a much different Japan than the one he had departed on the *China Clipper* in November 1941. His country would face the misery of a war it had started and ultimately a weapon never unleashed on a people anywhere on the planet before or since—the atomic bomb.

Gwen Dew, who'd also been exchanged at Lourenço Marques that same day, recalled her experience when she left fellow prisoners behind at Hong Kong. "Our hearts insisted on throbbing in our throats . . . as we went from friend to friend saying goodbye, for how long we did not know. For some, forever."

Once aboard the *Asama Maru* at Hong Kong, Dew looked into the faces of friends and strangers who were going home. Their faces reflected expressions of dull joy, afraid that at any moment the exchange would fail to happen and they'd be returned to a Japanese prison camp. "Among us were . . . men and women who were held in solitary confinement for months, barred from all communications with the outside world, with nothing to read, the floor on which to sleep, electric lights in their eyes at night." She described that many, including journalists, had been subjected to water torture, wrapped in barbed wire, slapped with bamboo, choked, and shocked with live electric wires.

Gwen Dew shared Phillip Harman's disdain for their captors and those being exchanged who'd been treated extraordinarily well by the US State Department. She expressed that there was "something enraging" about the difference in treatment of the Japanese and American prisoners. The Japanese diplomats, like Kurusu, businessmen, and newspapermen had been confined to "one of the most expensive hotels in the United States and received a large daily amount of spending money . . . with golf, tennis, and luxurious quarters." Dew also pointed out that while the treatment of those aboard the *Asama Maru* hadn't been much better than at Camp Stanley, the Japanese on the *Gripsholm* had "full privileges of the boat . . . the bar was open and the [Japanese] consumed 40,000 cases of beer; they had baths, laundry, movies, good food and service . . . yet always complained about something."

Much of Dew's bitterness melted away, however, and was replaced by unparalleled delight when she spotted several tankers and freighters arrive in Delagoa Bay that would be part of the MS *Gripsholm* convoy carrying her to New York. She described her feeling when she first observed them anchored in the harbor:

Flying from the mast of the first [ship] was the most beautiful sight the world could offer to our eyes—the Stars and Stripes floating proudly, gloriously, and freely in the winds of the sea! It was our first sight of it in eight months, and it represented all that we had been dreaming about so long—home, family, traditions, [and] standards of civilized living.

## CHAPTER 43

# REVENGE

A sole plane touched down on the deck of the *Akagi* around one o'clock that December 7 day, returning from a mission that had set in motion so many terrible things. Cmdr. Fuchida had been one of the last to return. He'd led the first wave of bombings on Pearl Harbor, and despite his plane having been hit several times by antiaircraft fire, Fuchida had continued to circle over the harbor until the second wave had completed its bombing runs.

"The air crews waiting impatiently for my return rushed to welcome me," Fuchida recalled. They patted him on the shoulders and back and shouted and cheered. He was their hero, and had instantly become a national hero.

When Fuchida returned to Japan aboard the *Akagi*, the Emperor of Japan wished to see him at his palace—an extraordinary honor. "I showed and described to him aerial photographs we had taken. His Majesty looked at the photos with great interest, turning them vertically and horizontally. Our allotted time was thirty minutes, but we ended up spending one and a half hours."

In addition to Fuchida, all of Japan considered Adm. Yamamoto a hero, "even a god-like admiral," Fuchida recalled. After all, it was his bold plan that had crippled the US Pacific Fleet. There was no more talk of his assassination from military radicals; only glorification. Yamamoto now planned other bold attacks to conquer the Pacific. Before he could claim new victories, however, the United

States surprised and embarrassed not only the great Adm. Yamamoto but Japan's Prime Minister Tōjō and his military machine. In a secret mission, the United States did what Japanese leaders said could never be done—bombed Tokyo. The bombing of the Japanese capital and five other military sites just four months after the attack on Pearl Harbor was led by Lt. Col. James "Jimmy" Doolittle in an effort to boost American morale and disgrace Japanese military arrogance. It worked.

To redress his public shame, Yamamoto immediately planned a retaliatory raid on Midway Atoll that would not only capture the US island base but lure the US aircraft carriers and battleships out of Pearl Harbor and into a Japanese trap. He believed that the large Japanese task force, similar in size to that which had attacked Pearl Harbor, would deal another devastating blow to the United States that would leave Hawaii open to capture and the North American West Coast vulnerable to attack. Thereafter, Americans would lose their willingness to fight in the Pacific, allowing Japan to move freely about the ocean and conquer at will. It would be the knockout punch that the attack on Pearl Harbor had failed to deliver.

Perhaps Yamamoto's plan could have worked, but US intelligence intercepted and decoded Japanese messages outlining the attack plan. Instead of Japan setting a trap in the Pacific, the United States did. The Battle of Midway in June 1942, just six months after Pearl Harbor, ended in disaster for Yamamoto and the Empire of Japan. Four of the six aircraft carriers in the Japanese fleet that had staged the air attack against Pearl Harbor (the other two were in drydock for repairs and couldn't take part in this battle)—*Akagi*, *Kaga*, *Sōryū*, and *Hiryū*—were all sunk, along with a heavy cruiser. Japan lost 3,052 men compared with the US loss of 362. The huge naval losses changed the tide of the war in America's favor, a debacle from which Japan would never recover.

Cmdr. Fuchida had been aboard the *Akagi* during the Battle of Midway. Assigned to lead the air attack as he'd done at Pearl Harbor, he instead had an emergency appendectomy aboard ship and was relegated to observing the battle from an upper deck. He watched helplessly as US bombs hit the *Akagi* and eventually sank her along with the other three carriers. Fuchida, who'd also sustained a broken leg during the attack, was among the survivors evacuated to neighboring ships. "This was the turning point, as the momentum in the Pacific War was reversed by this loss," Fuchida wrote.

The following year, after intercepting messages that Adm. Yamamoto would be aboard a plane heading to a Japanese base in the Solomon Islands, the United States implemented "Operation Vengeance" explicitly to shoot down Yamamoto's airplane. US Army Air Force P-38 fighter planes did just that in April 1943, killing the mastermind of the strike on Pearl Harbor. Upon learning of Yamamoto's death, Fuchida, who was then instructing pilots at the Japanese Naval Academy, "lost interest in engaging in any further . . . battle lessons . . . [because since] ancient times, the death of the leader of our entire force in action meant nothing short of defeat in the war."

In July 1944, Vice Adm. Nagumo commanded the Imperial Japanese Navy in its defense of the Japanese-held island of Saipan. Nagumo had led the Imperial Japanese Navy's carrier attack on Pearl Harbor. With the United States tightening its grip on Saipan, Nagumo committed suicide rather than suffer the shame of capture at the hands of his enemies.

A year later, Fuchida narrowly escaped the atomic blast that annihilated Hiroshima when he left the city one day before the horrific explosion. Though he lived to see the Japanese surrender firsthand aboard the USS *Missouri* in Tokyo Bay, he discovered that after the war, rather than remaining a hero, he was among those shunned by his countrymen. He was labeled a "professional soldier" and considered one of those responsible for Japan's having become a warmongering nation and for bringing death, destruction, and dishonor upon them.

"All the friends I had in the world cast me aside," Fuchida recalled.

Unable to obtain work, the brave and skilled pilot once hailed as a hero for leading the air attack on Pearl Harbor became "a peasant farmer with only three-quarters of an acre of land" and a hut for his family built by his own hands.

Nearing the end of his rope, Fuchida would convert to Christianity and eventually travel about the United States telling his story with Billy Graham and other well-known evangelical leaders of the time. He'd also meet US presidents like Truman and Eisenhower, and then vice-president Nixon, as well as US military icons like Nimitz, MacArthur, and Doolittle. He'd continue his travels, delivering his message about Christianity and speaking of the ills of war, even at the Pentagon and the US Naval Academy, where most wished to hear his firsthand account of the raid he'd led on Pearl Harbor that had started a war. He was warmly received.

"I enjoyed the friendly hospitality of worthy rivals during the Pacific War—just like the saying: 'Yesterday's enemy is today's friend.'"

## CHAPTER 44

# NEW YORK

View from atop Chrysler Building that housed Pan Am's headquarters. Pan Am
Historical Foundation, R. Fulton Collection.

Pan Am CEO Juan Trippe sat in his office and stared down at a report
from the US Navy as gigantic art deco stainless steel eagles stared
down at the city from each corner of the Chrysler Building. He'd

canceled all speaking engagements during December and into January and refrained from making public statements. Only his wife was noted for her charitable work during the Christmas holiday. Trippe and others at Pan Am constantly monitored all war developments that were of instant concern to Pan Am's operations, not only those across the Pacific and Atlantic Oceans but in Alaska, Africa, and Latin America. The whereabouts of the clippers still making their way home, as well as US military defense strategy, "made it imperative that every member of the company's personnel know what was happening and act accordingly." Thankfully, the *Anzac*, *Philippine*, and *Pacific Clippers* safely returned to the United States with their crews and the rescued Pan Am employees, as well as the crew of the strafed and burned *Hong Kong Clipper*.

Trippe's attention then turned to salvaging his airline—determining those routes Pan Am could continue to fly and those he had to give up, and which planes Pan Am could keep and which would go into military service. Pan Am lost its Boeing and Martin flying boats to the US military, which had wasted little time requisitioning them that December. The United States possessed only eleven B-24 bombers convertible to cargo use, which made Pan Am's flying boats extremely important to the war effort. The flying boats could traverse oceans with Pan Am's skilled crews at their helms, trained not only as pilots but as experts in navigation, radio, and meteorology.

The US government purchased Pan Am's planes for more than Pan Am had paid for them and then leased the planes back for one dollar so that Pan Am could operate and maintain the planes on behalf of the government. The US Navy received the Martin M-130 *China* and *Philippine Clippers* and the Boeing B-314 *Honolulu Clipper* that would continue to operate in the Pacific, primarily flying military brass to and from Pearl Harbor. The Navy also received the Boeing B-314 *Yankee*, *Dixie*, and *Atlantic Clippers* that continued operating over the Atlantic Ocean, along with the B-314A *Pacific Clipper* that had remained in New York following Capt. Ford's trek around the world. The US Army Air Forces procured the Boeing

B-314A *Anzac* and *California Clippers*, designating them C-98s, and moved the big seaplanes from the Pacific to the Atlantic Ocean, where they joined the *American* and *Capetown Clippers*; eventually they'd be transferred to the US Navy. Most of the planes on the Atlantic side shuttled men and materiel to West Africa, where they'd assist the Allies in the war against the Germans and Italians. As the war dragged on and the United States built more military transport planes and runways, the US Navy loaned a few of the clippers back to Pan Am to resume scheduled commercial flights.

The crews of the big flying boats were also transferred to the military. Most Pan Am crews were not drafted into the regular army or navy, but into the Naval Air Transport Service and the US Army Air Forces Air Transport Command where the crews exchanged their crisp Pan Am uniforms for khaki fatigues. Along with the services of Pan American Air Ferries Inc. and Pan American Airways-Africa Ltd., Pan Am made thousands of ocean crossings flying millions of miles ferrying men, lend-lease planes, and cargo to aid in the fight. Pan Am had already been training US Army Air Forces and Royal Air Force navigators in Miami to navigate the Pacific and Atlantic Oceans. Pan Am would be paid tens of millions each year during the war for its services, while earning millions more from its surviving commercial routes to Alaska, Mexico, South and Central America, and the Caribbean.

During this time, Pan Am CEO Juan Trippe not only continued to use the only flying boats at his disposal—the medium-range Sikorsky S-42s—to service commercial passenger routes from Miami throughout Latin America, but he also increasingly used unpressurized land planes like the Douglas DC-3 and later the DC-4. He also tried out a new plane, the Boeing B-307, dubbed the Stratoliner. It was the first pressurized commercial aircraft in use anywhere in the world that could fly passengers above wind gusts and storms, reducing the number of cancellations due to bad weather. With a range of 1,250 miles, however, it was not capable of spanning oceans but worked well for flights south of Miami.

Trippe principally had his eye on another pressurized plane that soon would carry passengers across the Pacific and Atlantic Oceans; and it would not be a flying boat with spacious dining rooms and passenger berths. The foresighted Trippe realized that with the war in the Pacific and in Europe, runways were being constructed seemingly on every island, in every valley, and on every mountaintop. Even Pan Am's own subsidiary, Pan American Airports Corporation, had contracts with the military to build runways and airports, which kept Mac busy. That meant that after the war, Pan Am would not have to rebuild the quaint Pan American Airways hotels on Midway and Wake or hire back hotel stewards and matrons to greet passengers of large flying boats with ice-cold drinks on Guam and Canton Island. At most, those islands would become mere refueling stations for pressurized land planes.

The plane that Juan Trippe truly desired was the Lockheed Constellation. Pan Am placed an order for forty such planes. With pressurized cabins, fifty-four seats, and the ability to fly over ocean squalls and typhoons at 345 mph and arrive at its destination in just hours, the Model L-749 Constellation would become the commercial airplane of choice. Although delivery of the Constellations would be delayed until after the war, the die had been cast. The golden age of the big, luxurious flying boats that had been interrupted on December 7, 1941, would come to an unceremonious end after the war. Pan Am completed its final flying boat flight on April 8, 1946, when the *American Clipper* landed in San Francisco from Honolulu. The future of aviation now lay in faster planes with more seats and inexpensive fares, and the Constellation would be just the beginning for Pan Am and its competitors.

———

Just days before the attack on Pearl Harbor, Clare Boothe Luce wrote in the November 1941 issue of *Life* magazine after having returned aboard the *Honolulu Clipper* from Hong Kong:

*For years from now people will look back upon a Pan American Clipper flight of today as the most romantic voyage of history.*

Indeed, the big flying boats had epitomized romance, elegance, and luxury in the air as well as adventure for those who embraced the novel form of international travel. And for those on the *Anzac, Hong Kong, Pacific,* and *Philippine Clippers* that fateful day in December 1941, romance and luxury transformed into a harrowing nightmare they'd not forget for the rest of their lives—lives that fortunately weren't cut short like so many others that December.

# EPILOGUE

From its inauspicious beginning with a ninety-mile mail route from Key West to Havana in 1927 to its close of business in 1991, Pan Am was the flagship of US international air travel, representing American capitalism and innovation to the entire world. Today, most remnants of Pan Am can only be found in museums and people's memories, or perhaps in film and television. Wake Island, Midway Atoll, and Canton Island are no longer tourist layovers with hotels, swimming pools, and tennis courts. They have become ghost islands ruled by gooney birds and hermit crabs amid rusted metal and crumbling concrete pylons, used occasionally by the US military for some obscure project, like the latest plan to install defensive missiles.

Of Pan Am's three Glenn Martin M-130 flying boats, all are gone. Besides the *Hawaii Clipper*, which disappeared between Guam and Manila in 1938, the *Philippine Clipper* crashed into a foggy California mountainside in 1943, killing all onboard. Two years later, the *China Clipper* ruptured its hull when it struck a submerged object, sinking off the coast of Trinidad. Only a propeller of the *China Clipper* is displayed at the Air and Space Museum in the Smithsonian and at SFO Aviation Museum and Library in San Francisco.

All of Pan Am's Boeing B-314 flying boats are gone too. The *Yankee Clipper* crashed in Lisbon, Portugal, in 1943, killing several

USO men and women. In 1945, the *Honolulu Clipper* developed engine trouble and made an emergency landing in the Pacific, only to be scuttled by the US Navy. After the war, the War Assets Administration sold the *American*, *Atlantic*, *Pacific*, *Dixie*, *Anzac*, *Capetown*, and *California Clippers* from a San Diego drydock for use by other airlines or for replacement parts. By 1952, all had been sold for scrap metal. None survive.

Juan Trippe's airline began calling itself Pan American World Airways in 1943, officially changing its name in 1950. Pan Am continued its innumerable firsts, like pressurized cabins, tourist-class seating, jets, 747s, computerized reservations, satellite messaging, and many others. Pan Am had grown into a conglomerate of not only its vast airline, but also Intercontinental Hotels, Forum Hotels, commercial real estate, business jets, helicopter service, and even a guided-missile range division. The airline hit its peak in the 1960s and early 1970s, at a time when many of the flying-boat captains were still pilots, albeit of Boeing 707 jets.

Pan Am's financial troubles began with the purchase of a large fleet of Boeing 747s not long before the 1973 OPEC oil embargo crippled the US airline industry and the world's economies. Pan Am attempted to merge with a domestic airline like Eastern, American, or United Airlines to boost its bottom line, but the Civil Aeronautics Board denied permission, believing it might contribute to a Pan Am monopoly in the skies. Deregulation of the US airlines industry in 1978 created huge problems for Pan Am. With no more government control of airline routes, any domestic airline that was capable could fly internationally, thereby severely cutting into Pan Am's revenues. Again, Pan Am attempted to enter the domestic market, this time by buying National Airlines, but that did not end well for either carrier.

To stay in the air, Pan Am commenced selling its land-based assets, such as the Pan Am Building, at one time the largest commercial building in New York, and its Intercontinental Hotel chain. When that wasn't enough, Pan Am cut wages, laid off employees, restructured debt, and sold routes and planes. Just about the time it appeared as if the airline might become profitable again, a terrorist bomb exploded in 1988 aboard Pan Am Flight 103 over Lockerbie, Scotland, ending 270 lives as well as Pan Am's chances of survival. Lawsuits and FAA fines cost Pan Am an estimated $500 million and precipitated the airline's decision to finally declare bankruptcy in 1991. Delta Airlines purchased most of Pan Am's remaining assets.

Juan Trippe had retired in 1968 and died in 1981, not living to see the death of the airline that he practically created single-handedly sixty-four years earlier.

When I was a boy, jet planes and space rockets provided excitement and wonder. With NASA's Apollo space program gobbling up the headlines and the fronts of cereal boxes, Pan Am began accepting flight reservations to the moon as part of a First Moon Flights Club, loosely planned for takeoff in the year 2000. "If anybody ever flies to the moon, the very next day Trippe will ask [the Civil Aeronautics Board] to authorize regular service," a former head of the Civil Aeronautics Board said before the first moon landing. This futuristic plan was incorporated into the 1968 film *2001: A Space Odyssey,* when the Pan Am *Orion III* space clipper traveled to the space station at the beginning of the film. I'd like to believe that had Pan Am's corporate destiny turned out favorably, I would have boarded a space clipper flight to the moon by now, complete with a drink tailored to my destination, like a Full Moon Martini, perhaps.

# ACKNOWLEDGMENTS

I am exceedingly grateful to my agent, Richard Curtis, with Richard Curtis Associates Inc. in New York City. He's a nice man and a knowledgeable and patient agent. I'm also grateful to Ryan Smernoff at Turner Publishing Company in Nashville, Tennessee, for believing in this project. Moreover, I appreciate the comments of Edward Trippe, a son of Pan Am founder Juan Trippe, who graciously read an early version of my manuscript.

During my research, I visited the Cradle of Aviation Museum at Garden City, New York; the SFO Aviation Museum and the National Archives Research Center in San Francisco; the Library of Congress, the Air & Space Museum at the Smithsonian, and the National Archives Research Center in Washington, DC, and in College Park, Maryland; and the University of Miami for its Pan American Airways Collection, the HistoryMiami Museum, and the Pan American Seaplane Base and Terminal Building in Miami.

I thoroughly enjoyed listening to recordings and reading transcripts of interviews with former pilots and crew members. My favorite part of researching was speaking and corresponding with family members of crews and passengers. Almost all proved helpful, courteous, and supportive throughout this project. They are proud of their grandfathers, fathers, uncles, and so on, and rightfully so. The men were pioneers of the sky during an age when the modern-day Oregon Trail meant flying over vast oceans in new and hopefully reliable machines thousands of feet above seemingly bottomless oceans. An overused comparison of Pan Am's clipper pilots is to Apollo astronauts, but the comparison is not necessarily far-fetched. The *China Clipper* made the flight in 1935 only eight years after Lindbergh's solo flight across the Atlantic, at a time before computers, satellite weather reports, pressurized cabins, and jet engines, where much of the Pacific Ocean was claimed by a hostile Empire of Japan.

# INTERVIEWS

I appreciate the time and generosity of those who spoke with me and replied to my messages without hesitation. They are incredible people. It's because everyone was so wonderful and kind to me that it is difficult to mention any one person above the others, but there were a few individuals who went above and beyond in my estimation. And though I thanked them at the time, I will gladly thank these amazing individuals once again:

Jane Barnett, daughter of Edward Barnett, Flight Engineer, *Philippine Clipper*.

Phillip A. Cooke, son of John Cooke Jr., Wake Island airport manager, evacuated on *Philippine Clipper*.

Terry Joan Dean, daughter of Edward Barnett, Flight Engineer, *Philippine Clipper*.

Bonnie Gilbert, granddaughter of Harry Olson, construction supervisor on Wake Island; author of *Building for War*.

Jock Hamilton, son of John Hamilton, Captain, *Philippine Clipper*.

Peter Hrutky, son of Ted Hrutky, First Radio Officer, *Philippine Clipper*.

Richard Hrutky, son of John Hrutky, Second Officer, *Philippine Clipper*.

Thomas Hrutky, son of John Hrutky, Second Officer, *Philippine Clipper*.

Sally Lacy Leonard, daughter of Edward Randolph Lacy, *Anzac Clipper* passenger.

Michael Mullahey, son of William Mullahey, "Mr. Pacific" and Auckland airport manager.

Monica Orton, daughter of Melvern Orton, First Radio Officer, *Hong Kong Clipper*.

John B. Parrish III, son of John B. Parrish Jr., Second Officer, *Pacific Clipper*.

Ronnie Sue Pfeiffer, daughter of Edward Randolph Lacy, *Anzac Clipper* passenger.

William Poindexter, son of John Poindexter, First Radio Officer, *Pacific Clipper*.

Gary Relyea, son of Charles Relyea, Purser, *Philippine Clipper*.

Grey Sellers, grandnephew of Cecil "Pop" Sellers, killed aboard *Samoan Clipper*.

Steve Steers, son of John D. Steers, Fourth Officer, *Pacific Clipper*.

Karen Marlow Torres, daughter of Doreen Frances Marlow and granddaughter of Frank "Mac" McKenzie, Pan Am engineer and *Philippine Clipper* passenger.

Dennis I. VanderWerff, PhD, friend of Cecile and Edward Barnett, Flight Engineer, *Philippine Clipper*.

I'd also like to acknowledge a 95-year-old man who witnessed the Massacre of Nanking atrocities as a boy. He remains nameless because it is still too painful after 85 years to discuss his experiences with me—a stranger. My request did, however, open up a dialogue between his son and him about those terrible memories he'd never before shared.

# RESOURCES

Tomohiko Aono, Registrar, SFO Museum, San Francisco International Airport, San Francisco, CA.

Elena Drayer, Department of Defense, United States Marine Corps, Pentagon, Washington, DC.

Molly Fulton, Public Services Manager, The John P. Holt Brentwood Library, Brentwood, TN.

Bonnie Gilbert, author of *Building for War*, containing information about Harry Olson and Pearl Harbor.

Michael Heinl, whose father, Jr. Lt. Col. Robert D. Heinl, wrote *The Defense of Wake: Marines at Midway* in 1947.

Nicola Hellmann-McFarland, Library Technician & Research Assistant, Otto G. Richter Library, University of Miami, Coral Gables, FL.

Suzanne Isaacs, Community Manager, National Archives Catalog, National Archives and Records Administration (NARA), Washington, DC.

Ivan Johnson, Chief, Reference Service Branch, NARA, College Park, MD.

Tom McAnear, Archivist, NARA, Washington, DC.

Doug Miller, Pan Am Historical Foundation, San Francisco, CA.

Nathaniel Patch, Archivist, NARA, College Park, MD.

Kevin Reilly, Archives Technician, NARA, New York City, NY.

Amy Reytar, Textual Reference Operations, NARA, College Park, MD.

Debbie Seracini, Archivist, San Diego Air & Space Museum, San Diego, CA.

Clay Skaggs, Archivist, NARA, San Francisco, CA.

Jay Sylvestre, Special Collections Librarian, Otto G. Richter Library, University of Miami, Coral Gables, FL.

Julie Takata, Curator-in-Charge of Collections Management, SFO Museum, San Francisco International Airport, San Francisco, CA.

Heather Thomas, Reference Librarian, Serial & Government Publications, Library of Congress, Washington, DC.

Vanderbilt University Library, Nashville, TN.

N. Adam Watson, Photographic Archivist, State Archives of Florida, Tallahassee, FL.

Alisa M. Whitley, Branch Head and Archivist, Archives Branch, USMC History Division, Alexandria, VA.

# NOTES

---

## PREFLIGHT BRIEFING

"There was a time": Lynwood Mark Rhodes, *American Legion Magazine*, "Those Magnificent Clipper Flying Boats," Vol. 99, No. 2, August 16, 1975, 20.

## PROLOGUE

"spread her silver wings": *San Francisco Chronicle*, "Giant China Clipper Hops for Manila," November 23, 1935, 1.

"World Pauses to Watch Sailing": *Times* (San Mateo, CA), November 22, 1935, 1.

"suggestive of the experience": *San Francisco Examiner*, November 22, 1935, 15.

"rivals the vivid imagination of Jules Verne": *Miami Herald*, "Roosevelt Praises Flight Over the Pacific," November 23, 1935.

"Like a hurricane out of nowhere": Mitsuo Fuchida, *From Pearl Harbor to Calvary*, 1953.

## CHAPTER 1: DESTINATION HONOLULU

The Golden Gate International Exposition celebrated the modern industrial West, including the recent completion of the Golden Gate and the San Francisco-Oakland Bay bridges. The nation had two competing world's fairs in 1939 and again in 1940, the principal one in New York City and the smaller one in San Francisco. Only New York's was sanctioned by the Bureau of International Exhibitions.

"[Like all the big Boeings] it is an elegant operation": *Richmond News Leader*, "Great Silver Bird," December 24, 1965.

"You'd holler": San Francisco Airport Commission Aviation Library Louis A. Turpen Aviation Museum, Oral History Program Interview Transcription: Sam John Toarmina, February 26, 1999 (SFOM Interview).

"You would be amazed": Bonita Gilbert, *Building for War: The Epic Saga of the Civilian Contractors and Marines of Wake Island in World War II*, 101.

"The Clippers have been the best international club": *Life*, "Life Flies the Atlantic: America to Europe in 23 Hours by Clipper," Vol. 8, No. 23, June 3, 1940, 17.

"A Clipper departure": *Pan American World Airways Teacher*, "By Flying Clipper to Australia and New Zealand," 1950, 2; University of Miami Libraries Special Collections—Pan American World Airways Inc. Records (U. Miami PAA).

"A Clipper had a personality": *American Legion Magazine*, "Those Magnificent Clipper Flying Boats," 20.

"Her interior was like": H. R. Ekins, *Around the World in Eighteen Days and How to Do It*, 1936.

Norman Bel Geddes was the father of actress Barbara Bel Geddes, who starred in film alongside Henry Fonda and James Stewart and most famously played Miss Ellie in the television soap opera *Dallas*.

"Setting the dining room": SFOM Interview: Sam John Toarmina.

"For a while everyone": *Life*, November 3, 1941, 99.

"Far behind us": Dorothy Kaucher, *Wings over Wake*, 14.

"Most of the time": Pan American Airways, "Your Clipper Trip," 1947, 4; U. Miami PAA.

"As roomy as the [zeppelin] Hindenburg": Ekins, *Around the World in Eighteen Days*.

CHAPTER 2: TROUBLE BREWING

"When carriers are not heard": Hearings before the Joint Committee on the Investigation of the Pearl Harbor Attack, Part 23, Proceedings of Roberts Commission, 1946, 659.

"I realize the difficulty": *Daily News* (New York), November 16, 1941, 41.

"I wish I could break": *The Boston Globe*, November 15, 1941, 1.

"the Government of Japan": US Department of State, Office of the Historian, Document 409, "Document Handed by the Secretary of State to the Japanese Ambassador (Nomura) on November 26, 1941."

"If this is the idea": US Department of State, "Papers Relating to the Foreign Relations of the United States, Japan, 1931–1941," Vol. II, 765.

"So long as the United States": *Philadelphia Inquirer*, November 29, 1941, 6.


CHAPTER 3: EAT, READ, AND DOZE

"PR chore": Ed Dover, *The Long Way Home: A Journey into History with Robert Ford*, 31.

"Presently you turn away": *Life*, November 3, 1941, 99.

Behind the cockpit, separated by a black curtain, was a gargantuan 9-foot × 21-foot operations room that included a 7-foot-long navigator's table in front of a panel jam-packed with sensitive instruments, the radio officer's station, and the flight engineer's station.

"Riding the Clipper": Gilbert, *Building for War*, 119.

"The food on the Clippers": *The Akron Beacon Journal* (Akron, Ohio), "The Roving Reporter," April 8, 1941, 12.


CHAPTER 4: PARADISE OF THE PACIFIC

"Paradise of the Pacific": *Pan American World Airways Teacher*, "By Flying Clipper to Hawaiian Islands," October 1955; U. Miami PAA.

"Red lights on high standards": *The Age* (Melbourne, Victoria, Australia), "Bright Lights & Gay Streets—Pearl Harbor Last Friday Night," December 12, 1941, 4.

The international banker and his wife were Louis and Caroline Cullings. He was VP of the First National Bank in New York (now part of Citibank), who'd headed the bank's foreign departments in India, Singapore, Sydney, Australia, and later Tokyo. Intriguingly, Mrs. Cullings would soon join the Office of Strategic Services (the OSS, the predecessor of the CIA), where she served not as a secretary, as was common at that time, but to conduct intelligence operations in the interior of China.

"And we were all prepared": "Clippers Turned Back—First-Hand Accounts of John Cooke, Bob Ford and Robert Hicks," Pan Am Historical Foundation, 1992.

"There was always lots": Autobiography of Henry (Hank) Anholzer, 1997, updated 2002.

"Aviation in itself": *Nashville Banner*, "Banner Publisher Sees Great Boon in Clipper Service," October 21, 1936, 8.

"Flying [on a clipper]": Ibid.

"Pan Am and I are old friends": *Look*, "A Visit with Hemingway," September 4, 1956, 24.

"We had the cream": Sanford B. Kauffman, *Pan Am Pioneer: A Manager's Memoir*, 45.

The original route called for the clippers to fly from Honolulu to Kingman Reef and American Samoa and then to Auckland (Britain would not grant an American airline landing rights in Australia at that time). Trippe selected Pan Am's number one master pilot, Capt. Ed Musick, to survey the proposed route. Musick's name was second only to that of Charles Lindbergh as an aviator. Musick flew a stripped-down Sikorsky S-42 called the *Samoan Clipper*. On his return trip to the United States, Musick discovered an oil leak minutes after taking off from Pago Pago. Knowing that he couldn't return with a seaplane full of gasoline, the master pilot hit the switch to dump fuel. The plane exploded, practically incinerating the plane and the six-man crew on board. It is believed that a faulty release valve caused fuel and vapors to seep onto a red-hot engine or into the fuselage, which was filled with sparking electrical connections.

CHAPTER 5: NEW YORK—PAN AM'S HEAD OFFICE

Being of Northern European descent, Juan Trippe never liked the name Juan and preferred being called J. T. He was the son of a wealthy investment banker. Living in New York City and spending his summers in East Hampton, a ten-year-old Trippe witnessed Wilbur Wright circle his aeroplane around the Statue of Liberty on September 29, 1909. Trippe never shook the wonder of that short flight. Later, Trippe walked away from his career on Wall Street and gathered some of his family's money and that of his enormously rich Yale buddies, such as Cornelius Vanderbilt "Sonny" Whitney (a descendant of both cotton gin inventor Eli Whitney and railroad and shipping tycoon Cornelius "The Commodore" Vanderbilt), and later William Rockefeller. After a few airplane company failures, Trippe became president of Pan American Airways System in 1927.

"the heaviest traffic": *San Pedro News-Pilot* (California), December 1, 1941.

"I could see that": *New York Times*, July 12, 1991, D5.

"My father saw an opportunity": *New York Times*, July 13, 1997, 8.

"They don't want a flying boat": William Stephen Grooch, *From Crate to Clipper with Captain Musick, Pioneer Pilot*, 133.

"Whether you wish": Lynn M. Homan and Thomas Reilly, *Images of Aviation: PAN AM*, 68.

"For total mileage": *Life*, "Juan Trippe: Pan American Airways' Young Chief Helps Run a Branch of U.S. Defense," October 20, 1941, 111.

"It's a stewardess": Pan American Airways, *Clipper News*, Vol. II, No. 1, January 14, 1941; U. Miami PAA.

"Trippe's astonishing ability": *Life*, "Juan Trippe," October 20, 1941, 116.

## CHAPTER 6: A REGULAR FELLA

The flight marked the *China Clipper*'s 174th voyage across the Pacific Ocean, covering roughly 1.23 million miles over open water—an astounding record for the time. Famous for opening the air route to the Far East six years earlier, it was unknowingly closing that same route for Pan Am's flying boats forever.

"[I am] usually happy": Gilbert, *Building for War*, 123.

"the nicest vacation": Ibid., 118.

"My window looks out": Ibid.

"Maxim Litvinoff [*sic*] is stretched": Ibid., 194.

## CHAPTER 7: DANGER IN THE VACANT SEA

"vacant sea": *The Atlantic*, "Pearl Harbor in Retrospect," July 1948.

## CHAPTER 8: ON TO MIDWAY

Those onboard the *Philippine Clipper* were Captain John Hamilton, First Officer William Moss, Second Officer John Hrutky, Third Officer Elwood Leep, Engineer Officer Edward Barnett, First Radio Officer Don MacKay, Second Radio Officer Theodore Hrutky, Flight Meteorologist Walter Nobs, Purser/Steward Charles Relyea, and passengers Frank McKenzie, 2nd Lt. Albert J. "Ajax" Baumler, Sgt. Henry Willcox, Lt. Col. John Tamraz, Maj. Thomas Harper, Freeman Hollis, Julius Ficke, Richard Hall, and Walter Smith.

"The heating": Pan American Airways, "Your Clipper Trip," 1947, 4; U. Miami PAA.

"he was a man of blue": Interview with Gary Relyea, September 29, 2021.

"Certain colors are conducive": Pan American Airways, "Color Engineer Decorates Planes," Vol. 7, No. 2, March 1936, 7; U. Miami PAA.

"jockey-sized youngsters": *New Horizons*, "Catering Aloft," February 1941, 27; U. Miami PAA.

"The job has always been considered": Ibid.

Six years earlier, two Japanese had attempted to sabotage the *China Clipper* at Treasure Island the night before its inaugural flight in November 1935.

"fiend that presides over all": Tobias Smollett, *The Adventures of Peregrine Pickle*, 1751.

"This black ball rose": SFOM Interview, Sam John Toarmina, 19.

"A good, capable man": Robert J. Cressman, *A Magnificent Fight: The Battle for Wake Island*, 2013.

"The young gooneys": William Stephen Grooch, *Skyway to Asia*, 68.

"a quaint colonial style inn": Kaucher, *Wings over Wake*, 25.

Jack Bramham was being relieved by Freeman Hollis, who'd been one of four Pan Am employees who'd disembarked from the *Philippine Clipper* that day.

### CHAPTER 9: YAMAMOTO'S PLAN

"sink to the extent that": Gordon W. Prange, *At Dawn We Slept: The Untold Story of Pearl Harbor*, 16.

"so difficult and so dangerous": Ibid., 19.

"The Division of Naval Intelligence places": Ibid., 33.

"If there were ever men": *The Honolulu Advertiser*, February 1, 1941, 1.

The America First Committee had around 800,000 members, mostly Republicans, many of whom possessed anti-Semitic and pro-German penchants, such as the group's highly celebrated spokesman Charles Lindbergh, who had visited Adolf Hitler three times since 1936. Though a good friend of Juan Trippe and an adviser for Pan Am, Lindbergh made statements viewed as pro-Nazi that kept him from being accepted as an officer or director of the airline.

### CHAPTER 10: THREE MORE CLIPPERS IN THE PACIFIC

The flight crew of the *Pacific Clipper* was composed of Captain Robert

Ford, First Officer John Henry Mack, Second Officer/Navigator Roderick Norman Brown, Third Officer James G. Henriksen, Fourth Officer John Delmer Steers, First Engineer Homans K. "Swede" Rothe, Second Engineer John Bertrand "Jocko" Parrish Jr., Chief Flight Radio Officer John "Jack" D. Poindexter, First Radio Officer Oscar Hendrickson, Third Radio Officer Eugene Roy Leach, Flight Meteorologist George D. Linklater, Flight Steward Barney Sawicki, Flight Steward Verne C. Edwards, and Flight Supernumerary Wilfrid E. Lessing.

The tiny isle of Palmyra Atoll had also been added only as a refueling stop between Honolulu and Canton Island.

"As we neared Suva": Sir Harry Luke, *From a South Seas Diary 1938-1942*.

"The colors are truly kaleidoscopic": *Pan American World Airways Teacher*, "By Flying Clipper to Australia and New Zealand," 1950, 2; U. Miami PAA.

"the place Adam and Eve": Pan American Airways "Dear Señor" Letters, Vol. 6, No. 20, December 7, 1941, 86; U. Miami PAA.

"One of the memorable hotels": James A. Michener, *The World is My Home: A Memoir*, 28-29.

Great Britain claimed the tiny uninhabited island of Canton Island as its own and forbade Pan Am from landing there. The United States dusted off the Guano Act of 1856 that stated that any US citizen who discovered bird manure (for fertilizer) on an unoccupied island could claim possession of the island on behalf of the United States. The United States immediately dispatched a handful of men to the atoll to scoop up bird droppings and place them aboard their boat flying the Stars and Stripes. The British government called it a ruse, but they had little recourse. Trippe had already received permission from the US Navy to send the SS *North Haven* to the island loaded with workers and construction materials to build a Pan Am base. The two countries settled on a unique joint ownership called an "Anglo-American condominium."

The flight crew of the *Anzac Clipper* was composed of Captain H. Lanier Turner, First Officer Edward F. Sommers, Second Officer Aubrey Lanham Charman, Third Officer Guy McCafferty, First Engineer Edward B. Abarr, Second Engineer R. H. Sanders, First Radio Officer Walter H. Bell, Second Radio Officer Charles John Wertman, Flight Steward Thomas Vincent O'Leary, Flight Steward Aubrey E. Harris, and Flight Supernumerary J. C. McDonald.

"The dream of aviators, businessmen": *South China Morning Post*, 1936.

Pan Am's ownership in CNAC was 45 percent; the Republic of China owned the other 55 percent.

The shuttle departed Manila every Sunday and Tuesday, flying to Macao and Hong Kong, and returning from Hong Kong (skipping Macao) every Monday and Wednesday. The Portuguese colony of Macao added twenty minutes to the flight. The *Hong Kong Clipper* simply tied up to buoys and unloaded passengers and freight at Macao without the crew members ever stepping off the plane.

Singapore had been added as a destination in May 1941.

The Sikorsky S-42B, registered NC16735, had completed its inaugural flight just seven weeks earlier in September, having replaced the previous *Hong Kong Clipper* S-42 that had flown the route since 1937. It would have been the clipper's eleventh roundtrip shuttle flight between Hong Kong and Manila. The S-42 was used primarily in the Caribbean, Alaska, and South America and, starting in 1937, shuttled passengers between Manila and Hong Kong. This particular S-42B had been in each of those places, starting out as the *Bermuda Clipper*, and then renamed the *Alaska Clipper*, before receiving its final moniker, the *Hong Kong Clipper* (sometimes called the *Hong Kong Clipper II*).

CHAPTER 11: NEXT HOP—WAKE ISLAND

"Actually there was little": Robert Hotz, *Way of a Fighter: The Memoirs of Claire Lee Chennault*, 105.

"tragedy of homesickness": *Brooklyn Times Union*, January 23, 1934, 3.

"I can stand the pain no longer": *Daily News* (New York), February 14, 1934, 6.

"shrub trees, brush and jumbled masses": Grooch, *Skyway to Asia*, 90.

"How the captain could find": Catherine Cotterman Hoskins, "A Dream Come True," 2007.

"Pan American . . . also functions": *Life*, "Juan Trippe," October 20, 1941, 111.

"Traveling on the Flying Clippers": *The Pacific-Alaska Flying Clippers*, "Wake Island," 1948, 7; U. Miami PAA.

Hamilton began working for Pan Am in 1933 as a mechanic at Pan Am's Miami marine base. By 1939, he'd worked his way up not only to pilot but to master pilot. A "Master Pilot of Flying Boats" at Pan Am had to be able to do the job of everyone onboard: pilot, navigator, radio officer, engineer, and even mechanic. A year afterward, Hamilton transferred to San Francisco to fly clippers across the Pacific Ocean.

On the Christmas 1937 flight of *Philippine Clipper*, the steward dressed as Santa Claus, showing the children onboard that Santa made stops everywhere, including moving airplanes over the Pacific Ocean.

### CHAPTER 12: FINAL PREPARATIONS FOR X DAY

"Young boys of the flying crews": Mitsuo Fuchida (translated by Douglas T. Shinsato and Tadanori Urabe), *For That One Day: The Memoirs of Mitsuo Fuchida, Commander of the Attack on Pearl Harbor*, 54.

### CHAPTER 13: BOAT DAY

"Boat day in Hawaii": *Knoxville News-Sentinel*, February 19, 1938, 7.

"The clipper leaves at noon": Bill McWilliams, *Scrimmage for War*, 2019, 16.

CHAPTER 14: WAKE ISLAND

"give those watching": SFOM Interview: John W. Strickland.

"This ecstasy of greeting": Kaucher, *Wings over Wake*, 108.

"These arrivals were the Wake Island": James P. S. Devereux, *The Story of Wake Island*, 15.

"I would walk down": Interview with Phillip Cooke, September 12, 2021.

"Wake sits on top": Eugene J. Dunning, *Voices of My Peers: Clipper Memories*, 144.

"Wake Island is a queer place": Gilbert, *Building for War*, 130.

"The beach is dazzling": Ibid., 62.

"[A young Chamorro man] bowed": Kaucher, *Wings over Wake*, 41.

"smelled as clean as the trade winds": Ibid., 42.

"It was fantastic": Ibid., 45.

"guaranteed to be free": W. Scott Cunningham, *Wake Island Command*, 37.

"Everywhere there was sound": Ibid., 38.

"being where the action is": Interview with Terry Dean, November 13, 2021.

"They proposed that I join": Oral History: William Justin Mullahey, Outrigger Canoe Club, an interview by Kenneth J. Pratt, May 9, 1980.

"The dock crew was intrigued": Grooch, *Skyway to Asia*, 111.

CHAPTER 15: PREPARATION FOR ISLAND INVASIONS

"malignant campaign": US Department of State, Office of Historian, "Papers relating to the Foreign Relations of the United States, Japan, 1931–1941," Vol. II, 778.

"this isn't getting us anywhere": United States Diplomatic Papers 1941, Volume IV: The Far East. Department of State Publication 6325.

"We [the United States] aren't looking": Ibid.

"This means war": *New York Times*, February 16, 1946, 1.

"No, we can't do that": Report of the Joint Committee on the Investigation of the Pearl Harbor Attack, 1946, 217.

CHAPTER 16: THE *PACIFIC* AND *ANZAC CLIPPERS*

"Spent most of the afternoon": Dunning, *Voices of My Peers*, 128.

"an old-fashioned shabby": *Courier-Mail* (Brisbane, Australia), May 24, 1941, 4.

"dazzling white motor yacht": Ibid.

In 1935, Heagney wrote a book titled *Are Women Taking Men's Jobs* and dedicated it to "the women of all lands whose aspirations and organization for equal status, equal pay and equality of opportunity are embodied in . . . women's work." She also would write a revolutionary book called *Equal Pay for the Sexes* before the decade was out. Heagney was quoted as saying "No longer can we adopt the viewpoint that a job is only an episode in a woman's life, and that marriage will be her career." She would die in poverty.

The previous owner of the yacht had been the late Cyrus Curtis, owner of the Curtis Publishing Company, whose successful publications at that time included *Ladies' Home Journal* and the *Saturday Evening Post*.

"I had wanted to drop in": Jim Slade, *Forty Minutes to Pearl*.

The crew slept on the upper level of the plane behind the cargo hold, on canvas cots lined side by side. Each crew member strapped a seatbelt across his midriff to prevent injury while he slept.

"As the moon shines": Diary entry of Edward Randolph Lacy, provided to author by daughters Ronnie Sue Pfeiffer and Sally Lacy.

CHAPTER 17: LOAD THE TORPEDOES

"At 39, my spirit was great": Fuchida, *For That One Day*, 54.

"We pray for our good fortune": Ibid., 83.

CHAPTER 18: GRIDIRON

"The Biggest Game": *Honolulu Advertiser*, December 3, 1941, 11.

CHAPTER 19: SEA SERPENTS

"'midget' submarines": US Navy, Naval History and Heritage

Command, "Japanese Midget Submarines Used on the Attack on Pearl Harbor," www.history.navy.mil.

## CHAPTER 20: FRIENDLY FIREWORKS IN HONG KONG

"I clippered to and from": Jan Henrik Marsman, *I Escaped from Hong Kong*, 5.

"fabulously rich and white-bearded": Ibid., 10.

"A thousand guests were invited": Gwen Dew, *Prisoner of the Japs*, 16.

"Hong Kong of yesterday": Marsman, *I Escaped from Hong Kong*, 5.

"Sunday was always a busy day": Dew, *Prisoner of the Japs*, 18.

## CHAPTER 21: TAKING OFF TO GUAM

## CHAPTER 22: CLIMB MOUNT NIITAKA

"Hawaii seems to be just like a rat": Prange, *At Dawn We Slept*, 463.

## CHAPTER 23: A LATE WARNING

"at 1:00 p.m. on the 7th your time": US Department of State, "Papers Relating to the Foreign Relations of the United States: Japan, 1931–1941," Vol. II, 786.

"If the negotiations with": Prange, *At Dawn We Slept*, 368.

## CHAPTER 24: THE CALM

"We had all been out": Gilbert, *Building for War*, 197.

## CHAPTER 25: TORA! TORA! TORA!

"The overwhelming sight": Fuchida, *For That One Day*, 83.

"We have to measure": Ibid., 86.

"I think it will work": Ibid.

"In my flying togs": Ibid.

"We flew through and over": Ibid., 89.

"I was full of enthusiasm": Ibid., 87.

"dropped depth charges": US Navy, Naval History and Heritage Command, National Museum of the US Navy, Action Report USS *Ward*.

"If things had been prearranged": Fuchida, *For That One Day*, 90.

"To, To, To": Ibid., 93.

"Tora! Tora! Tora!": Ibid., 94.


CHAPTER 26: THE STORM

"I awoke at six": Gilbert, *Building for War*, 197.

"I heard all this noise," Ibid.

"Nobody knew what was going on": McWilliams, *Scrimmage for War*, 27.

"found people standing outside": *Daily Independent* (Murphysboro, IL), January 15, 1942, 5.

"AIR RAID, PEARL HARBOR": Franklin Delano Roosevelt Presidential Library and Museum, Radio Alert, Doc. #1, received 1:28 p.m. in Washington, DC.

"HOSTILITIES WITH JAPAN COMMENCED": Ibid., Doc. #2.

"Like a hurricane out of nowhere": Fuchida, *From Pearl Harbor to Calvary*.

"As I observed the damage": US Naval Institute Proceedings, "I Led the Air Attack on Pearl Harbor," Vol. 78/9/595, September 1952.

"Suddenly a colossal explosion": Ibid.

"As my group made": US Naval Institute Proceedings, Ibid.

"Shortly after I left the house": Gilbert, *Building for War*, 197.

"Hello, NBC. Hello, NBC": *PBS News Hour*, "Hear the Breaking News Report from Pearl Harbor, 75 Years Later," Dec 7, 2016.

"sink to the extent that it could not": Prange, *At Dawn We Slept*, 16.


CHAPTER 27: ROOSEVELT RECEIVES WORD

"Mr. President": Franklin Delano Roosevelt Presidential Library and Museum.

"No!" *CBS News*, "Pearl Harbor: How FDR Responded to the 'Day of Infamy,'" December 4, 2016.

"We interrupt this broadcast": *Washington Post*, "WAR! How a Stunned Media Broke the Pearl Harbor News," December 6, 2011.

President Roosevelt received Soviet Ambassador Litvinov at the White House in the early afternoon of Monday, December 8. The president had just returned from the Capitol, where he had delivered his iconic address. Litvinov recalled that the president appeared "fatigued and preoccupied." Roosevelt had subtly inquired about a second front in the Pacific and if the USSR would "participate" in the war with Japan. A formal reply would come three days later—"It is impossible at present for us to go to war with the Japanese and we are forced to assume a position of neutrality." The United States would go it alone in the Pacific, while continuing to send billions of dollars in aid to the Russians and the British. *The American Experience in World War II: The Atomic Bomb in History and Memory* (Walter L. Hixon, editor, introduction), Vol. 8, 2003, 263.

Nearly 350,000 American women served in uniform, both at home and abroad, volunteering for the newly formed Women's Army Auxiliary Corps, the Navy Women's Reserve, the Marine Corps Women's Reserve, the Coast Guard Women's Reserve, the Women Airforce Service Pilots, the Army Nurses Corps, and the Navy Nurse Corps. They worked in office and clerical jobs, drove trucks, served as mechanics, radio operators, and lab technicians, rigged parachutes, and flew military aircraft across the US.

**CHAPTER 28: PLAN A**

"DECEMBER 7, 1941 EXECUTIVE MEMORANDUM 71": U. Miami PAA.

"President Roosevelt called Juan": Betty Stettinius Trippe, *Pan Am's First Lady: The Diary of Betty Stettinius Trippe*, 149.

"From that fateful Sunday on": *New Horizons*, "News Vigil," Vol. 12, No. 4, January 1942, 10; U. Miami PAA.

"a last minute system-wide coverage": Ibid., 11.

"Guam lost. One S-42 lost": Robert Daley, *An American Saga: Juan Trippe and His Pan American Empire*, 508.

**CHAPTER 29: THE *PACIFIC* AND *ANZAC CLIPPERS***

According to the fourth officer's flight log, the trip from Nouméa to Auckland took seven hours and forty-three minutes.

John "Jack" Poindexter was the First Radio Officer. He had filled in for a sick radioman for what Poindexter had thought would be a short flight from San Francisco to Los Angeles and back.

The trainee was Eugene Leach. "I had completed some modifications on radio equipment . . . at Nouméa . . . and was proceeding to Auckland." Dunning, *Voices of My Peers*, 112.

"About an hour out": Ibid.

"Radio operator listening in": Original log provided by Phillip A. Cooke; Dunning, *Voices of My Peers*, 133.

"At first, no one could": Dunning, *Voices of My Peers*, 128.

"It seemed incredible": Navy Times, *Aviation History Magazine*, December 21, 2018.

"The captain silenced the radio": Dunning, *Voices of My Peers*, 128.

"Our orders for future action": Ibid., 99.

"'Plan A' meant a lot": *Evening Sun* (Baltimore), December 15, 1941, 27.

Three Pan Am employees had departed from the plane earlier.

"an unusually low altitude": *Rodney and Otamatea Times* (New Zealand), December 10, 1941, 4.

"I had gone down below": Slade, *Forty Minutes to Pearl*.

"The island of Oahu": *Star Advertiser* (Honolulu, HI), December 14, 2014; *Honolulu Star-Bulletin*, January 4, 1936; KGMB station manager, Webley Edwards.

"[The first radio officer] informed me": Slade, *Forty Minutes to Pearl*.

"We were constantly on the alert": *San Bernardino Sun*, December 10, 1941, 4.

Captain Turner later told reporters: "We then followed a predetermined plan to land at an alternate port after making certain by radio that the alternate port was all clear." *Morning News* (Wilmington, DE), December 10, 1941, 6.

"We landed cautiously": Slade, *Forty Minutes to Pearl*.

"there was no panic": *San Bernardino County Sun*, December 10, 1941, 4.

CHAPTER 30: NO THOUGHT OF SURRENDER

In addition to the "Massacre of Nanking," the atrocities are also referred to as the "Rape of Nanking."

The crew of the *Hong Kong Clipper* consisted of Captain Fred Ralph, First Officer John W. Strickland, Second Officer Harry H. Shaw, Flight Engineering Officer Guy E. De Wees, Flight Radio Officer Melvern Orton, Meteorologist Wayne H. May, and Steward David Featherstone. Pan American personnel on the trip were Flight Meteorologist Walter C. Houghton and accountant Arthur Lawrence.

"there must be no thought of surrender:" *South China Morning Post*, Dec. 16, 2016; *Legion Magazine*, Mar. 1, 1996; *MacLean's*, July 1, 1968.

A radiogram from Russ Clark, Pan Am's airport manager and dispatch officer in Manila, instructed Capt. Ralph not to take off for Manila. Clark knew that Pearl Harbor had been attacked, yet to avoid British censorship which would not permit the use of US coded messages, Clark had sent the vague message "something was about to happen" to Pan Am's office in Hong Kong, believing that Fred Ralph would understand its meaning.

The director of civil aeronautics at Kai Tak Airport, British Lt. Albert "Papa" Moss, instructed Ralph not to fly to Manila and revealed that Japan had declared war.

"We have had so many flaps": Mary Monro, *Stranger in My Heart*, 24.

"I was in my hotel room": *Clarion-Ledger* (Jackson, MS), December 15, 1942, 1.

"I was in the Peninsula Hotel": SFOM Interview: John W. Strickland.

"We were at the little shack": Ibid.

"We were to board the bus": Marsman, *I Escaped from Hong Kong*, 12.

"We now present you urgent": Affidavit of Morio Tateno, International Military Tribunal for the Far East, Doc. No. 2543, July 24, 1946; Department of State, Foreign Relations of the United States Diplomatic Papers, 1941, The Far East, Vol. IV, 772; "Operations in Hong Kong from 8th to 25th December, 1941," Dispatch from Lt. Gen. C.M. Maltby to Secretary of State for War on November 21, 1945; *London Gazette*, supplement, January 27, 1948, 704.

"I advised Captain Ralph": *New Horizons*, Vol. 12, No. 5, February 1942, 10; U. Miami PAA.

"I was already sitting": *News Journal* (Wilmington, Delaware), July 27, 1942, 4.

"Get out! Get out!": Marsman, *I Escaped from Hong Kong*, 13.

"We piled out": Ibid.

Thomas B. Wilson was head of the American President Steamship Lines.

"I looked out the window": Marsman, *I Escaped from Hong Kong*, 13.

"The crew and I [planned] to": *Honolulu Advertiser*, "Clipper Set on Fire in Hong Kong Attack," December 9, 1941.

"Almost immediately planes": Ibid.

"Fortunately, nobody was aboard": *New York Times*, "Clipper Attacked by Swarm of Planes," December 10, 1941, 3.

"The horror of what I saw": Phillip Harman, *Hellions of Hirohito*, 54.

"Wham! Wham! Wham!": Gwen Priestwood, *Through Japanese Barbed Wire*, 14.

"A bomb made a direct hit": Dew, *Prisoner of the Japs*, 55.

"I saw planes diving in the distance": *Oakland Tribune*, July 27, 1942, 5.

"When the Japanese commenced": SFOM Interview: John W. Strickland.

"Back came the Japanese": *New Horizons*, Vol. 12, No. 4, January 1942, 22: U. Miami PAA.

"Bullets were hitting all around": SFOM Interview: John W. Strickland.

"There were at least a dozen": *New York Times*, December 10, 1941, 3.

"From my bed, I could see": Interview of Moon Fun Chin by Mauree Jane Perry of Making History Associates, 2004.

"The planes attacked the Kai Tak Airport": *Reporter-Times* (Martinsville, IN), July 31, 1942, 2.

"I got a little courage": SFOM Interview: John W. Strickland.

"It was a heart-sickening thing": Ibid.

"Words tumbled over one another": Marsman, *I Escaped from Hong Kong*, 14.

"When I returned to the field": *Honolulu Advertiser*, December 9, 1941, 9.

"I had gone outside to watch": Soldinski, "The Last Days of C.N.A.C.," 1941.

"subversive pamphlets": Bond, *Wings for an Embattled China*, 2001.

"I found craters on the runway": *New York Times*, December 10, 1941, 3.

"We're going to take you": SFOM Interview: John W. Strickland.

"I had a cable from Clarence Young": Bond, *Wings for an Embattled China*, 272.

**CHAPTER 31: SEEKING ANOTHER VICTORY**

**CHAPTER 32: SCUTTLEBUTT**

"Ah, life—it's wonderful": Gilbert, *Building for War*, 123.

"As the Manager for Pan Am": Dunning, *Voices of My Peers*, 92.

"As I walked to my pickup truck": Cunningham, *Wake Island Command*, 46.

"It just came in from ComFourteen": Ibid.

"[The radioman] looked at me": Ibid.

"This is no drill!": Devereux, *The Story of Wake Island*, 27.

"I returned to the radio-equipped launch": Dunning, *Voices of My Peers*, 92.

"We circled, dumped about": *Sacramento Bee*, January 14, 1942, 8.

"Pearl Harbor's been attacked!": Dunning, *Voices of My Peers*, 93.

"The commandant": *San Francisco Chronicle*, December 11, 1941.

CHAPTER 33: BEHIND THE SQUALL

CHAPTER 34: EVERY MAN FOR HIMSELF

"As I left his office": *San Francisco Chronicle*, December 11, 1941.

"Hey, you guys": *Kansas City Star*, March 22, 1942, 1C.

"I plunged into a shallow trench": Ibid.

"Shortly before reaching": Dunning, *Voices of My Peers*, 93.

"At that moment": *Sacramento Bee*, January 14, 1942, 8.

"Suddenly, there was a terrific explosion": *Boston Daily Globe*, January 12, 1942, 1.

"The Chamorro workmen": Ibid.

"this is it": *Kansas City Star*, March 22, 1942, 1C.

"some of the people": *Sacramento Bee*, January 14, 1942, 1, 12.

"I had rats up my sleeves": *AIR & SPACE Smithsonian*, August/September 1989, 71.

"Bombs were going off": "Clippers Fly thru War under Fire," *Pan American Clipper*, Vol. 25, No. 24, December 1, 1966, 9: U. Miami PAA.

"sand jammed under": Interview with Jock Hamilton, November 16, 2021.

"It was every man for himself": *Kansas City Star*, March 22, 1942, 1C.

"Dad positioned himself": Interview with Gary Relyea, October 1, 2021.

"The door opened inward": *Midland Journal* (Rising Sun, Maryland), March 23, 1945, 3.

"I glanced over beside me": SFOM Interview: William Moss. Later in the war, Col. Robert L. Scott echoed that observation. "I saw Captain Baumler do some of the nerviest things I've ever seen any man accomplish." *The Record Journal of Douglas County*, Mar. 23, 1945, 3.

"The island was shrouded": *Boston Daily Globe*, January 12, 1942, 8. Mac anonymously told a *Boston Globe* reporter when he returned to the mainland.

"I couldn't even find my": *Los Angeles Times*, December 27, 1941, 5.

Wally Call, a plumber employed by Pan Am, suffered a burst eardrum from a bomb concussion. Frank Loy, another plumber, wasn't harmed but had barely escaped death: a bullet had shattered the green celluloid sunshade on the white Pan Am hat atop his head.

"His trousers were so riddled": Interview with Gary Relyea, October 1, 2021.

"Ironically . . . he was tragic witness": Pan American Airways "Dear Señor Letter," Vol. VII, No. 2, December 15, 1941, 6; U. Miami PAA.

"The Pan American staff": *Boston Daily Globe*, January 12, 1942, 8.

"machine-gunned": Devereux, *The Story of Wake Island*, 31.

"but it never had a chance": Ibid.

"It had been an utter surprise": Cunningham, *Wake Island Command*, 52.

"Everybody seemed dazed": Gilbert, *Building for War*, 203.

"If we hadn't refueled": *Kansas City Star*, March 22, 1942, 1C.

"There went the hotel": Daley, *An American Saga*, 317.

"The evacuees had been instructed": Dunning, *Voices of My Peers*, 94.

"It seemed to me an unfortunate time": Cunningham, *Wake Island Command*, 53.

"Throw everything overboard": Dunning, *Voices of My Peers*, 95.

"When the [Japanese attacked] Wake": Hotz, *Way of a Fighter*, 118.

"When we counted noses": Dunning, *Voices of My Peers*, 94.

"We are hoping to get in the air": Ibid.

"After the bombing stopped": *AIR & SPACE*, August/September 1989, 72.

"I've never regretted it": Ibid.

"It struck me as a rather drastic": Devereux, *The Story of Wake Island*, 35.

One passenger would avoid capture by boarding the clipper by "mistake"—Thomas Leo Cleary—a nineteen-year-old member of the defense contractor's crew. He'd flown to Hawaii for surgery and had returned to Wake on the *Philippine Clipper* the day before. As he went to see the plane take off, he was mistaken for a passenger and told to "come aboard." The young man didn't ask questions and jumped on the plane. He was not included in Cooke's plane manifest. No one noticed.

"It was a painful parting": *Kansas City Star*, March 22, 1942, 1C.

"It was hell to go away": *Boston Daily Globe*, January 12, 1942, 8.

"My God it's heavy": SFOM Interview: William Moss.

"Keep on throwing everything": Dunning, *Voices of My Peers*, 95.

"The Flight Engineer advised": Ibid.

"I shouted to Hamilton": Ibid.


CHAPTER 35: THE *PACIFIC* AND *ANZAC CLIPPERS*

Whereas Qantas and Tasman Empire Airways would continue flying for the moment, the governments had already commandeered planes and given priority to those flying on behalf of the military. Australia and New Zealand were more concerned about the conservation of fuel.

"I am quite sure": *The Age* (Melbourne, Victoria, Australia), "Bright Lights & Gay Streets—Pearl Harbor Last Friday Night," December 12, 1941, 4.

The first radio officer was Walter Bell.

Auckland lies on an isthmus near the tip of the North Island of New Zealand.

"Always just one hop ahead": *Australian Women's Weekly*, December 20, 1941, 7.

"We pushed [the clipper] up": Slade, *Forty Minutes to Pearl*.

"In the old days of barnstorming": Ibid.

"The premier of Burma": *The Spokesman-Review* (Spokane, Washington), "Early seaplane pilots tell tales of choppy days," September 14, 1986, 36.

"Yesterday, December 7th, 1941": Speech by Franklin D. Roosevelt, New York (Transcript), AFC 1986/022: AFS 24,312, folder 22.

"[The flight had not been] out of the ordinary": *San Francisco Examiner*, December 10, 1941, 4.

"The fact that I had delayed": Slade, *Forty Minutes to Pearl*.

Randolph Crossley had chosen to travel an hour away and stay at the Volcano House that sat on the rim of the Kīlauea Crater farther inland.

Capt. Turner placed a telephone call to Pan Am's operations manager, Bill Eldridge, at Pearl City. "I was talking to him and he was describing to me the blowup of some of our naval vessels just as if I were looking right at it." Slade, *Forty Minutes to Pearl*.

**CHAPTER 36: ESCAPE FROM HONG KONG**

"I was pretty well tired": William M. Leary Jr., *The Dragon Wings: The China National Aviation Corporation and the Development of Commercial Aviation in China*, 145.

"It took the judgment of Solomon": Theodore H. White, "China's Last Lifeline," *Fortune*, May 1943.

"We have three planes remaining": Bond, *Wings for an Embattled China*, 272.

"embattled information desk": Marsman, *I Escaped from Hong Kong*, 16.

"Staff and families fly out tonight": Gregory Crouch, *China's Wings*, 243.

"Night fell and bedlam broke loose": Zygmund Soldinski, "The Last Days of C.N.A.C. in Hong Kong," *Wings Over Asia*, Vol. II, 40.

"assassination, highway robbery": Marsman, *I Escaped from Hong Kong*, 19.

"War," Gwen Dew of the *Detroit News* wrote, "it swings its blood-drip-ping scythe, and there is death all about you. . . . It is your flag coming down and someone else's flag going up. It is crashing and violent and overwhelming. . . . Why did the Japanese want to kill Chinese by the millions, and the British and Canadians and Australians and Americans and Dutch? Why?": Dew, *Prisoner of the Japs*, 22.

"The [Japanese] pulled a gigantic surprise": Mary Monro, *Stranger in My Heart*, 24.

War correspondent Joe Alsop Jr. later claimed that his seat, the last seat, was taken by "Mme. H. H. Kung's very large, well-fed dog." Charles Schafer, the Pan Am district traffic agent in Hong Kong, volunteered to stay behind and direct the last CNAC flight out of Hong Kong.

"Under double cloak of darkness": *New Horizons*, Vol. 12, No. 5, February 1942, 10; U. Miami PAA.

"I had no idea, they just said": SFOM Interview: John W. Strickland.

In addition to the crew, Walter Houghton, a Pan Am meteorolo-gist who was vacationing in Hong Kong, hopped on the out-bound plane, as did Arthur Lawrence, a Pan Am accountant. Capt. Fred Ralph took one of the CNAC planes directly from Hong Kong to Chungking, leaving First Officer Strickland in charge of the crew at Namyung. The entire crew reunited at Chungking. SFOM Interview: John W. Strickland; *New York Times*, December 15, 1941, 10.

"as dark as the inside of a whale": *New Horizons*, Vol. 12, No. 5, February 1942, 11; U. Miami PAA.

"My husband is a resourceful man": *Pasadena Post* (California), "Escape from Hong Kong Told by American Mine Executive," March 7, 1942, 1.

"With air raid alarms, shelling, bomb explosions, antiaircraft, and sporadic fire from the looted areas making the night hideous," Marsman wrote, "sleep was hard to woo and almost never won.

But worst of all were the oppressive periods of silence in that pitch-black, crowded room—sometimes a full half hour waiting for whatever new brand of terror could come out of the night surrounding us." Marsman, *I Escaped from Hong Kong*, 19.

"We're circling some place": SFOM Interview: John W. Strickland.

The crew spotted a five-story building near the top of the gorge. The building served as CNAC's headquarters called the Pink House. It was so called because of its pink color, particularly when most structures in Chungking bore no color at all, just weathered wood or stone. The men also observed caves scattered along the side of the cliff. The depths of one cave stored parts and equipment for servicing the planes. Other caves served as bomb shelters. It was unsophisticated, almost beastlike, yet necessary due to the relentless bombing.

"Entire clipper crew now in": Bond, *Wings for an Embattled China*, 274.

"the sweetest job of flying": *Arizona Republic* (Phoenix), January 11, 1942, 2 (Section 2).

CHAPTER 37: A WILL-O'-THE-WISP

"That night and the following day": *Boston Daily Globe*, January 12, 1942, 8.

"Twenty-two pairs of eyes": Ibid.

"By this time a certain optimism": Dunning, *Voices of My Peers*, 95.

"Our spirits soared": Ibid., 96.

"Approaching Midway": SFOM Interview: William Moss.

"The burning buildings": Dunning, *Voices of My Peers*, 96.

All those onboard chipped in later and presented Capt. Hamilton with a wristwatch for delivering them to safety.

"When we landed": *Boston Daily Globe*, January 12, 1942, 8.

Branham had been relieved by Freeman Hollis, one of the four Pan Am employees who'd flown in on the *Philippine Clipper* just two days earlier.

"This time we had to take off": *Boston Daily Globe*, January 12, 1942, 8.

"Dawn came with the stench": Ibid.

"operational scenario [would] be determined": Dover, *The Long Way Home*, 58.

"The officers kept calling Honolulu": *Boston Daily Globe*, January 12, 1942, 8.

"There was speculation of a terrible disaster": SFOM Interview: William Moss.

"8 DEC 41 . . . PAN AMERICAN CLIPPER": NARA, San Francisco. RG181 Records of Naval Districts and Shore Establishments, Fourteenth Naval District.

"After eleven and a half hours": SFOM Interview: William Moss.

"PANAM CLIPPER DUE": U.S. Navy Bulletin, December 7, 1941, NARA, San Francisco, RG181, Declassified Records of Naval District and Shore Establishments, Fourteenth Naval District, Boxes 1-7.

"As we circled over it": *Boston Daily Globe*, January 12, 1942, 8.

"We could see smoke rising": SFOM Interview: William Moss.

"We flew past Ford Island": Ibid.

"It was the worst thing": *AVAN*, Issue 223, February 2012, 5.

CHAPTER 38: MARTIAL LAW

"I have called upon": *Honolulu Advertiser*, December 9, 1941, 9.

"that every male citizen": *Honolulu Advertiser*, December 14, 1941, 1.

"a total blackout": *Honolulu Star-Bulletin*, December 8, 1941, 2.

"Motion picture houses, theaters": *Honolulu Advertiser*, December 9, 1941, 1.

"We're happy to help": *Honolulu Star-Bulletin*, December 8, 1941, 18.

"this means that you may buy": Ibid., 2.

"Japanese exterminators": Maj. Gen. Thomas H. Green, *Martial*

*Law in Hawaii: December 7, 1941 to April 4, 1943*, Library of Congress.

"Me Chinese": Ibid.

"And it is a sad and terrible sight": Gilbert, *Building for War*, 212.

"You know it is only a miracle": Ibid., 250.

"small harem": Ibid., 237.

**CHAPTER 39: HOMEWARD BOUND**

"We've heard from the boys": SFOM Interview: William Moss.

"Pan American Airways base": *Boston Daily Globe*, January 12, 1942, 8.

"Condition Seven": Pan American Airways, *The Clipper*, "Eldridge Returns to Pacific Coast," September 18, 1946, 1: U. Miami PAA.

"Adm. Kimmel requests Captain Hamilton": *AIR & SPACE*, August/September 1989, 71; Interview with Phillip Cooke, October 17, 2019.

"We were tired and in shock": SFOM Interview: William Moss.

Cecile Barnett would be imprisoned by the Japanese in March 1942.

"We've gained twenty pounds each": *Oakland Tribune*, May 13, 1945, 10-C.

"Honolulu Spends Anxious Night—Many Alarms": *Honolulu Star-Bulletin*, December 9, 1941, 2.

"thousands of complaints": Ibid.

"Attention, all cars. Arrest anyone": Ibid.

"There were plenty of amateur air raid": *Boston Daily Globe*, January 12, 1942, 8.

"At Fort Russy": Ibid.

"[Relyea] is making very satisfactory progress," Letter from George Gardner, Pan Am public relations manager, to Frank Martin, dated December 18, 1941; Gary Relyea collection.

"I couldn't think of anything appropriate": *AIR & SPACE*, August/September 1989, 71; Interview with Phillip Cooke, October 17, 2019.

"It was unnerving . . . the worst thing that I'd ever seen": *AVAN*, Issue 223, February 2012, 5.

"The Captain said they may take": Gilbert, *Building for War*, 211.

"[We] were prepared to land anywhere": *San Francisco Examiner*, December 10, 1941, 4.

"Last night there were planes": *Daily News* (Los Angeles), December 10, 1941, 23.

"Nearing the Pacific coast, we learned": *San Francisco Examiner*, December 10, 1941, 4.

"The radio which brought": *San Bernardino County Sun*, December 10, 1941, 4.

"We were not to tell anybody": SFOM Interview: William Moss.

"routine": *New York Times*, December 11, 1941.

### CHAPTER 40: CHRISTMAS IN WASHINGTON

"I am thankful that [Providence] has": Jewish Virtual Library, "Adolf Hitler: Speech Declaring War against the United States," December 11, 1941.

"Being saturated and satiated": The National WWII Museum, New Orleans, "The Declaration of the United Nations in the Aftermath of Pearl Harbor," January 2022.

"We could review the whole war plan": *HUMANITIES*, "Christmas at the White House with Winston Churchill," Fall 2016, Volume 37, Number 4.

"Our strongest weapon in this war": *Chicago Tribune*, "Churchill, Roosevelt Texts for Tree Lighting Ceremony," December 25, 1941, 14.

"two turkeys and a Christmas tree": *Detroit Free Press*, "Japs in Capital Celebrate, Too," December 25, 1941, 3.

"When Ambassador and Mrs. Litvinov were lunching with me alone," Joseph Davies memorialized that evening, "word came of the Japanese attack. Litvinov asked me how I felt about it. I replied that it was a terrible thing, but it was providential. It assured unity in this country." Davies mused in his memo that the "question . . . will arise as to whether it is better to try to get the Soviets to attack and aid us or not. We might win the battle," Davies continued, "but hazard the war. If the Soviets should be defeated by an attack on two fronts; or if they should lose heart [like they had in World War I], it might affect the ultimate issue." US Department of State, "Papers Relating to the Foreign Relations of the United States, Diplomatic Papers, 1941, The Far East, Vol. IV, Doc. 545, Memorandum by Mr. Joseph E. Davies of Conference Had With Ambassador Litvinov Upon His Arrival, December 7, 1941.

CHAPTER 41: *ANZAC* AND *PACIFIC CLIPPERS* REACH HOME

"thrilling dash though a war zone": *San Francisco Examiner*, December 11, 1941, 5.

U Saw's former secretary, Tin Tut, who'd flown with him aboard the *Anzac Clipper*, later a deputy to Gen. Aung Sun, had avoided assassination by U Saw's henchmen only to be murdered when a grenade was tossed into his car a year later.

"pig, poi, coconut pudding, and all the trimmings": *Honolulu Star-Bulletin*, July 30, 1942, 11.

"[Juan Trippe and] the Navy," Hawaiian-reared Bill Mullahey recalled, "was a little 'kanalua' [hesitant] about letting the plane come back through Pearl Harbor." Oral History: William Justin Mullahey, Outrigger Canoe Club, May 9, 1980.

"Strip all company markings": Dover, *The Long Way Home*, 66.

"With the captain, we went down": Oral History: William Justin Mullahey, Outrigger Canoe Club, May 9, 1980.

"I had no information about his whereabouts": Interview with Steve Steers, son of John D. Steers, October 7, 2019.

"We gave the people there about one hour to get packed—one small bag apiece—and get aboard," Fourth Officer Steers remembered. "We took 22 men, women, and children and a considerable amount of gas—we were really overloaded." Dunning, *Voices of My Peers*, 129.

"We expected, as did the French": Ibid., 99.

"crossing some of the most desolate country": Ibid., 100.

Unable to locate 100-octane aviation fuel, Ford's men employed a clever idea. They isolated the plane's aviation fuel into two tanks by means of the plane's fuel pumps and filled the remainder of the tanks with automobile fuel, which had an average octane level of 77. They'd use the powerful aviation fuel for takeoff and then switch to automobile fuel as they cruised to Trincomalee, Ceylon. "We switched to the automobile gas and held our breaths. The engines almost jumped out of their mounts, but they ran." Ibid., 102.

"There was a launch that had come out": *AVAN* (Australian Vintage Aeroplane News), "Around the World Saga of Pan-Am 'Pacific Clipper,'" Issue 223, February 2012, 9.

While there, Ford met a young officer off the USS *Houston*. "He approached me with the request that I take the portrait of himself . . . to his father in New York." Dunning, *Voices of My Peers*, 102. Ford accepted the young man's request. He learned later that the Japanese sank the *Houston*, and the young officer was among those lost.

"All night I kept thinking": Ibid.

To defend against the raids, the Chinese maintained a reliable system of spotters along the countryside to warn Chungking and small villages by shortwave radio of an oncoming formation of bombers. It has been reported that the Japanese carried out 268 sorties that dropped thousands of tons of bombs, mostly incendiary, on Chungking and its inhabitants.

"The Saudis had already caught": *AVAN*, Issue 223, February 2012, 10.

"Leopoldville is just 4 degrees": Dunning, *Voices of My Peers*, 131.

"That was one of the high": *AVAN*, Issue 223, February 2012, 11.

"LaGuardia Tower, Pan American Clipper": *Hawaii Tribune-Herald*, March 2, 1942, 2.

"the water splashed up": Dunning, *Voices of My Peers*, 132.

"The coldest temperature of the Winter": *New York Times*, January 7, 1942, 21.

"He was gone for nearly six weeks": *Chicago Tribune*, December 3, 2000, 417.

"This was only my father's second trip": Ibid.

### CHAPTER 42: THE EXCHANGE

First Officer Strickland later recounted that Capt. Ralph was not in Namyung with the rest of the crew, but had flown from Hong Kong directly to Chungking.

"Marsman, this is the toughest spot": Marsman, *I Escaped from Hong Kong*, 192.

"There were friends and more friends": Ibid., 238.

"I was a little late for Christmas": Ibid., 248.

On August 14, 1945, Emperor Hirohito announced to the Japanese people that their country had surrendered to the Allies. President Harry S. Truman also announced the surrender to White House reporters that evening. However, the surrender wasn't formally signed until September 2, 1945, aboard the USS *Missouri* in Tokyo Bay.

After forty-four days in Camp Stanley, Gwen Priestwood escaped. "I got so hungry I couldn't stand it another day," she later wrote. "Even death at the hands of the Jap soldiers would have been better than slowly starving in that filthy, wretched camp." Gwen Priestwood, *Through Japanese Barbed Wire*. She sneaked away one night and made it all the way to Chungking after a 24-day, 675-mile trek across mountains and valleys. With word that a lone British woman had escaped from Camp Stanley, her presence in Chungking was celebrated with lunches and dinners held by Chinese heads of state and various ambassadors and dignitaries.

"When my feet touched": Harman, *Hellions of Hirohito*, 204.

"I realized that he was Mr. Saburō Kurusu!": Ibid., 207.

"It must seem absurd to you": *Austin American-Statesman*, "Kurusu Says Jap Plan Not Shown Him," November 19, 1945, 6.

"Mr. Kurusu . . . I was beaten nearly to death": Harman, *Hellions of Hirohito*, 208.

"Our hearts insisted on throbbing": Dew, *Prisoner of the Japs*, 283.

"Among us were . . . men and women": Ibid., 293.

"something enraging": Ibid., 296.

"Flying from the mast of the first [ship]": Ibid., 308.


CHAPTER 43: REVENGE

"Instead of something soft to sleep on": Melvern Orton Interview. "Pan Am—The Early Years," July 14, 2000.

"Someone came by and woke us up": SFOM Interview: John W. Strickland.

"a dirty, filthy, rat-infested dump": *Wings over Asia: Memories of CNAC*, "Playtime in Chungking," Vol. IV, 25.

In Lagos, Foy Kohler, who was a member of the American Foreign Service stationed in Cairo, boarded with his wife, Phyllis. Kohler had been recalled to Washington, DC, as the war with Germany and Italy had grown more intense in Egypt.

"The air crews waiting impatiently": Fuchida, *For That One Day*, 103.

"I showed and described to him": Ibid., 109.

"This was the turning point": Ibid., 155.

"lost interest in engaging": Ibid., 159.

"All the friends I had": Ibid., 211.

"I enjoyed the friendly hospitality": Ibid., 285.


CHAPTER 44: NEW YORK

"made it imperative that every": *New Horizons*, Vol. 12, No. 4, January 1942, 10: U. Miami PAA.

"For years from now people": *Life*, November 3, 1941, 99.


EPILOGUE

"If anybody ever flies to the moon": *Life*, October 20, 1941, 116.

# BIBLIOGRAPHY

## BOOKS AND PERIODICALS

"2 Clippers Land Here, Third Due," *San Pedro News-Pilot* (California), December 1, 1941.

"A Visit with Hemingway," *Look*, September 4, 1956.

"Adventures of Clippers When the War Broke Out," *Hawaii Tribune-Herald*, March 2, 1942.

Allen, Roy. *The Pan Am Clipper: The History of Pan American's Flying-Boats 1931 to 1946*. New York: Barnes & Noble Books, 2000.

Altschul, Selig, and Marylin Bender. *The Chosen Instrument: Juan Trippe, Pan Am, the Rise and Fall of an American Entrepreneur*. New York: Simon and Schuster, 1982.

"Anzac Clipper Completes Round Trip to Hawaii without Spotting War," *San Bernardino County Sun*, December 10, 1941.

"Around the World Saga of Pan-Am 'Pacific Clipper,'" *AVAN* (Australian Vintage Aeroplane News), Issue 223, February 2012.

Baldwin, James Patrick, and Jeff Kriendler. *Pan American World Airways Aviation History through the Words of Its People*. St. Augustine: Bluewater Press LLC, 2011.

"Banner Publisher Sees Great Boon in Clipper Service," *Nashville Banner*, October 21, 1936.

Berke, Donald A., Don Kindall, and Gordon Smith. *World War II Volume 5: Air Raid Pearl Harbor. This Is Not a Drill. Day-to-Day Naval Actions December 1941 through March 1942*. Dayton, Ohio: Bertke Publications, 2013.

"Blazing Trail for Passenger Air Line to China." *Popular Mechanics*, July 1935, 5.

"Boeing Builds Largest Flying Boat for Transatlantic Service in 1938," *Life*, Aug. 23, 1937, 38–41.

Bond, W. Langhorne; edited by James E. Ellis. *Wings for an Embattled China*. Cranbury, New Jersey: Associated University Presses Inc., 2001.

Boothe, Clare. "Destiny Crosses the Dateline: Report on a Flight Across the Pacific." *Life*, November 3, 1941.

Bowers, Peter, "The Great Clippers: Part II," *Wings*, Vol. 7, No. 6, December 1977, 10–23, 46–52.

"Bright Lights & Gay Streets—Pearl Harbor Last Friday Night," *The Age* (Melbourne, Victoria, Australia), December 12, 1941.

Brock, Horace. *Flying the Oceans: A Pilot's Story of Pan Am 1935–1955*. New York: Jason Aronson Inc., 1978.

*Brooklyn Times Union*, January 23, 1934.

Busch, Noel F. "Juan Trippe: Pan American Airways' Young Chief Helps Run a Branch of US Defense." *Life*, October 20, 1941.

Chapman, Frances Allan. *Talking to the World from Pan Am's Clippers*. Newton, New Jersey: Carstens Publications Inc., 1999.

Chennault, Claire Lee; Robert Hotz, editor. *Way of a Fighter: The Memoirs of Claire Lee Chennault*. New York: G. P. Putnam's Sons, 1949.

China National Aviation Association Foundation. *Wings Over Asia, Vol. I–IV, A Brief History of China National Aviation Corporation*. Birmingham, AL: CNAC Heritage Foundation, 1972.

"Christmas at the White House with Winston Churchill," *Humanities*, Fall 2016, Volume 37, Number 4.

"Churchill, Roosevelt Texts for Tree Lighting Ceremony," *Chicago Tribune*, December 25, 1941.

"Clipper Accomplishments and New Plans," *Airpost Journal*, June 1937, 3–9.

"Clipper Attacked by Swarm of Planes," *New York Times*, December 10, 1941.

"Clipper Set on Fire in Hong Kong Attack," *Honolulu Advertiser*, December 9, 1941.

Cohen, Stan. *Wings to the Orient: Pan American Clipper Planes 1935 to 1945, A Pictorial History.* Missoula, Montana: Pictorial Histories Publishing Company, 1985.

Conde, David W., 1906–1941. The University of British Columbia. International Military Tribunal for the Far East; Prosecution documents and exhibits. University of British Columbia Library Rare Books and Special Collections. Vancouver: University of British Columbia Library. http://rbscarchives.library.ubc.ca/index.php/ex-1200-1251-japanese-american-relations-attacks-on-u-s-bases-dec-7-1941 Ex.1200-1251. Japanese-American relations. Attacks on US bases, Dec. 7, 1941.

Conrad III, Barnaby. *Pan Am: An Aviation Legend.* Emeryville, CA: Woodford Press, 1999.

Cooke, Isyl J., "Escape from Wake Island = A Miracle of the War's Beginning," *Kansas City Star*, March 22, 1942, 1C–2C.

Cressman, Robert J., *A Magnificent Fight: The Battle for Wake Island.* Annapolis, Md.: Naval Institute Press, 1995.

Crouch, Gregory. *China's Wings.* New York: Bantam Books, 2012.

Cunningham, W. Scott. *Wake Island Command.* New York: Popular Library, 1962.

Daley, Robert. *An American Saga: Juan Trippe and His Pan Am Empire.* New York: Random House, 1980.

"Daughter's Death Drives Man to Kill Wife, Self," *Daily News*, February 14, 1934.

Devereux, James P. S. *The Story of Wake Island.* Philadelphia: J.B. Lippincott Co., 1947.

Dew, Gwen. *Prisoner of the Japs.* New York: Alfred A. Knopf, 1943.

Dover, Ed. *The Long Way Home: A Journey into History with Captain Ford*. Self-Published, 2008 (Revised Edition).

Dunning, Eugene J. *Voices of My Peers: Clipper Memories*. Nevada City, California: Clipper Press, 1996.

"Escape from Hong Kong Told by American Mine Executive," *Pasadena Post* (California), March 7, 1942.

Ekins, H. R., *Around the World in Eighteen Days and How to Do It*. New York: Longmans, Green and Co., 1936.

"FAM-22," *Airpost Journal*, Vol. XIII, No. 3, Issue 140, December 1941.

Francillon, Rene J. *Japanese Aircraft of the Pacific War*. Annapolis, MD: Naval Institute Press, 1970.

"Giant China Clipper Hops for Manila," *San Francisco Chronicle*, November 23, 1935.

Gilbert, Bonita. *Building for War: The Epic Saga of the Civilian Contractors and Marines of Wake Island in World War II*. Philadelphia: Casemake Publishers, 2012.

Glines, C. V., "At this time in 1941, a Clipper plane was trying to get home the hard way—flying around the world!" *Aviation History Magazine*, December 18, 2018.

"Governor's Proclamation," *Honolulu Star-Bulletin*, December 8, 1941.

"Great Silver Bird," *Richmond News Leader*, December 24, 1965.

Green, Maj. Gen. Thomas H. "Martial Law in Hawaii: December 7, 1941 to April 4, 1943."

Grooch, William Stephen. *From Crate to Clipper with Captain Musick, Pioneer Pilot*. New York: Longmans, Green and Co., 1939.

Grooch, William Stephen. *Skyway to Asia*. New York: Longmans, Green and Co., 1936.

Grosscup, Luann, "World Travelers: Pearl Harbor bombing turns a routine Pan Am Pacific Clipper flight into a 31,500-mile odyssey," *Chicago Tribune*, December 3, 2000, 1, 5.

Hager, Alice Rogers, "Hell on Wake Island!" *Boston Daily Globe*, January 12, 1942, 1, 8.

Harman, Phillip, narrated by Eric Heath. *Hellions of Hirohito.* Los Angeles, California: DeVorss & Co., 1944.

"Hawaii Martial Law Proclaimed by Army," *Honolulu Advertiser,* December 9, 1941.

Heinl, Lt. Col. Robert D. Jr. *Marines at Midway.* Historical Section, Division of Public Information, 1948.

Hill, John H., and Mark Cotta Vaz. *Pan Am at War: How the Airline Secretly Helped America Fight World War II.* New York: Skyhorse Publishing Inc., 2019.

Homan, Lynn M., and Thomas Reilly. *Images of Aviation: Pan Am.* Charleston, South Carolina: Arcadia Publishing, 2000.

"Honolulu Clipper Evades Jap Raids," *Morning News* (Wilmington, DE), December 10, 1941.

"Huge Clipper, Strafed by Japs, Safe in S.F.," *San Francisco Examiner,* December 11, 1941.

"Insists Jap Raiders Off L.A., S.F.," *Daily News* (Los Angeles), December 10, 1941.

"J. N. Bramhams Tell of Experiences during Jap Attack in Pacific," *Daily Independent* (Murphysboro, IL), Jan. 15, 1942.

Jackson, Alice. "Always Just One Hop Ahead of Danger in Thrilling Dash Home," *Australian Women's Weekly,* December 20, 1941.

"Jackson Miner Gives Vivid Story of Attack on Wake Island," *Sacramento Bee,* January 14, 1942.

"Jap Bombs Fire Clipper," *Arizona Republic* (Phoenix), January 11, 1942.

Japlonski, Edward. *Sea Wings: The Romance of the Flying Boats.* Garden City, NY: Doubleday, 1972.

"Japs in Capital Celebrate, Too," *Detroit Free Press,* December 25, 1941.

Kaucher, Dorothy. *Wings over Wake.* San Francisco: John Howell Books, 1947.

Kauffman, Sanford B. *Pan Am Pioneer: A Manager's Memoir, from*

*Seaplanes to Jumbo Jets*. Lubbock, Texas: Texas Tech University Press, 1995.

"Keesler Private Saw Japs Strike," *Clarion-Ledger* (Jackson, MS), December 15, 1942.

Klaas, M. D. "Clipper Across the Pacific: Part One." *Air Classics*, December 1989.

Klaas, M. D. "Clipper Across the Pacific: Part Two." *Air Classics*, January 1990.

Krupnick, Jon E. *Pan American's Pacific Pioneers: A Pictorial History of Pan Am's Pacific First Flights 1935–1946*. Missoula, Montana: Pictorial Histories Publishing Company, 1997.

"Kurusu, in Capital, Gives Peace 'Fighting Chance,'" *Daily News* (New York), November 15, 1941.

"Kurusu Lands; 'Touchdown,' For Peace His Goal," *Boston Globe*, November 15, 1941.

"Kurusu Says Jap Plan Not Shown Him," *Austin American-Statesman*, November 19, 1945.

Leary, William M. Jr. *The Dragon Wings: The China National Aviation Corporation and the Development of Commercial Aviation in China*. Athens, Georgia: The University of Georgia Press, 1976.

"Life Flies the Atlantic: America to Europe in 23 Hours by Clipper," *Life*, Vol. 8, No. 23, June 3, 1940.

Lohr, Steve, "A Symbol of U.S. Business Prowess," *New York Times*, July 12, 1991.

Luke, Harry. *The British Pacific Islands*. Oxford University Press, 1943.

Marsman, Jan Henrik. *I Escaped from Hong Kong*. New York: Reynal & Hitchock, 1942.

McWilliams, Bill. *Scrimmage for War: A Story of Pearl Harbor, Football, and World War II*. New York: Open Road Integrated Media Inc., 2014.

McWilliams, Bill. *Sunday in Hell: Pearl Harbor Minute by Minute*. Guilford, Connecticut: Stackpole Books, 2019.

Michener, James A. *The World is My Home: A Memoir*. New York: Random House, 1992.

Miles, Sherman. "Pearl Harbor in Retrospect," *The Atlantic*, July 1948.

Monro, Mary. *Stranger in My Heart*. London: Unbound, 2018.

"New Fleet Command," *Honolulu Advertiser*, February 1, 1941.

Nissen, Edward M., ed. *Pacific 97 Handbook*; and Healey, Barth, ed. *The Congress Book 1997*. The American Philatelic Congress Inc. (1997).

"Operations in Hong Kong from 8th to 25th December, 1941." Dispatch from Lt. Gen. C.M. Maltby to Secretary of State for War on 21st November 1945. *London Gazette*, supplement, 27th January 1948.

"Pan Am Airways Shifts to War Role," *Evening Sun* (Baltimore), December 15, 1941.

"Pan American Airways Wins Collier Trophy Pacific Plane Service," *Life*, August 23, 1937, 36–37.

Prange, Gordon W. *At Dawn We Slept: The Untold Story of Pearl Harbor*. New York: McGraw-Hill, 1981.

Priestwood, Gwen. *Through Japanese Barbed Wire*. London: George Harrap, 1944.

"Pursued Ships: Here's What Happened to the Pacific Clipper," *Boeing Magazine*, Vol. XII, No. 1, January 1942, 8–9.

Pyle, Ernie, "Lei is an Expression of Personality," *Honolulu Advertiser*, February 6, 1938.

*Reporter-Times* (Martinsville, IN), July 31, 1942, 2.

"Residents Must Build Shelters," *Honolulu Advertiser*, December 14, 1941.

Rhodes, Lynwood Mark. "Those Magnificent Clipper Flying Boats," *American Legion Magazine*, Aug. 1975, 20–24, 39–41.

*Rodney and Otamatea Times* (New Zealand), December 10, 1941, 4.

"Roosevelt Praises Flight Over the Pacific," *Miami Herald*, November 23, 1935.

Scheppler, Robert R., and Charles E. Anderson. "The Martin Clippers." *Journal of American Aviation Historical Society*. Vol. 10, No. 3, Fall 1965, 172–182.

Scammell, Henry. "Pan Am's Pacific: The Clippers that spanned the world's largest ocean left many lives realigned in their broad wakes." *Air & Space Smithsonian*. August/September 1989.

Scott, Robert L. "God Is My Co-Pilot," *Midland Journal* (Rising Sun, MD), March 23, 1945.

SFO Museum. *China Clipper*. San Francisco: San Francisco Airport Commission, 2013.

Sheinis, Zinovi. "Roosevelt-Litvinov: Man to Man Talk: History of U.S.-Soviet Diplomatic Relations," *Soviet Life*, February 1969, 21–23.

Shinsato, Douglas T., and Tadanori Urabe (translators). *For That One Day: The Memoirs of Mitsuo Fuchida, Commander of the Attack on Pearl Harbor*. eXperience inc., 2001.

Singley, Richard L. "The Orient Views First P.A.A. Clippers," *Airpost Journal*, June 1937, 12–15, 32.

Slade, Jim. "Forty Minutes to Pearl."

"Sneak Raid Through Sewers Helped Japs Take Hong Kong," *News Journal* (Wilmington, DE), July 27, 1942.

"Some at Wake Evacuated," *New York Times*, December 10, 1941.

"The Roving Reporter," *Akron Beacon Journal*, April 8, 1941.

Thomas, Lowell, and Rexford W. Barton. *Wings Over Asia*. Philadelphia: John C. Winston Company, 1937.

Trautman, James. *Pan American Clippers: The Golden Age of Flying Boats*. Boston: Mills Press, 2007.

Trippe, Betty Stettinius. *Pan Am's First Lady: The Diary of Betty Stettinius Trippe*. McLean, Virginia: Paladwr Press, 1996.

"Trippe's Clipper Hailed in the Afterglow," *New York Times*, July 13, 1997.

"U.S. Breaks Peace, Tokyo Radio Claims," *Philadelphia Inquirer*, November 29, 1941.

"Visiting Grid Players Given Police Duties," *Honolulu Star-Bulletin*, December 8, 1941.

"When Sudden War Caught American Clippers in Mid-Air," *Kansas City Star*, Dec. 21, 1941.

White, Theodore H. "China's Last Lifeline," *Fortune*, May 1943.

Wilson, Richard C. "Japs Sneak Attack Described by Correspondent," *Oakland Tribune*, July 27, 1942.

"Wings Over the Pacific," *Popular Mechanics*, June 1935, 862–864.

"World Pauses to Watch Sailing," *Times* (San Mateo, CA), November 22, 1935.

# ARCHIVAL

"Adolf Hitler: Speech Declaring War Against the United States," Jewish Virtual Library, December 11, 1941.

Ancestry.com.

California Digital Newspaper Collection.

"Clippers at War." International Historic Films. 1985 (DVD).

Declassified Top Secret document: Midway, NARA Project No. NND 868130, 1–16.

Department of State, Foreign Relations of the United States Diplomatic Papers, 1941, The Far East, Vol. IV, 772.

"Dispatch from Lt. Gen. C.M. Maltby to Secretary of State for War on 21st November 1945," *London Gazette*, supplement, January 27, 1948.

Fairfax Media, Sydney, Australia.

Franklin Delano Roosevelt Presidential Library and Museum.

Hong Kong General Chamber of Commerce, Report for the Year 1940.

"Hong Kong: Gateway to China." Andre De La Varre; The Screen Traveler. 1938 (Film).

Melvern Orton Interview. "Pan Am—The Early Years," by Ralph Conly. July 14, 2000 (DVD; provided by Monica Orton).

National Archives and Records, San Francisco, RG181, Declassified Records of Naval District and Shore Establishments, Fourteenth Naval District, Boxes 1–7.

Newspapers.com.

New Zealand National Library.

Oral History: William Justin Mullahey, Outrigger Canoe Club, an interview by Kenneth J. Pratt, May 9, 1980.

Pearl Harbor Attack: Hearings Before the Joint Committee on the Investigation of the Pearl Harbor Attack, 79th Congress, First Session, Parts 15 and 26. US Government Printing Office, 1946.

San Francisco Airport Commission Aviation Library Louis A. Turpen Aviation Museum, Audio Cassette Tape: Interview with William Moss, 1999.

San Francisco Airport Commission Aviation Library Louis A. Turpen Aviation Museum, Oral History Program Interview Transcription: John W. Strickland, 1997.

San Francisco Airport Commission Aviation Library Louis A. Turpen Aviation Museum, Oral History Program Interview Transcription, Robert Ford.

San Francisco Airport Commission Aviation Library Louis A. Turpen Aviation Museum, Oral History Program Interview Transcription: Sam John Toarmina, February 26, 1999.

Soldinski, Zygmund. "The Last Days of C.N.A.C. in Hong Kong," 1941, *Wings Over Asia*, Vol. II, 40.

Text of Report Made Jointly by Pan American Airways and 12th Naval District Public Relations Office, at San Francisco, December 10, 1941.

"The Declaration of the United Nations in the Aftermath of Pearl Harbor," National WWII Museum, New Orleans, January 2022.

Trove Australia/New Zealand.

United States Diplomatic Papers 1941, Volume IV: The Far East.

Department of State Publication 6325. Washington, DC: US Government Printing Office, 1956.

University of Miami Libraries Special Collections—Pan American World Airways Inc. Records. "Ashore," *New Horizons*, December 1940, 22–23.

University of Miami Libraries Special Collections—Pan American World Airways, Inc. Records. "Catering Aloft," *New Horizons*, February 1941, 25–27.

University of Miami Libraries Special Collections—Pan American World Airways Inc. Records. "Pan American Features Biggest Working Exhibit at New Clipper Base at San Francisco's World's Fair," *Pan American Air Ways*, May/Jun. 1939, 1–2.

University of Miami Libraries Special Collections—Pan American World Airways Inc. Records. "Pan American to Build Mid-Ocean Hotels," *Pan American Air Ways*, Jan/Feb. 1936, 1, 9.

University of Miami Libraries Special Collections—Pan American World Airways Inc. Records. Pan American Airways Inc. Cab Docket Nos. 851 et al. "History of the Transpacific Air Services to and Through Hawaii," August 12, 1944.

University of Miami Libraries Special Collections—Pan American World Airways Inc. Records. "Ten Thousand Times Around the World," Pan American World Airways. 1944.

University of Miami Libraries Special Collections—Pan American World Airways Inc. Records. "The Fleet," *New Horizons*, April 1942, 20–21.

University of Miami Libraries Special Collections—Pan American World Airway, Inc. Records. *New Horizons*, January 1942.

US Congressional Record, 77th Congress, 2nd Session. Appendix Vol. 88, Part 8. (1942).

US Congressional Record, 80th Congress, 2nd Session. Appendix Vol. 94, Part 10. (1948).

US Department of State, Office of Historian. "Papers relating to the Foreign Relations of the United States, Japan, 1931–1941."

US Navy, Naval History and Heritage Command, National Museum of the U.S. Navy, Action Report, USS *Ward*.

Wake Island National Historic Landmark. Historic American Landscapes Survey. National Park Service, US Department of the Interior, HALS No. UM-1, May 2011.

"Weight Frets Prison 'Angels,'" *Oakland Tribune*, May 13, 1945.

# INDEX

# ABOUT THE AUTHOR

**PHILIP JETT** is a retired corporate and tax attorney living in Nashville, Tennessee. He has represented multinational corporations, CEOs, and celebrities from the music, television, and sports industries. He is a member of various boards and organizations, including a founding member of the Nashville Writers' Council. His first nonfiction book, *The Death of an Heir: Adolph Coors III and the Murder That Rocked an American Brewing Dynasty*, was released in September 2017 and was named one of the best true crime stories of the year by the *New York Times*. His second book, *Taking Mr. Exxon: The Kidnapping of an Oil Giant's President*, was released in 2021. Mr. Jett has two sons and he often volunteers for children's causes.